So Much To Do
So Little Time

MEMOIRS

OF

STANLEY KENNETH JENKINS

*To my wife Barbara
and our four daughters
Nicola, Caroline, Nina and Alison*

Willow Press
Ferring

First published in Great Britain in 2000
by Willow Press, 1, Beehive Lane,
Ferring, Worthing, West Sussex,
BN12 5NL

ISBN   0-9538827-0-5

Cover design by Julie Dene

Printed by:
RPM, 2-3 Spur Road,
Quarry Lane, Chichester,
West Sussex. PO19 2PR

CONTENTS

ACKNOWLEDGEMENTS

I acknowledge with thanks the considerable help I have received in the preparation of this book, especially from my wife Barbara, who undertook much of the research and proof-reading. Her memory of events, dates and venues never ceases to amaze me. Like her ancestors she is one of those who never throws anything away and when it came to meeting her wishes that I should write this book, this trait was of inestimable value. Nonetheless, much of my writing is from memory and I apologise for any inaccuracies attributable to the passing of time.

Thanks must also go to my children, brothers and friends for their contributions, and to those called 'nerds' who are responsible for the indispensable help my computer has given: without it I most certainly would not have begun.

vi

PROLOGUE

On many occasions when I found myself recounting incidents from the past, I was asked why I did not put my life story on paper. I was never quite sure how to interpret this - had I gone on talking too long and my audience thought they could more easily lay the written word aside? The idea of writing memoirs seemed too pretentious for me, and it was some time before I was finally persuaded to begin typing on my computer keyboard.

My story falls conveniently into five separate parts, each covering a phase of my life, and each spent in sharply contrasting environments. I spent my early years, which spanned the period following the end of the First World War to the start of the second, in a small and relatively isolated Welsh township. During the Second World War, following a period of military training in the UK, I was posted to West Africa, India and Burma, where I served with West African troops.

My time in the army was followed by a frenetic four-year period as a student leader, when I found myself immersed in the Cold War in Eastern Europe. This opened the door to a fascinating career in the Diplomatic Service that lasted twenty-eight years, but it would take more than one book to tell all of that story, and probably more authorisations than I could ever get. After that I enjoyed a long period 'in retirement' in a Sussex village.

Looking back over what seems an eternity, I've had more than my share - a veritable cocktail - of tragedy, travel, excitement, hardship, love, hard work, enjoyment, satisfaction, responsibility, triumph and failure, good health and bad. In the words of the old song 'Who could ask for anything more?'

So Much To Do
So Little Time

• • • • • • • •

Part I

The Early Years

CHAPTER ONE

WHICH ONE ARE YOU THEN?

'It is only rarely one can see in a
little boy the promise of a man.'

Alexandre Dumas, fils.

To judge from newspapers published on 25th November 1920 – the day I was born – this was not a date of any particular importance. *The Times* of that day carried a report on a parliamentary debate on Ireland that included accusations of Sinn Fein fundraising for 'the assassination of policemen or soldiers'; there were numerous advertisements for domestic staff and manservants, and a lady advertised her 1915 Rolls-Royce for 2,000 guineas, but there was nothing to suggest that this was a significant day or one of any special interest in any part of the world. Perhaps it was for my parents, but having two daughters and five sons already, they may have had mixed feelings! For me, it marks the beginning of my story.

The First World War that had not long ended, had left Britain battered in every sense, economically drained and desperately short of young men; so many had perished in the conflict. Governments faced a daunting task and it was to take several years before the nation began to make gradual and often painful steps towards recovery. But I was much too small to be concerned about any of that.

Historians in my family have traced my forebears back over four generations to 1787, and have established that my paternal grandfather, Benjamin Jenkins, born in 1855, had already developed a successful building business in west Wales when, in order to expand his enterprise, he tendered successfully for

1

some long-term contracts for work at the Brecon barracks, some thirty miles away. This provided him with the opportunity he was seeking and, in 1880, at the age of 25, he moved his base and family from Llandeilo to the old market town of Brecon, which became the home for our family firm.

Brecon, the county town of Brecknockshire – renamed Powys after the parliamentary boundary changes of 1992 – lies between two major mountain ranges, the Brecon Beacons and the Black Mountains. Fortunately, the relative remoteness of the town, due mainly to poor communications, had spared it from many of the ravages of war. The town which had been granted a Borough Charter by Philip and Mary in 1556 had grown over centuries at the point where the rivers Usk and Honddu merge, before meandering in a south-easterly direction as a single watercourse to the sea at Newport. When I was born it had a population of some five thousand predominantly God-fearing souls.

Built mostly of red sandstone, with Welsh slate roofs, the town had a sombre cast. Apart from a few Georgian buildings there were few of architectural merit to commend it. Its old Benedictine Priory of St. John, dating back to 1096 – which became a Cathedral in 1923 as the seat of the Bishop of Swansea and Brecon – crowned the hill behind the broken-down remains of a Norman castle, while the town centre, built around the parish church of St. Mary, provided for most of the needs of the residents.

Across an ancient stone arched bridge over the river Usk stands Christ's College, founded in 1541 as a boys' public school, but now co-educational. But Brecon is probably best known as the base, established in 1873, for the 24th of Foot (South Wales Borderers), whose men won eleven Victoria Crosses in the Zulu Wars in the 1870s, and as the birthplace of the famous dramatic actress, Sarah Siddons, born there in 1755, who made her debut as Portia in the Merchant of Venice and had her first major success as Isabella in Garrick's version of Southerne's 'The Fatal Marriage'.

The area's economy, so dependent on extractive industries, had virtually collapsed after the 1914-18 war. The mining valleys, in particular, had suffered greatly and their economies had been painfully slow to recover. In the many depressed valley towns there were high levels of unemployment, and menfolk could be seen throughout the day idling at street corners looking dejected, with expressions of hopelessness on their faces. Children were mostly dressed in little more than rags and some had no shoes. Seeing them in that state it would have been easy to forget that these were a proud and indomitable people who asked only to work and rebuild their own communities. Many families had lost their only breadwinner in the war, there was little hope of jobs for school-leavers and many households lived under the burden of debt. I often thought in later life how much these people must have empathised with their contemporary Russian revolutionaries and longed for a Moses (or even a Lenin) to deliver them from their misery. These were places where slagheaps substituted for mountains and coal dust pervaded life itself.

Brecon, lying to the north of the valleys, was more fortunate. The fact that it was located in an agricultural area and was self-sufficient in most of the essentials of life had helped it overcome the scarcities following the war. There was less unemployment than in the depressed towns to the south and, as the years passed, standards of living had begun to rise.

Prodigious rainfall in the area ensures that the countryside around Brecon is always lush and green. The patchwork of fields, mostly stocked with sheep and cattle, penned in by dry-stone walls and orderly oak post-and-wire fences or neatly layered hedges, gives the landscape the seal of being well-managed farmland. In almost every view from the town there is a background of mountains and trees. Not surprisingly, in 1957, much of the Brecon Beacons, including the highest peak, Pen-y-fan (2906 feet), an area of 519 square miles, was designated a National Park.

When my grandfather first arrived in Brecon to start his new building contracts he occupied a small yard off Free Street, near the centre of the town. But this soon proved inadequate and he moved his thriving business to an established stonemason's yard conveniently sited opposite the Brecon barracks, which became the base for the enterprise over the next several decades.

From our knowledge of his achievements it is clear that he was a capable and industrious businessman. Having acquired certain running rights on the Brecon to Newport canal, which constituted one boundary of his storage yard, he used this for the transportation of some of his building materials from the seaports to the south-east. And to house his growing family he built, on a site adjoining his land, a substantial house, 'Maesllan', ('church in a field' – there was once a church near the site) – adding two more as his sons grew up. It was in one of these named 'Lynwood' that I was born.

My father, named Benjamin after his father, was born in 1884, and was sent as a boarder to Carmarthen Grammar School. But his school days were cut short when his father died suddenly at the age of forty-four, and he had to take on the heavy responsibility of running the firm – now renamed 'Benjamin Jenkins and Sons' – with his widowed mother. Within a few years his younger brother Stanley, after whom I was named, joined him.

My mother who was also born in 1884, and christened Ethel Jane, was one of a family of nine, the daughter of George Hicks Edwards who came to Brecon when he was appointed to head the post office established in Lion Street in 1889. He was descended from a line of mariners, his father, when he left the sea, becoming harbour master of Swansea. My parents married in the Priory Church, Brecon, in 1905. My mother was of slight build but had an amazing inner strength and abundant energy. By sheer example she instilled into her family the best of Victorian virtues and was, undoubtedly, a major influence on the lives of all her children.

In later years she told me that when she and my father had first decided to get married, her mother-in-law-to-be summoned her to attend at her house daily for a week to be instructed in the duties of a housewife. She had to demonstrate that she could cook, wash, iron and run a home efficiently. Apparently she passed the tests, though it seems there was no such instruction for the male member of the partnership!

I was last but one of the nine children of Benjamin and Ethel – two girls and seven boys. Winifred, the eldest, was born in 1905, followed by Trevor, Betty, Leslie, Harry, Mervyn, Fred, (I believe he should have been Frederick, but my father was said to be confused by his celebrations *en route* to the registry office), myself, and finally David, the youngest, born in 1923. We were spaced almost evenly at two yearly intervals and were each given two Christian names, except Fred. Mine was Kenneth, but I have no trace of any family connection with that name.

After my paternal grandfather died in 1899, my grandmother, a tenacious woman of marked business acumen, carried on the family firm with the aid of two of her sons, whom she trained and directed. She was essentially a lady of the Victorian era and was held in considerable awe by all who knew her. On market days she would ride 'in state' from her home to the town centre driving herself in a pony-drawn trap. If we, the grandchildren, were deemed to have been very well behaved, we were sometimes allowed, as a special treat, to ride with her. In her declining years the old lady was obliged, through infirmity, to take to her bed, but even then she continued to influence and supervise the conduct of the business. She liked her grandchildren to line up at her bedside every Friday to receive a few pence pocket money and these were occasions none of us missed. One of few memories I have of the remarkable old lady is of her sitting up in bed wearing her lace nightcap distributing her pennies.

In spite of the deprivation of the period between the two great wars, families tended to be large, and ours was no exception: there was much ignorance about sex and none of the modern contraceptive methods was available, nor was there any general wish to reduce or control population. Six to ten children per family was not at all unusual and I knew of one family of eleven living in a two roomed house – one room up and one down – with a small landing that was used for sleeping, and with only a lean-to at the rear for cooking and washing. Many houses had only outside toilets and these were often some distance from the house at the end of a long garden path – hence the chamber pot under every bed.

Few of those lucky enough to be in work took home wage-packets sufficient to meet the needs of such numbers: there was widespread unemployment. From those with no wages and with virtually no social security back-up, the local workhouse claimed many victims. Our parents frequently spurred us to greater effort in our school work with warnings of ending up there ourselves, resorting to such threats of dire consequences – biblical or otherwise – to ensure effort and compliance.

When I was three years old my widowed grandmother moved into the smaller house we occupied and we moved next-door into what had been her home, 'Maesllan', which was more commodious for our growing family, and this became my home for the next nineteen years. It was a roomy semi-detached building with five bedrooms, attics and large chilly cellars, laid out with slate slab shelves that had been used by my grandmother as a dairy. Her rotating milk churn was still there, and was occasionally used to produce cream and butter for the family. It took considerable energy to rotate the drum by hand, but with our mother, our living-in maid and we children, all taking turns, milk would, miraculously, be turned into cream or butter.

The cellar would occasionally flood in winter after heavy rain, and the water would rise steadily to the top of the cellar stairs. Only a wooden door separated the ground floor and the 'lake' below. When the water subsided, the cellar, the slate slabs and the churn had to be carefully cleaned before they could be used again, a mammoth, exhausting and unwelcome task. As the house dried out the damp could be felt throughout the whole building and the process could last well into the following summer. We gave little thought to the health risks, but they must have been considerable.

For the successful management of households the size of ours, it was essential that a fairly disciplined regime should be followed. In our home there was a recognised and predominantly repetitive order of life. Monday was washday when the large drum-boiler built into our back kitchen was stoked with logs from the timber yard before we children were roused from our beds. The day involved an incredible amount of physical exercise for the womenfolk, with much beating, rubbing and mangling of clothes. The nappies would stretch for yards on the lines in the garden, for there were none of the disposable variety then, and the ironing, which was regularly done on Tuesday by one or more of the womenfolk, lasted all day. The clothes then had to be aired in our huge airing cupboard heated by a vast kitchen range, which was cleaned and black-leaded every Wednesday. On other days there was always a programme of cooking and cleaning in train and, when the children were asleep, the women would sit and knit socks or pullovers and mend our clothes. The pile of mending awaiting attention allowed no time for reading or rest.

After my grandmother's death in 1926, when I was six years old, the family business passed to her two sons, Benjamin, my father, and his younger brother Stanley. They became partners and retained the same name for the firm they had inherited. Both were proud, industrious and honest traders who built up a highly successful business on the foundations their parents had laid down.

My father was a fairly easygoing entrepreneur – always addressed as 'boss' – but my uncle ruled with a firmer hand. It was not unusual for him to stand, with watch in hand, at the entrance gates to the yard, waiting for the men to clock on for the daily shift. To arrive even a few minutes late could cost a man his job: there were many waiting to fill any vacancy. I recall one serious and distressing consequence of this practice, when he dismissed a workman who had been in his employ for many years, for being late for work, and the man died of a heart attack on his way home to inform his family. Cause and effect, who knows? These were hard times for many.

Not only were we builders, coal, slate and lime merchants, we were also timber merchants, buying up and converting locally grown timber and importing lumber from many parts of the world, principally Scandinavia. The firm also enjoyed a thriving trade in pit props used by the thousand in the many coalmines in the neighbouring valleys. There was always a bustle of activity in the yard where we played. Horses and carts were constantly coming and going from dawn to dusk, loading and unloading building supplies, while horse-drawn carts and later lorries, transported building materials, coal and firewood to every corner of the town.

My father was renowned for his ability to view a piece of woodland from a distance, estimate accurately the useful timber content, and give a competitive quotation out of his head. The trees – mostly oak, beech, elm and pine – were felled and hauled by his men and stacked and seasoned in the yard before being processed in our sawmill.

At its peak the family firm employed over two hundred workmen, spread over building sites in and around the area, and in extensive workshops where craftsmen were engaged in making specialist joinery for buildings under construction, and producing handcarts, wheelbarrows, gates and hurdles to supply the never-ending demand of the local farmers. Skilled craftsmen, aided by their apprentices, manned each workshop and the machines they housed. In wooden sheds and outbuildings lathes were constantly turning to shape wheel hubs and spokes, baluster rails and newel posts and all the other wooden artefacts required by a rural community. This afforded us hours of instruction and entertainment.

The firm also provided undertaking services, and its joiners made coffins in a workshop lit only by candlelight, where the men would work late into the night, scraping and polishing oak coffin-boards and pouring pitch to seal the joints and cracks so that, as the foreman carpenter once told me, 'the occupants wouldn't get their feet wet.' Magnificently finished coffins, covered with a black sheet, were taken out of the yard and delivered discreetly after dark on a handcart. As children this morbid process fascinated us and we often helped the men to secure the soft cotton wool coffin linings and thin brass nameplates that were meticulously polished before the coffins were delivered.

We owned a number of fields around the town where we often played, some alongside the river Usk and others on the hillside to the north of the town. The hay they produced was gathered each summer to feed the horses throughout the winter months and the haymaking was a great event when all the firm's employees would be mustered. We children joined in and rode with the men to and from the fields on the horse-drawn hay wagons, ('gambos', as we knew them) clutching large earthenware jars of beer and cider, so essential to the optimum functioning of the harvesters. The ripe golden hay was then transported and hand-pitched into lofts over the stables, to be fed sparingly to the horses via chutes leading to their feeding racks below. It was warm up there over the horses and we found it a congenial place to play when it was raining outside, as it so often was.

Our house backed onto the builder's yard with its stacks of timber logs, a steam driven saw mill and stocks of all manner of building materials. With all of these heaven-sent facilities we were never short of a sandpit to play in, or scraps of wood to fashion into push-carts, or rafts to navigate the Brecon to Newport canal which ran at the bottom of the yard. The canal had been little used for many years, but it provided us with a perfect opportunity for rafting and boating, in a variety of craft we pieced together out of planks lashed to empty oil drums. Perhaps it was this experience of water that later persuaded us not to follow in the steps of our maternal mariner forebears, for many were the times we fell overboard into very cold, if shallow, water.

With a family of such a range of ages we proved a magnet for other local children and were never short of playmates. We used to construct swings, seesaws and roundabouts from the timbers in the yard and chase over the huge stacks of logs awaiting their demise in the sawmill. Indeed we made our own theme park and I have memories of many happy hours playing there with my brothers and our young friends. It may have been a builders' yard, but for us it was a playground of splendid proportions, ample provisions and inexhaustible opportunities for our enjoyment.

One of the attractions of the yard was the large steam-driven engine, bought second-hand from a colliery when it was well past its 'sell-by date'. It had a huge brass ball-governor that rose and fell to control the running speed and it hissed, creaked and groaned as it powered saws and other machines through a network of intertwined, twisted and dust laden belts driving a series of shafts under the floor of the sawmill. These delivered power to the lathes in the joiners' shops and saw benches in the main shed where machines had replaced the old hand-saw pits used in earlier times for cross-cutting logs and rendering them into planks. At the very end of the line, the drive shaft was connected to a mortar-making machine, which threw up clouds of dust as its huge rollers ground ashes, bought from the local gas works, with lime slaked in vats in the yard, to produce building mortars and wall renderings which were bound together with horsehair. Portland cement was yet to come. To keep the engine fuelled, a stoker, as old and creaking as the engine itself, was continuously employed feeding its boiler with timber off-cuts, sawdust and coal. Regardless of the considerable dangers, we used to play in the workshops where all the unprotected machinery was operating, and in the sweet smelling sawdust below the sawmill floor, where the drive shafts and belts transmitted their power to the many machines on the floor above – a practice that would have appalled any present-day Health and Safety Inspector, but in those days inspections were rare.

With so many young boys playing in the yard it was perhaps understandable that our parents discouraged us from traipsing through the house to use the bathroom, and instead, encouraged us to relieve ourselves at a conveniently sited rainwater gully near our back-door. I remember an occasion when this caused my uncle Stanley acute embarrassment. He was having a business discussion with a few elderly lady customers when six of us proceeded to relieve ourselves at the family watering hole, in their full view. The pleasure we had in achieving the maximum range was entirely lost on him and his clients. He must have felt glad he had no children of his own.

We had a team of horses, used for timber and general haulage, stabled in the yard behind our house, and my brothers and I regularly helped ourselves to the manure, piled outside in the stable yard, to improve the soil in the vegetable garden we all helped to cultivate. The Thomas brothers, Jack and Albert, tended the horses late into the night, by the light of flickering hurricane lamps, feeding, watering and cleaning them down after a hard day's toil, and preparing them for an early start the next day, when they would be hauling in the timber, felled by men armed with axes and cross-saws. Heavily loaded wagons would return at dusk causing considerable noise and excitement.

One route home to the yard was impeded by a steep hill in the middle of the town called Ship Street (a corruption of Sheep Street). Without additional horsepower it was impossible to haul the heaviest of the loaded wagons up the slope and it was necessary to add at least one or two horses at the bottom of the hill to reinforce the teams. With great skill the hauliers would negotiate a sharp twist at the top of the hill, first to the left and then again to the right. The lead horse was trained to pull sharply left and then right and, on one memorable occasion, this manoeuvre caused the second horse to stumble and fall. Disaster was averted by the men running with the wagon, who pushed blocks of wood under the wheels to prevent the load careering back down the hill. The horse that fell had to be destroyed and for days this was the talk of the town.

Many of the men the firm employed were delightfully colourful characters and, in true Welsh custom, were usually known by nicknames associating them with their distinctive trades or parentage. Children were denied an identity of their own until much later in life and were generally known as Evans' boy or Bill Williams' girl. I was known locally as 'one of Ben's boys', and sometimes more intimately as 'Leslie's brother'. From an early age I remember sensing this loss of identity and deciding that I was not forever going to be known as 'one of Ben's boys'. There were rather a lot of them anyway.

I have no recollection of ever having spoken to my father or him to me apart from one occasion when I asked my mother about some problem in arithmetic with which I was struggling, and she suggested that I should ask my father about it. I approached him with some trepidation as he sat in what we called 'the breakfast room', though I never remember having breakfast there. This was a room where my father usually sat alone to smoke his cigarettes, and when I put my question he turned and, through the tobacco haze, asked me 'Which one are you then?' Hardly the stuff on which sound filial relations are built! Perhaps when a younger man he had found more time for his many children, but I came too late for that.

The large stonewalled army barracks across the road that

had brought my grandfather to Brecon in the first instance, and where many of his men worked, became very much a part of our lives. From the 1870s it was the military centre for the counties of Brecknock, Radnor, Montgomery and Monmouth, from which most of its soldiers were recruited, and the main base and training centre for the South Wales Borderers Infantry Regiment. Our family firm was to be employed there constantly over some eighty years – building new accommodation and maintaining the existing structures – until it abandoned army contract work in the 1970s. Living as we did just across the road from the barracks, we woke each morning to the bugle call of 'Reveille', followed throughout the day by 'Come to the cookhouse door' and finally 'Lights-out'. The sentries on duty at the main gate through the daylight hours marched to and fro, stamping their feet as they 'about-turned'. Little traffic passed by and the 'stamp-stamp-stamp' of feet could be clearly heard some distance away. Every two years or so it fell to our firm to renew the concrete at the point where the stamping feet had pitted the surface to form a hole into which the rain collected, refining 'stamp-stamp-stamp' into 'splash-splash-splash'.

On Sundays, headed by the regimental band, the troops would march from their barracks to church, and children and adults from all around would assemble to follow the parade. The troops on the barrack square formed up with the Catholics on the left, C. of E. in the centre and Nonconformists on the right. There was a point to this. As they approached the centre of the town the main column would divide, without so much as breaking step. The Catholics on the left would proceed up Glamorgan Street to the Catholic Church; the Nonconformists on the right would branch up Lion Street to the right, and those in the centre would go through the town to either the parish church of St. Mary or to the cathedral. The C. of E. brigade always retained the band. The return parade was similarly

14

planned so that the three columns would join at the top of what was known as the 'Watton Pitch', where the three roads converged, to march in column down the Watton to their barracks. We children marched with them, swinging our arms and stamping our feet as we mimicked the soldiers.

The nonconformist building boom, which had provided so much opportunity for my grandfather when he first moved to Brecon, was on the decline by the 1930s, by which time the family firm had contributed many public buildings to the old town. One such, the Plough Congregationalist Chapel, its ornate woodwork galleries sculptured in our family workshops is still regarded as one of the finest examples of church joinery in the Principality. The firm also built the Watergate Chapel and Libanus Church and extensive housing in various parts of the town and its environs.

In the 1920s and 1930s the roads were still lit by gas lamps, ignited at dusk by a man wielding a long taper and extinguished by hand at dawn. In my early years there was little traffic on the roads and children, released on completion of their homework, could be seen in the streets playing late into the evenings in relative safety, enjoying home-made toys, bowling old bicycle wheels and tyres as makeshift hoops, or kicking the daylight out of empty cans for want of footballs. I recall when a visit by a local circus had started a craze for walking on stilts, which prompted me to make a pair on which I strode through the town and joined in the street games.

Cars were still relatively uncommon and though tourism was to grow, as cars and buses became more popular in the 1930s, bringing in anglers and hikers to enjoy the countryside, the townsfolk of my childhood did not travel far afield. Journeys to Cardiff and Swansea involved crossing the Beacons and for those few who had cars these were ventures that required some planning and were not lightly undertaken. My journeys through the Brecon Beacons and beyond the Black Mountains to the east were thus infrequent, but whenever I made the crossing I could not fail to notice the sharp visual contrast between the placid necklaces of reservoirs and pine forests that clad the hillsides and the grey depression of the coal mining areas that lay just beyond.

The better-off children in schools in Brecon were frequently reminded of the plight of the less fortunate when their teachers would ask them if their parents could spare any old clothing, or footwear, for others who had none. I remember my brothers coming home from school with such requests, and my mother searching for discarded items, of which there were few, for the art of passing things down in our family was already highly developed. Any contributions, no matter how badly worn, were welcomed by the teachers and distributed to pupils in need. It was not uncommon for tramps to call at the house begging for food and I remember my mother handing them bread crusts that she liberally spread with dripping she kept in a jar in the larder. There were no refrigerators then. And there were times when we children had bread and dripping for supper and vied for the salty meat jelly that settled to the bottom of the jar.

In a town where nothing much seemed to happen, one of the most interesting events was the advent of the Assizes, bringing local miscreants to trial. There was always the chance that someone might be 'up for murde'. We believed – or were we led to believe – that all those sentenced to hang were despatched behind the walls of the local gaol, their bodies being buried in lime. Hangings in earlier times were in public, but the last public hanging at the local gaol, recorded as having been witnessed by some 3,000 people, was in 1861. We were spared such morbid scenes, but few knew what still went on behind those sinister prison walls and this was the stuff that gripped our imagination when we were young.

The quarterly Assizes also served as a timely reminder that crime did not pay. Indeed, as I remember it, crime was rare, though I vividly recall the shock that followed the imprisonment of a local trader caught defrauding the Revenue, especially for me as he had been my tennis partner in a recent match! Crimes of sex and violence were sufficiently rare to be savoured in full when they did occur, but means of communication were not adequate enough to spread news widely and our knowledge of such things was limited. (The Assize Court closed in about 1971, but a complete replica of the court scene has been kept for posterity in the Brecon museum).

My memories of Brecon are, of course, of the 1920s through to the early part of the 1940s. Living there then it was hard to imagine that anything had ever changed. But a report on the Health of Towns published some eighty years earlier by a Dr. Lyon Playfair, a Commissioner appointed by Her Majesty, showed the contrast, and just how much had altered. His report highlighted that:

'Much of the town was subject to severe flooding......A penalty of 2s. is incurred for each pig, by parties permitting swine to wander about in the streets...... A penalty of 20s. may be levied for throwing ashes and filth upon the foot-ways.......The inhabitants are compelled to sweep the footpaths before their houses.....and may have the sweepings as their own property......There are no sewers in the town, with the exception of a small one 2ft. in diameter in Castle Street......The drainage of the town is effected very inefficiently by means of small surface-drains, and many of them are much too small to take the surface-water away during heavy rains........'

'The houses of the middle and upper classes are

17

provided with proper water-closets or necessaries; but for the poorer order one is made to serve for several houses, and these are in many instances placed in exposed situations, in others, close to dwelling houses in confined courts. There are many cottages entirely without such conveniences. The necessaries empty generally into open cesspools, which are cleansed by manual labour, and the contents carted away for manure. The only houses in the town where the necessaries empty into the sewer are situated at the northern end of the Struet and in Berkeley-place and Castle-street, and these sometimes emit offensive smells from the want of being trapped.....A few of the respectable houses have drains communicating with the drains in the streets, but the inhabitants of the cottages almost invariably throw their refuse waters into the streets, more especially those at the lower end of the Struet, Llanfaes, the Watton, and the smaller streets.'

'The Mayor of Brecon, a Mr. Bevan, reported to the Commissioner that 'all the liquid refuse is carried into the sewers and by them into the rivers Usk and Honddu.'

That must have sounded entirely satisfactory at the time.

It would seem from this report that I was indeed fortunate not to have been born just eighty years earlier, and can rejoice in not having shared the doubtful pleasures of using such 'necessaries' or being allowed to share the 'sweepings'. In spite of the legacies of the First World War that influenced my earliest days, my childhood memories are of much happier times.

CHAPTER TWO

TRAGEDY STRIKES

'We participate in a tragedy;
At a comedy we only look.'

The Devils at London.

In my childhood years there was no National Health Service, and all medical care had to be paid for. The reforms introduced in 1909 by Chancellor of the Exchequer, Lloyd George, in what he described as 'The people's budget' had yet to make any serious impact on the poor. There was considerable discussion of such controversial matters as the introduction of a new surtax of 6d. in the £ on those with incomes over £5,000 per annum, and an income tax rate of 9d. in the £. The Beveridge report of 1942, which formed the foundation of the welfare state, lay in the future.

Preventative medicine was in its infancy and infections spread quickly. Measles, mumps, chickenpox and diphtheria were prevalent and could and often did prove fatal. There was rarely a time when one or more of our family was not suffering from some malady and sometimes we were all afflicted at the same time. I remember a period when there were five of us ill in bed, and my mother and our maid had to keep fires going in three or more bedrooms, for this was long before the days of central heating. Coal and logs had to be hauled upstairs to fuel our bedroom fires and whenever a door was opened the down-draught from the chimney would engulf the room with acrid smoke. Fresh air was very much in vogue as the cure for all children's ailments and, whatever the weather, windows had to be kept wide open.

I suffered more from the many childhood illnesses prevalent

at the time than did my siblings, and consequently missed much of my schooling. As I recovered from one indisposition I invariably succumbed to another and the more school lessons I missed the more difficult it became for me to rejoin classes at the appropriate level. This became a vicious circle from which it seemed I could never break free.

Fortunately for me, my sister Winifred, who had taken up teaching, helped me with my schoolwork whenever she was available, and I learned to read and write ahead of my age group. I loved my books and spent many months in bed, while convalescing, reading mainly comics and adventure travel stories, and later, books on other subjects that caught my interest. This developed in me an ability to teach myself, which was to prove my salvation in later life, for having been without tuition for most of my formative years I needed to be self-sufficient. Subsequently, whenever I wanted to learn something, I would seek out the appropriate books or someone who could assist me, and progress to the best of my ability. The only school report I have been able to trace relates to my infancy and records that 'he never wastes a minute'. With my health record it was perhaps not surprising that I always valued my time so highly.

My brothers were more fortunate with their schooling. They all attended Brecon Mount Street Primary School – which was built by my grandfather – and later the Boys' Grammar School, established on Cradoc Road in 1902. The siting of the boys' school on a hill at one end of the town and the girls' school on a hill at the other extreme was surely no coincidence. In those days boys and girls were kept as far apart as possible and there was quite a strong taboo governing every aspect of sexual relationships. It was some years later that the boys' and girls' schools were merged on a new site above the town, where they enjoyed much improved educational and recreational facilities.

As our family grew up, the older ones began to fly the nest and my eldest brother, Trevor, was the first to leave home. At sixteen he went to Newport to learn the trades of carpenter and joiner in readiness to join the family firm. This was typical of the formal training given to those who managed the building industry in those days. He was apprenticed to an elderly joiner who, it later transpired, was suffering from the highly infectious disease, pulmonary tuberculosis (TB). Trevor fell ill after a few years away and returned home having contracted the disease from his mentor. The infection spread quickly through our family.

It was not long before my sister Betty was diagnosed as having it and then Leslie, who was despatched to a sanatorium at Talgarth, some seven miles from Brecon, where he found conditions so intolerable that he discharged himself. When I was just eight years old, having attended school only intermittently for the previous three years, I too caught the disease, as did my brother Mervyn. We spent about a year under treatment by a local doctor before both Mervyn and I were admitted to the King Edward VII sanatorium at Talgarth, where Leslie had been a patient, to rest and, hopefully, to recover. A little later my youngest brother, David, as a preventative measure, was sent to a home in Llandrindod Wells in central Wales.

At that time there were no drugs, and no certain cure, for TB, which was fairly prevalent in South Wales. The only hope lay in rest and fresh air. Wealthier parents sent their children to resorts in Austria or Switzerland, but that was not for us. Each child in the Talgarth sanatorium, where Mervyn and I were patients for nine months, was isolated and confined to bed in a very small cubicle, barely 8 feet x 6 feet. There was no heating and, apart from a few hours schooling each day, we were only allowed to walk to the dining hall for our meals. We were there

21

to rest, and rest. There were few recreational facilities and I could never get enough to read. I remember being desperately lonely and unhappy. We longed for visitors, but with little public or private transport it was not easy for my parents to make the journey from Brecon, except by the occasional district bus. My eldest brother, Trevor, was confined to bed at home by this time, and I remember only a few visits by my mother in all the months I was there – who could blame her, with all she had to contend with at home? – and none by my father who was unwell. On one of her visits she brought news of Trevor's death. The fear of infection kept others away.

Mervyn and I seemed to spend an eternity in those bleak sanatorium conditions. I assumed that we had been sent there to end our days and the news of Trevor's death did little for our morale. Miraculously for us, however, the fresh-air-and-rest cure worked and, in due course, we were sent home to continue our convalescence.

My sister Betty was not so fortunate. After a spell in Craig-y-nos sanatorium she was sent home, as there was little prospect of her regaining her health. I remember lying awake at night when she was ill, listening to her coughing in the next bedroom as she haemorrhaged herself to death She died in 1931, aged just twenty-two. By now Winifred, who had been teaching at a Welsh village primary school, was also stricken, and was admitted to a sanatorium in Denbigh in North Wales. She made no progress and was soon discharged and sent home, where she was confined to her bed with little hope of recovery.

Since we were a reasonably affluent and well cared for family, it was perhaps surprising that we were so hard hit by tuberculosis, but we were by no means the only family to suffer; there were many in similar situations, and the specialist TB doctor's surgery in the town was always crowded.

Through all the family crises, life went on. There were always many mouths to feed and rarely fewer than eleven appetites to satisfy at meal times. There was enough food for those who could afford it but meat was never cheap and poultry was usually only available for special occasions. We ate a lot of rabbit bought from a man who used to call at the house once a week with a pole over his shoulders supporting strings of the animals he had either bred or, more probably, poached. We then had to skin them: they made excellent soups. The younger children usually ate in one room and the adults in another; perhaps this is, in part, why I have so few memories of my father. Swelling the numbers further, we always seemed to have children from a large family of neighbours sitting down to eat with us. In particular two daughters of a local family, whose stepfather worked for the family firm as a plasterer – Betty and Flossie Armstrong – spent a lot of time with us. They substituted as sisters to a large extent, ensuring that we boys did not grow up in a too exclusively male society. Both were vibrant personalities and they greatly enriched our lives. Additionally, members of our extended family – for my mother had five sisters and three brothers, who seemed to reproduce in large numbers – were frequent visitors to our home. I marvel today at the capacity of the housewife and mother in the 1920s and 1930s to feed and nurture progeny in such numbers. Yet I cannot recall my mother ever complaining about anything, whatever burdens were thrust upon her. Just imagine routinely cooking and washing-up after preparing meals for a dozen or more, with none of the facilities that became available to the housewife a few decades later.

Even then, when domestic work was still an acceptable occupation for young people, it was not always easy to get help locally, but we were fortunate in having a living-in maid – a young girl, Anne Gibson, who joined us from Bargoed – one of the valley towns with exceptionally high unemployment. Her younger sister, Maud, later succeeded her. Domestic servants worked incredibly long hours, had little or no time off and were paid a mere pittance. But Anne and Maud were always cheerful and to a large extent they shared their lives with us.

Life in Brecon in my childhood days moved at a leisurely pace. Our lives were punctuated by little more than routine events such as the weekly market days, a focal point in the lives of the local farmers, as were the many taverns. In those days it seemed necessary to have at least one public house per hundred of the population! They were institutions of primary importance to the Welsh people, rivalled only in numbers, if not perhaps in following, by the proliferation of churches and chapels established in all parts of the town.

The main market, held each Friday, was devoted to the sale of farm and home-baked produce in the purpose-built market hall. As a small boy I was overawed by the crush, keeping close into my mother's skirt as she moved from stall to stall buying eggs, butter, fruit and cakes from the farmers' wives, while picking up all the news from the farms around. But much more exciting for me was the Tuesday market for sheep and cattle that had been driven along roads and tracks from farms as much as six miles away, and herded into little pens surrounded by narrow walkways traversed by the auctioneer, whose speed of speech enchanted me. It was on these market days that one was most likely to hear Welsh spoken by farmers and their wives who came into town to sell their produce. Otherwise English was the predominant language, the teaching of Welsh having been discouraged since the reign of Henry VIII, by governments anxious to anglicise Wales. On these two main market days, most people came into the town by pony and trap and every inn offered stabling for horses.

Twice a year a funfair came to Brecon and, occasionally, a

circus. The fair virtually closed off the whole central area of the town, to the chagrin of the shopkeepers. But it was a popular event with young and old alike, and one for which we usually saved up our pennies, and pondered long and hard as to which stalls to patronise, or rides to take, so that we would get the best value for our money.

We also had our own local Eisteddfod (the Welsh festival of arts and music) in the market hall, with poetry, dancing, and singing. As a seven-year-old I remember competing in a maypole dance, and on another occasion offering a recitation. If I ever won a prize, I would surely have remembered it. All I can recall is the distress of a member of our maypole troupe who never failed to confuse clockwise with anti-clockwise, with disastrous consequences for us all. I was not in the least bit musical and, I am ashamed to admit, have no knowledge of the Welsh language. Having to sing the Welsh national anthem, 'Mae Hen Wlad fy Nhadau' (Land of my fathers) in school, always caused acute embarrassment for those monoglots speaking no Welsh. Anything after the first line of the anthem had to be mouthed surreptitiously in the hope that no one would notice!

We used to wander unescorted far into the countryside in search of entertainment or adventure using our feet or bicycles for transport and would think nothing of riding the five miles to Llangorse Lake to bathe or go boating. The lake was about two miles long, a mile wide and deep in parts and one day two friends and I decided to try to swim its length. I remember seeing my two companions and childhood friends, Peter Leonard and Eric Thomas, who were both strong swimmers, disappearing across the water, while I struggled with a limited breast stroke to make any headway. Fortunately for me the place we had chosen for the crossing was shallow enough to enable me to keep at least one toe on the bottom for much of the way. We never gave a thought for our safety and nothing gave rise to the fears that came to haunt parents fifty years on. I don't think ours had any idea where we were much of the time, and can only surmise that they called the roll silently at bedtime.

When not at school we were mostly left to play outside by ourselves. But it must have been bedlam in the house on those many wet days when we could not be outside and we crowded into the family kitchen to keep warm before the great iron range. It would be a travesty to say that our home was ever quiet. Like all large families of that period, long before the advent of television and such distractions, we each had our pets, hobbies and interests. We had cupboards full of board games and playing cards but, to a large extent, we created our own toys and entertainment, and shared to some degree in the domestic chores. There was also some devolution of labour where the older children were assigned roles involving supervision of their younger siblings. On the whole we seem to have been a well-ordered and integrated family, but we were not without our boisterous and cantankerous moments either.

We had no television or radio but these were the pioneering days of 'the wireless' and my eldest brother, Leslie, was adept at constructing primitive radio receivers and adjusting coils that screeched and occasionally emitted an unintelligible signal. When he succeeded in making a set work we crowded round and listened intently for any scraps of news, or to listen to popular music. When he wasn't tinkering with his electronic gadgets, he was practising the piano or experimenting with his chemistry set: he was later to become a pharmacist. Fred was learning to play the violin and we would wait expectantly while he paused to find F sharp – a note that always proved elusive. I accumulated a stamp collection, which, in later years, I passed on to my godchild, Susan, for her 21st birthday. We learned a lot from one another's interests.

We often had relatives staying with us, and very occasionally took holidays with them. But mostly our treats were of a different kind. For us, a special event was something like a trip on the local railway, which played an important role in the economy of the town. It linked Brecon with Newport to the south-east, Aberystwyth in the west, and Builth Wells to the north Another line ran north-east to Hereford, which we considered the gateway to England. An outing for us would be a return journey, costing a few pence, to the next station, Cradoc, just four miles away. The train whistles of arriving and departing steam trains could be heard over much of the town and their time-keeping was highly dependable. Sadly, the local railway service, along with thousands of miles of track throughout the United Kingdom, was axed in the 1960's by Dr. Beeching and, with the closing of the railway some of the character of Brecon changed too.

It was a great thrill for us, and for other children in the neighbourhood, when the family firm acquired its first motor lorry in the early 1930s – a significant advance on the era of the horse and cart. Our prized open vehicle, fitted with temporary bench seats, was soon brought into use at weekends to take us, neighbours included, to the seaside – Porthcawl, Barry Island or the Gower Coast being the most popular resorts. Day trips such as these often substituted for annual holidays. On one of our excursions it rained all day and poured when we reached the sea, but in spite of all the discomfort – not to mention the sand in the sandwiches – we made our own fun and thoroughly enjoyed ourselves. Looking back it seems that society was altogether more contented then than it became half a century later, when thresholds of expectation had risen significantly.

Brecon, like most small Welsh communities at that time, offered a wide choice of local activities, through clubs and societies matching a variety of interests, each with their own devotees, and in most cases having an attachment to one or other of the local churches or chapels. Apart from the women's institutes, scouts, cubs, guides and so on, which have long contributed to the fabric of our society, we had a lively local amateur dramatics group into which I was recruited when I was a teenager. Although I hated it at the time, it probably did me a lot of good as a confidence builder.

In my early days there were no indoor or outdoor swimming pools available to us, and the local children used to bathe and learn to swim in a pool created beside the Brecon promenade on the river Usk. Many of us turned out to watch the opening ceremony for a new pavilion the Borough Council had built near the weir, when the Mayor of Brecon, Cllr. Captain Stanley Francis, emerged from the pavilion wearing, to everyone's surprise, his swimming trunks. We watched as he climbed ceremoniously onto the new high diving board to open the project officially, and dived into the river. When he did not come up immediately it was realised that something was wrong and he was rescued suffering from mild concussion and rushed to hospital, where, fortunately, he made a good recovery. The river was clearly much too shallow at that point for a diving board of that height. This was my first encounter with local government ineptitude. I was to experience much more of it in retirement.

When I was fourteen, my parents gave me a pedigree smooth-haired fox terrier bitch for my birthday. I named her 'Perky' and I remember my surprise when she produced a litter of puppies. My knowledge of sex and reproduction was minimal, and I doubt whether my brothers knew more or even cared; birds and bees and such matters were not even discussed in our family. I raised the puppies and when they were a few months old sold them for a handsome profit. A local grocer friend had docked their tails with his penknife and checked the bleeding with sawdust. Next time we found Perky a more suitable partner and her litter of pedigree pups fetched a much better price! Things were looking up, and my commercial instincts were aroused. Carried away by the success of this enterprise I placed a large advertising board on the wall of the builders' yard, inviting those wanting to buy my puppies to apply to Stanley Jenkins. I had overlooked that this was also my uncle's name and, as a prominent local dignitary, he was not amused and demanded that I take the board down. I began to question whether I was cut out for commerce after all.

Undaunted I then started to keep chickens that I bought from local farmers and transported home in a basket on my bicycle. I used to sell the eggs to my mother to earn a little pocket money, and employed my brothers to clean the hen houses for me. An early diary I kept records that I paid them each 6d. (2.5p) per week! I can still remember the individual hens and their names. The Barred Plymouth Rock was Barrie, the Rhode Island Red was Rosie, and so on, each named after the breed or some other characteristic. Another note in my diary, for May 1937, records that I sold eight fowls to a local farmer for fourteen shillings, realising a profit of two shillings. At this early age these commercial instincts were beginning to look either ominous or promising, whichever way you looked at it. My meagre cash surpluses went mainly to pay for a weekly visit to the 'pictures', or the 'flicks' as we knew them, when I took my mother for just about the only outings she ever had during the course of her weekly toil. Later, my diary records that I was giving up keeping hens, because 'I had insufficient time to care for them properly' – I never seemed to have time for all that I wanted to do, and I clearly was not making an adequate profit on the poultry business!

With all our pets and individual hobbies we learned to share and share alike. If one was ill someone would step into the breach and look after the others' animals, or assume their duties. Large families soon learn that if life is anything it is a medley of compromises.

By the end of 1934 my father was seriously ill with kidney trouble, but he would not go to his doctor. He was a chain smoker and had become a heavy beer drinker by the time he was fifty, both of which would have contributed to his condition. It is doubtful whether his patronage of the national brewing industry was enough to influence share prices, but he did much to sustain them. I often wondered what bearing his health had on his drinking, rather than the other way round. Before his illness he worked hard over long hours in all weathers, getting up early to go out with the timber hauliers to bring the round timber back to the yard, where it would be converted into sawn planks or farm timbers. But on the way home he would be drawn into one, or many, of the twenty or more public houses that lined the streets of Brecon at that time, particularly one of the ten that graced the long road called 'The Watton' – where we lived..........at the very end! He would have argued that this was an essential form of what would be called 'corporate entertainment' today. Many of his farmer customers were notorious for not paying their bills and he would often return home with the satisfaction of having squeezed at least a payment on account out of a long standing debtor.

I was fourteen when, in January 1935, my father, after being bedridden for six months, died of kidney failure. He was 51. My mother was devastated but I cannot remember myself feeling the loss deeply. She still had her large family to care for and there was, initially, some doubt as to whether we would have the financial means to stay in 'Maesllan', the family home. My uncle Stanley turned up trumps with an allowance from the family firm and this sustained us for a number of years in relative comfort, but with little to spare. My father had not been able to save a fortune in his short lifetime, but we each got a small inheritance in a variety of investments that grew over the years to provide us with some security.

In spite of the burdens of her life at home, and as if she had not enough problems of her own, my mother usually found time, when cooking for her family, to make extra bread or cakes, to deliver each week to a few old folk she would support in different parts of the town. As a young lad I accompanied her on a number of these visits and, some fifty years later, when I revisited Brecon, I met a lady who remembered my mother who said to me, 'She was a saint, you know'. I've never doubted it; she certainly had saintly qualities, and her deep Christian faith must have been a considerable strength and solace to her in those hard and troubled times.

My sister, Winifred, died of consumption seven months after her father. In just a few years our large family had suffered the loss of my only two sisters, both vivacious and lovely girls, my eldest brother and my father. While we younger children were sheltered from the suffering of these bereavements to a large extent by our elders we, nonetheless, felt the losses of a brother and two sisters very deeply. My mother was all too aware that funerals, especially when of loved family members, were particularly painful for children and, thankfully, I was not required to share in any of these traumatic experiences. When told of the death of my sister, Winifred, who had been very close to me, I remember being instructed to go and play in the yard, to pray and be good. I was told that 'God moves in mysterious ways, his wonders to perform', but for a grieving child this simply was not good enough: with each loss I felt that another prop had been kicked

31

from beneath the platform of my faith.

That we lived a largely open-air life in an idyllic country atmosphere undoubtedly helped us to leave each of the family tragedies behind. Our little town comprised our whole world and for me, growing up, it was home and I loved it. As George Eliot wrote 'we could never have loved the earth so well, if we had had no childhood in it'.

To us the outside world seemed remote and did not enter our thoughts on a daily basis, but some external events did leave a mark. I distinctly remember the widespread sympathy for the participants in the Jarrow March of 1933, and the excitement of the record-breaking land speed record achieved by Malcolm Campbell at Utah in 1935 (301.7mph.), but we were mainly preoccupied with local news – or scandal – and we made the most of whatever there was of that.

CHAPTER THREE

WELSH TRIALS.... AND TRIBULATIONS

'One religion is as true as another'

Burton.

In my formative years the society in which we lived was largely dominated by our elders and was much more rigidly structured than it is today. Our family life was, as were the lives of those living throughout most of Wales, particularly in the Welsh speaking areas, greatly influenced by the churches and chapels and all they represented. In matters of ethics, morality and social behaviour, religion provided much more than a framework. A consequence of this was that there was often tension and friction between the different religious factions and between their respective devotees. The affiliation of each family played a significant part in determining the relationships of everyone in the community. Brecon, as I remember it, was essentially parochial. Even marriage outside one's own religious sect was a matter for comment and, for the families involved, concern. I can still hear my protestant aunt saying of an acquaintance 'He's been going out with a Catholic girl you know'. Such a remark would draw a gasp.

As a child, growing up in this environment, I always had a keen sense of being supervised – watched by someone for most of the time. Word travelled fast. To be seen by an aunt talking to a girl would be news likely to reach home, with overtones, long before I did, even if, as was probably the case, I was arranging nothing more significant than a game of tennis. What people thought of us was of primary importance and this probably made us unduly concerned about our own image. It seemed impossible to do anything without being seen and reported on, and none of us would have wanted to incur the

33

slightest criticism. This was a feature of society that undoubtedly played a key role in ensuring that individuals toed the line and observed at least the principal conventions. Apart from a brief courtship of my elder sister by a Franciscan monk, whom I remember pursuing her around the carpenters' shop, I cannot recall any other member of our family risking the gossip that would have attended even a potential attachment to a member of the other sex. But perhaps there were, indeed there must have been, 'goings-on' of which I was unaware.

Over the years we built up a strong family association with our parish church of St. Mary, where we were all christened and later confirmed. If my mother could leave her chores at home on a Sunday we were taken there for the morning or evening service and it was not surprising that we all adopted our mother's faith without question. The family firm did all the necessary building and maintenance work on the church and on the cathedral for a number of generations. My maiden aunt Gwladys, a staunch member of the church, is suitably commemorated in St. Mary's by an oak choir stall screen and my grandfather by a finely carved altar rail in the side aisle.

But we relied heavily on the chapels, most of which had an annual calendar of musical events, for much of our externally generated entertainment. The Welsh have long been a nation of religious dissenters and it was probably their religion that inspired their music and especially their love of singing. Periodically choirs and orchestras brought the town to life. The Plough Congregational Chapel was a regular home for impressive musical productions and their Easter performance of Handel's Messiah, with leading guest soloists and a massive local choir, could be relied upon to fill the chapel to the back balcony seat.

While my father's life had been devoted to his work, civic

duties had fallen in plenty to my uncle Stanley, his business partner, who was active in many local organisations. He was a pillar of rectitude and respectability in our little town, something of which we were reminded whenever we did anything wrong. When chairman of the local Chamber of Trade, he played a leading part in the introduction of electricity to Brecon. In 1924 he sent a circular letter to members of the Chamber inviting their views on the provision of a municipal supply. In spite of a strong objection from the local gas company, of which he was a director, and another from a tradesman who had already installed a generator and was supplying a few shops and businesses, the Borough Council agreed to the measures proposed by the Chamber. Until we had electricity we managed with gas lamps, which we lit with matches or tapers. Electricity was a great novelty at first and a vast improvement on the fragile gas mantles we had known. By the time I was about ten years old we had electric light in the streets and in many houses. We had the telephone installed in our office and in our house some years later.

After serving as a borough councillor (and later alderman) for many years, my uncle was Mayor of Brecon in 1937, the Coronation year of King George VI. He and my aunt were both presented to their majesties at the City Hall, Cardiff. The event was celebrated locally with a drumhead service in the army barracks in the morning, a gymnastic display on the playing fields of Christ's College in the afternoon, followed by tea and a dance in the cattle market, concluding with fireworks on the Promenade in the evening. There were also street parties in abundance. In our small community these were exciting events, and we would have been loath to miss any of them.

At the time when we each approached the age when decisions about careers had to be made, there still widespread unemployment throughout Wales, and I recall the consternation and discussion within the extended family about what each of us could or should do for a living. Progress through the teenage years seemed to have been punctuated with youthful notions of sensation and sensuality rather than the hard realities of life, but after my father's death, with no other breadwinner in the family, it was time for hard choices. Further progress now depended on we children finding employment.

On leaving school my eldest brother Leslie had begun an apprenticeship with a local pharmacist, but was not paid during those years and had nothing to contribute financially to support the family. My brother, Harry, felt that he could no longer be a burden on the home and one day, as a teenager, he crossed the road to the army barracks and joined the Royal Corps of Signals, without telling anyone until after the event. He sailed for India in 1937, and we were not to see him again for seven years. On leaving school, Mervyn joined the family firm, while Fred decided to make a career in the Royal Air Force and joined as an apprentice.

As I moved into my late teens I began to appreciate the consequences of having had so little formal schooling, no more than a few years in all, and that in intermittent periods. To make good some of my missed education, my father's sister Gwladys, herself a teacher at a local primary school, had volunteered to contribute five shillings a week, which she paid to a colleague, Victor Jones, to tutor me for two hours a week. He encouraged me to study on my own and later taught me to drive a car and to learn shorthand and typing. I remain to this day grateful to him for the latter in particular. I soon became a proficient touch-typist; a skill that was to serve me well throughout my life, especially when, in later years, I had to draft reports and despatches, often working against the clock. While other office colleagues dictated and waited for their scribbles to be typed, my drafts were ready as they emerged from my machine. This facility with a typewriter was to prove as significant for me as the later advent of the word-processor to the world at large.

I used to wonder what would become of me. In spite of my tutor's efforts I had lost ground and felt ill qualified for anything. Moreover, I was physically in poor shape. While pondering my future, my uncle Stanley found me a post locally with the Borough Surveyor, Hugh Llewelyn Griffiths, an old friend of his, and I stayed in that job from 1935 until the war began in 1939. My employer was made an allowance of £50 per annum by the Brecon Borough Council to employ an assistant, and this was my total remuneration over the next three years. I was not paid for my two weeks holiday, because the allowance he got was £50 not £52, but I felt lucky to get even that. I was fortunate in that he took a paternal interest in me and gave me every encouragement and guidance. I owe him a great deal, not least for stimulating my love of grass-court tennis. He had one of the first privately owned grass courts I had seen, and to be asked to play on it was a very special treat, in spite of its undulating surface. I vowed to have one of my own – a level one - some day.

On leaving school, my youngest brother, David, took an appointment with the National Provincial Bank in Hay, and moved away from home. It was then, with most of my brothers gone, that I began to feel particularly responsible for my mother. She was lost without her large family and began to lead a less hectic life at home while still caring for others in need. My earnings left me with little more than enough to pay for our weekly visit to the local cinema – the highlight of my week – to see the great and mostly romantic films of that period: 'The Lives of a Bengal Lancer', 'Everything's in Rhythm', 'Rose Marie', 'East Meets West' and 'The Girl Friend'. Those evenings, in the cosy atmosphere of the cinema, were moments of sheer escapism and what pleasure they gave.

In the summer months my friends and I walked in the mountains and played tennis at our local club. I remember how carefree we felt. On long walks in the countryside and the Beacons we wandered for miles, stuffing ourselves with hazelnuts and blackberries, that grew everywhere in profusion, and sometimes raiding apple or pear orchards to pack our saddlebags with forbidden fruit.

The Brecon Sports Club became the centre of my teenage existence. As secretary of the tennis section, I spent many happy days organising games and playing matches against other clubs. We undertook most of the grass court maintenance ourselves, or rather, some of us did. As always there were a few workers and those who expected everything to be done for them. I have special reason for remembering those days at the club, if only because of my falling from the pavilion roof when painting it one summer afternoon – I was always a 'hands-on' man! Each Saturday we enjoyed playing or watching tennis, cricket and bowls matches and I have the fondest memories of delicious teas organised by the ladies who seemed to vie with each other to produce the best sandwiches, cakes and scones. In retrospect, the sun always seemed to shine.

In 1937, I made my first trip to the lawn tennis championships at Wimbledon. My brother Mervyn and I had just bought our first car – a tiny Austin Swallow with a dicky seat at the rear – for the princely sum of £25, but we were dissuaded from taking it on the long journey to London and went instead with a local grocer, Mr. Hogarth, whose vehicle was considered more likely to make the journey there and back. Arriving at Wimbledon at around midnight on the last Friday of the tournament, we queued for twelve hours before the gates were opened to allow us to rush to the centre court and secure a place in the standing room area. Play began at 2 p.m. and we stood until play ended as the light failed at about 9 p.m., when we began the long drive home. No sporting occasion has ever impressed me so much as the atmosphere and play on that day. We saw Donald Budge at the peak of his career. On the same day he won first the men's singles final when he beat the German, Baron Gottfried von Cramm 6-3, 6-4, 6-2, followed by the mens' doubles final, and lastly the mixed doubles final; the first time this 'triple' had ever been achieved. We also saw Dorothy Little (Round) winning the ladies' singles final against the Polish player Miss J Jedzejowksa. Since that time, whenever I have been in England during the Wimbledon fortnight, I have done my best, and usually managed to get there somehow.

We considered ourselves a middle-class family, and in Brecon at that time, class was all pervading. This was highlighted for me by the existence of another tennis club in the town called 'The County Club'. As the name implied, this was exclusively for those who were categorised in some mysterious way as 'county people', i.e. the upper classes. It was not easy in those days to cross the social barriers. Absurd as it now seems, our tennis fixture list at the Brecon Sports Club did not include matches with this other club because of the class divide. Both clubs were closed on a Sunday, which was considered a special day, quite different from the rest of the week. Our parents were not over-strict about this, and we were allowed to play in our yard and even to play cards on the Sabbath.

My great passion as a teenager, however, was table tennis; I loved the game as it was then played. There were about a dozen table tennis clubs in our little town, each linked with one or other of the many churches or chapels, all of which competed in a lively Churches' Table Tennis League, of which, for three years, I was the champion singles player and secretary. We had the use of church halls for so many nights a week, and there was usually one where we could get a game. Competition between the clubs was fierce. In part, this was based on the inherent conflict between the diverse religious sects, and in part it had its roots in local bigotry. On one occasion our Church of England vicar protested to my parents because I, one of the leading local players, was playing for the Plough Congregational Chapel's team! My mother dealt with him robustly. Similar narrow perspectives were exemplified by the attitude of local people to one club where I played, the 42nd Club, which had the best players and table, but was owned by a local publican and the premises where we played were at the rear of his public house. Being attached to anything other than a church or chapel meant that the club was not eligible to join the local Churches' League, and this presented a moral dilemma of some magnitude for the parents of the players. Mine, fortunately, took a tolerant stance, and allowed me to play there, but the narrow outlook of a few parents excluded some of the players.

Playing for the 42nd Club I competed against a number of clubs throughout the Welsh valleys in a District League and my standard of play improved immeasurably as a result. After a long evening drive over the Beacons we would frequently find ourselves searching in some run-down area for the miners' hall where our match was to be played, and then playing in dimly-lit, smoke-filled rooms crowded with spectators cheering on their home side, playing darts or drinking quietly in a corner.

One of my treasured memories of those years was a trip I made to Cardiff in 1937 to see an exhibition played by the three top table tennis players in the world, including Victor Barna the reigning and five times world champion. We sat there, open-mouthed, having witnessed nothing like it before.

Today young people can see and learn from experienced players in any sport, by watching them live or on television. We had none of those advantages. The journey from Brecon over the Beacons to either Newport or Cardiff was an adventure in itself: to watch players exercising such skill and dexterity left us spellbound and the effect on our own game was dramatic. From then on we were streets ahead of contemporaries who had not had the privilege of seeing the game played at that level.

My Welsh league play culminated in an invitation to play in the trials for the Welsh team. As my car was not reliable enough to traverse the Beacons I was entirely dependent on friends for getting to the event, in particular Messrs. Jones, (my tutor), and Hill, (the local greengrocer), both of whom had cars. This fell to Victor Jones and, as so often happened in those days, his car broke down crossing the Beacons and we arrived in Cardiff when the event was almost over. I think I played only one match, but the door was now ajar and, had it not been for the war, I had high hopes that I might well have got my 'cap' the following year. Sadly, the war put paid to that, and many of my, and millions of others', dreams.

Another highlight of my table tennis days was the draw for the Welsh Open Championships held in Cardiff in 1938. In the first round I actually drew my hero, Victor Barna. My excitement knew no bounds. I still have the printed draw showing me through to the second round. Although this looks impressive, it actually resulted from Barna withdrawing, after damaging a finger in the railway carriage door on his journey to Wales. In the next round I fell to Eric Bubley, the reigning English champion. I had had my day, but my ambitions remained intact – after all Fred Perry had gone on from world table tennis champion to Wimbledon champion. It was a long shot, but there was still hope! It is good for the young to dream

41

and I had many such dreams. At another exhibition in Cardiff in 1938, I saw the world table tennis champion Vana, and at Swansea in 1939 the tennis players whose names were to become legends of the game: Budge, Vines, Tilden and Stoefen, playing an exhibition at the St. Helens Ground.

With the net 6¾ inches high, table tennis was much more of a spectator sport than it became when the net was lowered to 6 ins. In the days when I played, it was usual for one player to be at the table driving the ball, while the opponent stood well back, returning the ball almost from floor level. It was then a great game to play and a joy to watch. By comparison the modern game leaves me cold.

In May 1937, my mother's parents celebrated their diamond wedding in Chippenham, Wiltshire and my mother, brothers and I motored there from Brecon for what was a remarkable family occasion, if only because all my grandparents' 9 children and 26 out of 28 surviving grandchildren were present.

Perhaps, surprisingly, against a background of illness and family tragedy, I recall my teenage years as a happy time. We youngsters had little chance to compare our lot with that of others, and in our childhood setting we thought of ourselves as better off than most. Like all large families we attracted many friends of all ages. (It was years later when I regaled the girlfriend who was to become my wife, about the advantages of large families and how sorry I felt for the single child, that she revealed to me that she was one). We children made our own amusements and, in the bosom of a large family, we felt secure. It is said that individual characters are rooted somewhere in the soil of childhood: I am especially conscious of the part my upbringing played in my personal development.

By 1939, my hometown, unlike many of the towns in the

neighbouring mining valleys, had largely recovered from the trauma of the First World War, the rural economy had picked up and much had been done to improve the nation's health There were fewer unemployed, the standard of living for most people was rising, and they generally felt better off than at any time during the preceding twenty years.

But by this time Germany was mobilising her armed forces and threatening and subjugating her neighbours in Europe: the danger of another conflict loomed larger by the hour. The years 1920 to 1939 that spanned my childhood and youth were, as it turned out, but a brief respite between two major world wars that were to change the course of history.

CHAPTER FOUR

DIG FOR VICTORY

'An army is a nation
Within a nation.'

Alfred de Vizany.

A s a family of young men, all of military age, we lived in an atmosphere of bewilderment and foreboding as the Second World War grew closer. The inexorable drift towards another conflict seemed incomprehensible to us, and we prayed that it could somehow be averted. We also knew that the nation was by no means ready for another confrontation with Germany and were aware that, if war came, we were all bound to be involved. Reminders of World War I – men who had lost limbs and sight – were still sufficiently present, even in a town as small and isolated as Brecon. These were anxious days and there was nothing we could do to influence events.

Our apprehension was worsened because we had little news or interpretation of what was going on elsewhere in the world. Rumours about the invincibility of the German air force, the Luftwaffe, fanned by the Spanish Civil War, were frightening enough, as were the newsreels showing in our local cinema, of the Japanese invasion of China. I cannot remember our family having newspapers, and if they did, none of us read much about the world at large. Anyway, table tennis was, for me, a more tangible option and I remained heavily involved with that.

In the summer of 1939 I had again been ill, this time with a persistent middle ear infection, which led to a minor operation on my left eardrum. As soon as I was well enough, in late August 1939, my mother took my brother David and me to

Weston-Super-Mare for a holiday, but within days of our arrival my uncle telephoned in alarm from home to advise us to return immediately, as war seemed imminent. We sacrificed our holiday, went home and I returned to work. We did not have long to wait.

On that fateful day, Sunday, 3rd September 1939, normally a rest day, I was working in the Borough Surveyor's office in Brecon when the telephone rang and the clerk to the council invited me to join him in his office in the town hall, to hear a broadcast by Prime Minister Neville Chamberlain. All the council staff were at their posts that day making last minute preparations for what we feared inevitable, in spite of assurances of 'peace in our time' which Chamberlain had recently given to the nation on his return from talks with the German Chancellor, Hitler, in Munich. We crowded expectantly into the clerk's office to hear the broadcast by the prime minister announcing that we were at war with Germany. I was eighteen and, health permitting, likely to be called to the colours in the first round of military conscription. There was a lot of speculation as to how long we would have before our call-up papers landed on the mat.

Advice had already been given in newspapers, and on the radio, about air raid precautions, and after organising the blackout of all our windows we started constructing bunks in our cellars and erecting timber props to prevent the roof from collapsing on top of us if ever we had to sleep there. We gave little thought to the prospect of our cellars flooding, as we knew they sometimes did.

Although my mother, with memories of her brothers' involvement in the Boer War and World War I, was distraught when war was declared, she remained as stoic as ever as she faced the prospect of seeing her last four boys called up. Harry and Fred were already in the armed forces in India.

We began to speculate as to what our respective roles in the war would be. Britain at that time had the largest merchant shipping fleet in the world and the largest and most powerful navy. Thus, it was not unnatural that many young men still sought careers at sea, but none of our family felt attracted to the navy. I was no hero and had little stomach for war. I also doubted whether I would ever pass a medical examination for the armed forces, and that would have meant my staying at home for the duration, and I did not relish that prospect either.

As we waited, my brothers and I felt we were doing something useful by joining the Dig-for-Victory campaign, a national drive to encourage everyone to plough up any vacant land and maximise food production. We had a large garden and turned our hands to growing vegetables – with increasing raids on the stable manure-heap and the lime shed – as we strove to improve the fertility of the soil, following the instructions of that early radio gardener, Mr. Middleton. Without many books on gardening we relied heavily on our radio guru and before long were growing a full range of produce that made a useful supplement to the food rationing that had been introduced.

It was a busy time for everyone and especially for the family firm and trade boomed. Not only were there more army contracts to fulfil than ever before, but building materials were scarce as preparations for war were intensified. Patriotism abounded and only the 'spivs' gave any thought to exploiting the situation for financial gain, though there were copious opportunities for black marketeering for the unpatriotic.

Leslie, the eldest of my brothers, was the first to be called up, but he failed his medical because of a minor heart problem, and continued to practice as a pharmacist in London. Mervyn enlisted soon after the outbreak of war in 1939 and David would join up in 1942, on coming of age. For my part, it was decided – I had little say in such matters – that I should leave the Borough Surveyor's office and replace Mervyn in the family firm, which I duly did. I soon became engrossed in contract work for the Ministry of War, work that included army camp construction at Derring Lines, Brecon, and at Sennybridge and Crickhowell. These were important army camps and they played a major role in the training of British troops. Consequently their construction and maintenance was considered vital war-work and, when the postman brought my first call-up notice in 1940, my uncle contested it on the grounds that he could not carry on his army contract work without my assistance. I was duly accorded deferment, but for only a month at a time.

The spirit of euphoria resulting from the salvation in 1940 of the remnants of the defeated British expeditionary force – some 334,000 men – from the beaches of Dunkirk, by a flotilla of 800 little craft, swept through the nation and welded it together to an astonishing degree. There was certainly no anti-war faction then as there was at the time of the Falklands War some forty years on, and the later intervention in the Balkans. The British had their backs to the wall and, to a man, knew the dangers they faced. Dunkirk was especially vivid for me because my brother Mervyn was one of those safely evacuated.

Soon afterwards the Local Defence Volunteer Force (LDV) was formed; it soon changed its name to the Home Guard. This was a volunteer civilian force, created from those not already conscripted, to augment the armed services and strengthen national defences. There was a rush to join. Initially we had no uniforms, turning up for drill dressed in whatever we had – an incongruous group of 'civvies' with only our LDV armbands and boxed gas masks for uniform. For months we had no weapons, and it was hilarious to see men of all ages lined up for drill, carrying broomstick handles as substitutes for rifles. Our sergeant-major, Joe Pallardy, a tall and forbidding character with a typical sergeant major's bark, was an experienced soldier from the First World War who completely matched the caricature for the part. The more he shouted at us the more we laughed quietly to ourselves. There is, after all, something bizarre about presenting arms with a mop handle. We had little perception of the reality of war, but, nevertheless, were very serious about it, for the threat of invasion was real enough. The Home Guard has since been immortalised in the BBC's series 'Dad's Army'. Our 'preview' of the civilian army was every bit as comical.

Home Guard training taught us little more than the basic elements of infantry weaponry and drill, but participating made us feel better about staying at home, when all the able-bodied had already left. When uniforms became available we had time to get used to them gradually. But how very uncomfortable they were and how I hated those shirts. We were taken on map reading and other navigational exercises in a landscape shorn of any road signs or finger posts: they had all been removed, so as to confuse any invading force. One exercise, when a visiting company of Indian infantrymen were billeted in a local mansion on the south side of the River Usk, involved me being sent as a lookout to give advance warning of any approaching enemy. I had recently seen the film 'The Four Feathers' so I disguised myself as a Sikh and hid in a tree overlooking the town. The whole exercise well illustrates how unrealistic our approach to war was at that time. I was to signal across the river, by means of a mirror, to warn of any enemy approach, but all day the sun stayed behind the clouds and I saw nothing of the adversary. When evening came, I still clutched my dubious warning device and, getting colder and hungrier as I clung to my perch, I kept very quiet when a young couple settled down in the grass below me: the appearance of a Sikh up the tree might have alarmed them! But, as a loyal member of the Home Guard with the safety of my hometown in my hands, it was not for me to desert my post. It was dark when my platoon commander, having a pint in his local, remembered his lookout and sent someone to call me in. Fortunately the threat to the town never came nearer in reality.

The family firm was exceptionally busy in the early part of the war fulfilling military contracts, but it suffered from the loss of workmen, especially the craftsmen, as they were called to the colours. I found myself working long hours on campsites by day and on paperwork during the evenings. We had a decidedly dingy Victorian office and I resolved to do something to bring it into the twentieth century. But I knew there was likely to be opposition to any change from my uncle, who was a man of few words – an economy born of a hatred of waste – and decidedly set in his ways. His idea of a conversation was a nod or a reluctant smile. I was somewhat apprehensive when I decided, without telling him, to make a gesture towards modernisation by dispensing with the high double-sided desk and stools on which he and the former clerk, Lewis Lewis, had perched, facing one another for much of their working lives. I decided to make a modern oak desk for my uncle and a similar one for myself, and to move them into place one day when he was away. To suggest such a change would certainly have been met with a refusal and comment 'Oh I think it's fine as it is, leave well alone boy'. He always addressed me thus, as perhaps his father had him. I went ahead, however, and made the desks. We were all versatile with our hands having imbibed many skills as we watched craftsmen at work in their various trades in the yard. When all was ready I took a saw to the old office desk, sliced it into small pieces and hauled it out of the room.

My polished new oak desks, with dovetailed drawers and leather-inlaid tops, were in place when my uncle arrived the next morning. I elected to keep a safe distance, and saw him park his car, walk into the office and, after a moment come out, get back into his car and drive home. I feared the worst. However, he returned after talking to my aunt, who must have calmed him down, for he went into the office, sat down at his new desk and carried on as though nothing had happened. He never mentioned the change to me then or later, and to this day I do not know how he felt about it, but he never could get his long legs under that little desk.

As conscription to the armed forces bit deeper, there was an acute shortage of manpower, especially on the land. Large numbers of women were encouraged to join the Women's Land Army to mitigate this problem and as they arrived in Brecon they were assigned to neighbouring farms. Their arrival highlighted the shortfall in the male population, and put fresh and sometimes welcome demands on the young males who had not yet enlisted, but I was not interested and far too busy to become involved.

My mother's father, who had been the head postmaster of Brecon at the outbreak of the First World War, was by now in retirement living with my grandmother in Chippenham, Wiltshire. They were both in their mid-eighties and though my grandfather retained all his faculties, my grandmother was extremely deaf and almost blind. They could not go on living by themselves, and so my mother brought them to live with us at 'Maesllan' in 1941. At the same time, with the prospect of even heavier bombing of London and other cities, the government had started to evacuate children to safer places in the country. Although we had already decided to have the grandparents to live with us we still had space for evacuees and just before the old folk arrived, we were required to take in a family from Liverpool, a city suffering from heavy bombing. This was compulsory billeting and we did what we were told. A young mother and two small children duly arrived and we made them welcome, giving them a large room of their own to share. It seems my mother was destined to carry far more than a fair share of life's burdens.

This was the first time our evacuee family had lived outside a city and they found the quiet of the countryside almost terrifying. It was certainly not to their liking and within a week they had packed their bags and made their way back to face the nightly air raids; the relief for us was welcome. But three unaccompanied little girls soon replaced them. The father of one was a radio operator in the merchant marine and he was glad, on his few hours of leave, to enjoy the peace of the countryside. On one of his rare visits he brought his daughter a chameleon, which we let make its home on the wash drying-frame hanging from the kitchen ceiling. It thrived on flies that seemed to be with us throughout the year. The father of the other two was a typical London 'spiv' who came to Brecon on occasional weekends, partly to see his family but mainly, we thought, to see what he could buy cheaply to sell in London. I had grown a bed of prize onions that he tried to buy from me: he would have found a ready market for anything like that in the city where rationing cut more deeply than in the countryside.

The austerity of war taught us to economise on everything. We saved tiny scraps of soap, crushed them together, and reused them in small wire holders; the ends of loaves were used to make bread and butter puddings; we learned to turn off taps when not in use, though there was never any shortage of water. Nothing was left to waste. We were taught, in the words of Dr. Johnson, that 'without frugality none can be rich, and with it very few would be poor'. Habits learned then, like turning off lights whenever I left a room, boiling only the amount of water required and never washing under a running tap, stayed with me, and would often amuse our children, until years later, when such 'economies' assumed a new significance in terms of conserving natural resources.

In 1940 I was still having intermittent health problems, and when suffering from a persistent ear infection, was sent to see a consultant in Swansea. I travelled by train, not knowing, until I approached my destination that, on the previous night, the German Luftwaffe had dropped tons of bombs on the city. As we drew near I saw huge fires and clouds of smoke engulfing the whole area. The train stopped short of the devastated town and was turned back. It is hard to describe what a great city looks like, enveloped in flames and smoke, just hours after an air raid of that magnitude. The attack, of which I saw only the immediate aftermath, had been preceded a few weeks earlier by raids on three consecutive nights. Swansea had a small dock area but it was never clear why it was singled out for such a ferocious blitz. Whatever the reason, the city paid a terrible price.

The deferment of my call-up was repeated monthly for a year. When it seemed that postponement was unlikely to be extended, the District RE Chief Engineer intervened, and claimed that he too would be in difficulty if I left. He proposed an ingenious plan to make me a Royal Engineers' civilian staff member, in which capacity I continued to work for both my uncle and the Royal Engineers simultaneously, an arrangement that lasted until I was called up in April 1942 to, perversely, not the Royal Engineers, but to the Army School of Artillery, at Larkhill in Wiltshire.

Playing so much table tennis during the period while my military service was deferred had made an astonishing difference to my physique and general health and, to everyone's surprise, when I attended my medical board the army gave me an A1 rating. (Many of us thought that to be able to stand erect was sufficient to be cleared for enlistment!). I was now to train as a soldier and this was not a prospect I savoured, though being of military age, and not in the forces, was not made pleasant either. The nation expected young men to be in one of the services and those deemed to be malingerers, however unjustified, were subject to taunts; some even had white feathers pinned to them. Because of my deferments, by the time I left home, I was one of very few of my age to be seen out of uniform.

One of my few companions at that time was a young man of my age, Albert Fensome, with whom I spent many of my leisure hours. Together we explored every mile of the Brecon Beacons, played tennis and, for a time, attended ballroom dancing classes. He had failed his medical for the armed forces and, sadly, died at an early age.

The life I had lived in Brecon – a somewhat closeted family existence – had ill-prepared me for the outside world, while poor health for most of my childhood and a chequered education had left me decidedly insecure and lacking in self-confidence. It was thus not surprising that I approached the next phase of my life with apprehension.

Brecon Town Centre c. 1900

The family firm – 1920 Letterhead

The whole family picnic at Barry Island 1928

Back row: Mother, Father, Leslie. Middle: Betty, Harry, Winifred, Trevor, David. Front: Fred, Stanley, Mervyn

A day by the sea
Porthcawl – 1934

In the builders yard with
my little dog Perky

The Mayor, my uncle Stanley, with the cup he presented to the 42nd Club table tennis team – 1937. Self on his left

So Much To Do
So Little Time

. . . .

Part II

We're In The Army Now

CHAPTER FIVE

SQUAD 'SHUN

'Boots-boots-boots-boots,
Marching up and down again.'

Rudyard Kipling.

The hutted camp at the Royal Artillery School in Larkhill on Salisbury Plain, where I first reported for army service in April 1942, was a bleak place with very few comforts. We were twenty-four men to a hut, sleeping in wooden double bunks, sharing toilets and washing facilities housed in ablution blocks some fifty yards from where we slept. I think we all felt the lack of privacy in varying degrees. The little heating there was came from circular iron stoves fuelled by wood and coke, which belched as much smoke into the room where we slept as up the chimneys, and my 'oppos' smoked as much as the chimney itself. I seemed to be one of very few non-smokers and the atmosphere was sometimes suffocating. But nothing would have stopped me sleeping soundly under the training regime that was about to commence.

We must have looked a ragged bunch of reluctant mortals when we first assembled on the tarmacadam drill-square where we were to spend many gruelling hours over the next six months. We were something of the tail-end of the conscription drive, with a high proportion of the 35-45 age group, and I was the youngest of the intake. For the first time I found myself addressed variously as 'a shower', 'a shambles' or 'a rotten lot'. Under the watchful eye of a sympathetic and kindly sergeant Simms, we trained and drilled for hours and attended innumerable lectures, to become soldiers and gunner surveyors. Some of us had undergone a brief training of sorts in the Home Guard, but for most there was still much to learn about weapons and military ways. In a short time we had to be turned from raw civilians into soldiers, and there was no time to lose.

I found the routine and physical aspects of army life particularly arduous at first and generally disagreeable, but soon became reconciled to getting up at crack of dawn and making my way, whatever the weather, to the washrooms and mess huts; and to shaving in cold or tepid water. Army boots tormented my feet and my skin never fully adjusted to the coarse fabrics from which our clothing was made. The evenings were long and lighting in the huts was never good for reading. We had little to cheer us except for those invaluable individuals who come into their own on these occasions, men with a quick wit, the natural comedians, the musicians and other born entertainers. I envied those with such talents, and wished I had something to contribute. When off duty I, and my fellow rookies, used to find refuge in the Women's Voluntary Service and YMCA canteens where we would listen to Vera Lynn and her sentimental songs or to Arthur Askey's and George Formby's comedy on radio. There was little else.

The technical survey training was interesting enough combining a study of orography and the solar system and we spent hours at night on Salisbury Plain, trying to recognise stars and identify constellations, measuring their altitudes, determining their orientation and working out gun-bearings and distances. As this was long before pocket calculators or computers, we wrestled and calculated with cumbersome six-figure logarithm tables. Fortunately, I was quick with figures and had no difficulty with any of that, except that my knowledge of mathematics was really not up to scratch, and I worried about the examinations pending at the end of the course. I remember borrowing books on arithmetic and geometry and sitting within the circle of Stonehenge stones trying to understand what our instructors had been attempting to teach us, while wondering who first studied trigonometry on that historic site.

Throughout this early period of my army days I had the invaluable friendship and support of a few fellow recruits, one in particular, Reggie Underwood, whom I had met on the train coming to Larkhill, and who enlisted on the same day. He was some ten years my senior and a man with deep religious conviction, eternal optimism and an enviable sense of humour. He became something of a father figure to me, or perhaps more accurately, a substitute elder brother, who remained a good friend for life. (It was a sad occasion for me to attend his funeral some fifty years later.)

As far as keeping abreast of world events was concerned, Larkhill was not dissimilar to my early days in Brecon. We had little news of what was going on in the war, of which we now felt very much a part. We had no access to radio and saw no newspapers, apart from any we could grab in our mess room or read in the civilian canteens we visited when off duty. This was probably just as well, for from what we did hear we appeared to be suffering setbacks on every battlefront. Only in the sky over Britain did we see anything of the action, and even there our prospects did not seem good. Each night we heard the throbbing of enemy aircraft passing overhead, carrying devastation to another of our cities. The armies of our allies in Europe had failed to stop the Axis powers. How could we succeed?

It was not long before we tired of training, much of which seemed repetitive, pointless and tedious, while the ambivalence of many aspects of army life often confused and irritated us. In spite of that we maintained what, on the evidence available to us at the time, seemed totally unjustifiable optimism. Yet not one amongst us ever believed in our heart of hearts that we would lose the war: perhaps that was too awful an outcome to contemplate. The uplift provided by our victory at Alamein in 1942 did much to boost our morale and we clung to the hope, held out by Prime Minister Winston Churchill, in his many inspirational speeches, that we would eventually triumph. He galvanised the nation, rekindled our resolve and infused into the hearts of all those who heard him the will to fight on. For young soldiers this was a testing time, but the spirit of comrades-in-arms is very real and it sustained us.

Some six months after my call-up I heard that my mother was ill, but news was scarce and the life of a trainee soldier left little time for worrying. Then my mother's youngest brother, Jack Edwards, a Lt. Commander RN, telephoned my unit seeking permission to pick me up to visit her in hospital in Oxford. Only when we arrived did I learn how serious her condition was. She had developed a brain tumour and was dying. We paid a brief visit to her in hospital but she did not recognise either of us, and soon afterwards she was returned to Brecon where she died a few days later, aged 58. She was buried at Brecon cemetery in the family grave where her husband and three children had earlier been laid to rest. I was given two days leave to attend the funeral and was utterly devastated: it seemed then that my last link with home had gone. My brothers were scattered around the world and, for the moment I had lost contact with them. My mother had been the central pillar of my life and pivotal to our family, and I thought it very sad that she had died so young and that none of her children had been with her at the end.

It was perhaps only now that I realised the extent of the burden my parents, particularly my mother, must have carried. I wondered how she must have felt as her sons were called up and left home. My lifelong regret is that she did not live to enjoy whatever her many children might, in later life, have been able to do for her. It seemed to me that she had borne the entire load and reaped none of the reward. Another plank of my faith was kicked away on that very sad day. When I returned to Larkhill I felt totally dejected, but my good friend Reggie Underwood proved a tower of strength, raised my spirits and helped me through the traumatic weeks and months ahead.

Back in camp I resumed and completed my RA surveyor training, but just when I was relishing my new-found health and the prospect of leaving the harsh training regime behind, I felt ill and attended a sick parade. Attending these parades was an ordeal: it seemed as though they were calculated to deter the malingerer rather than treat the sick. We were required to queue before breakfast often in a cold room until the doctor could see us, whatever state we were in, and we used to say that to report sick was sufficient of itself to ensure a medical condition. I was admitted to hospital in Salisbury with bronchitis.

After a few weeks I was allowed out to wander in the city streets while convalescing; my hospital blue uniform, mandatory for patients, worked miracles and brought out the very best in the British people. I spent hours in canteens – there was nowhere else to go to keep warm – and rarely had to pay for anything. I would visit cafes and order meals and drinks, only to discover when I came to pay, that someone had already paid the bill without telling me and they would leave without letting on who my benefactor was. I should have liked to say 'thank you'. These were times when people really did think more of others than themselves.

On being discharged from hospital I was delighted to rejoin forces, quite fortuitously as it happened, with my old friend Reggie as we queued at Salisbury bus station for the Larkhill bus. When I went into hospital, he had been sent on some course or other and we were both returning to our old unit. He was to be instrumental in shaping the next phase of my life.

We were dismayed to discover that, in our short absence, our unit had been posted to Africa to join the 8th Army commanded by General Montgomery and was already engaged in battle with the Afrika Corps under the redoubtable General Rommel. Someone must have been looking after my interests, as the company was virtually wiped out in their first encounter with German armoured divisions in the desert. I learned afterwards that my former colleagues, who were out in front of our guns giving gun-bearings and distances to the artillery, caught the full force of the counter-fire. Casualties were heavy and only a handful of my original intake of some fifty men survived. News of the demise of so many fine young men brought home to me the horror of war as nothing previously had done. But for us in Britain the desert campaign signalled our first real military victory of the war. Montgomery had shown that the German army was not invincible and morale that had sunk to an all-time low began at last to rise.

Reggie and I were having coffee in camp one morning while waiting to learn what was to become of us, when he remarked that he had seen a notice in the battery office inviting recruits to apply for officer training. We were both pretty fed up at the time. Life in barracks offered little joy, and to make matters worse we now had to share our hut with Canadian gunners, who seemed to do little training and sat up smoking, as though to compete with the heating stove, while playing cards late into the night. Their language was not appealing either.

We submitted applications and in due time presented ourselves at Winchester to be assessed by a War Office Selection Board. Following two days of tests of our intelligence, physical condition and officer aptitudes we were both accepted and began six weeks of basic infantry training at a pre-OCTU (Officer Cadet Training Unit) in Wrotham, Kent. It was my good fortune that Reggie lived at Otford, some seven miles from Wrotham, and I was able to accompany him on those weekends when he went home. I remember that we were, and felt, so physically fit as a result of the training, that we would run the seven miles along the Pilgrims Way and back. Reggie's wife Marjorie was an angel, never failing, in spite of rationing, to stoke us up with wonderful meals before we had to return to camp. But perhaps the greatest treats of all for me were wonderful hot baths in an English home. How much we missed the simple things in life.

The Underwoods had what I saw as an idyllic home and I was attracted to their place in the Kent countryside and the loving relationship between the parents, and their small children. I thought then that perhaps, after the war, I might achieve something like that - my own home and family, but this seemed an almost unattainable dream at the time. Our visits to the Underwood menage were necessarily short, and all too often, after a bath and a good lunch I would fall asleep in front of a log fire. I felt mean leaving Reggie to tidy up the garden, trim the hedges, etc. before we returned to camp, but I was usually 'out for the count'. (Because of my Welsh origin my army mates nicknamed me 'Taffy', as Reggie's family still know me to this day. But the Welsh accent I had on leaving home, I lost entirely in my army days. Now I find it creeping back on those rare occasions when I visit Brecon and hear it all around me.)

When we finished our pre-OCTU training in mid-1943, Reggie was despatched to a training centre to prepare for commissioning in the Pioneer Corps – which I thought a terrible fate at the time. The artillery officer who interviewed me was disgusted when I opted for the Royal Engineers, but in due course I was sent to the RE OCTU at Newark. Here the individual powers of leadership of the cadets were developed and honed so that we would at least be less likely to commit the blunders of some former military commanders, and at best, be able to lead our troops well and effectively in battle. It was a tough course but the quality of the instruction was superb. On completion of my officer training, in late 1943, I had the honour of being selected to take the passing-out parade for my Class 107. This was a special occasion for me, in that my youngest brother David had, coincidentally, just arrived at Newark as an officer cadet, and was on parade that day. Later, he too would be commissioned in the Royal Engineers. Reggie was commissioned in the Pioneer Corps and I was to see little more of him until after the war.

While every soldier's life was, of course, at risk, I was to have a few lucky escapes in my subsequent army days. The first of these was during a training exercise off Skegness, my first posting as a second lieutenant, where we were preparing sappers for the invasion of Europe. After a beach assault we had to clear a minefield, where dummy charges were exploded to simulate the real situation. One of these went off too close to me for comfort and I counted myself lucky to have escaped with little more than a few burns. Some of my colleagues were not so fortunate and ended up in hospital. On another exercise I was riding a motorcycle when the driver of a huge army truck decided to reverse into me. I only escaped by leaping from my bike into a hedge before my vehicle was completely crushed. I had some explaining to do at the Inquiry into the loss of my motorcycle. On another exercise I was involved in a head-on crash with another army vehicle. I was not driving, but technically I was in charge. At the Inquiry both drivers told the examining officer that they had been on the correct side of the road, which prompted the question 'why had the vehicles not therefore passed each other?' The case might have dragged on for hours but my driver observed, 'But sir, the road was only wide enough for one vehicle'. In the absence of evidence to the contrary, we got away with it. There were more lucky escapes to come.

While still a subaltern I was sent, in 1944, on a few interesting training courses. The first of these was to prepare officers to take part in the Army Bureau of Current Affairs (ABCA) programme where I learned a great deal about presenting course material and public speaking that I practised when I visited units to present ABCA lectures. I was impressed by the quality of the teaching on these courses, and particularly by the visual aids prepared for officers to use. A course I attended at Matlock in Derbyshire dealt with army field intelligence and another, at an RE centre at Longmoor in Hampshire, trained us to maintain and run railways – not a subject that was to prove of much use to me, though I felt more entitled, in later years, to give voice to my opinions on British Rail's inadequacies than I might otherwise have done.

After only a few months in Skegness, where we were housed in Butlin's holiday camp, devoid of all the customary holiday facilities (perhaps that is why I have never visited one since), I was promoted and posted as a lieutenant to Wooller in Northumberland where we continued training troops for D-Day in Europe. We marched for days, we ran for miles and when we were thoroughly exhausted, we built Bailey bridges in rain-sodden clothes. We climbed in the Cheviot Hills until we were ready to drop into our bivouacs under the stars. We were tasked to train our men to test the limits of their endurance, and to observe them for leadership and other qualities, on which we duly reported. It was hard on officers and men alike but I loved being in the mountains, had never been more fit, and felt I could do anything. My confidence had grown and I was a very different person from the diffident young man who had joined the army only twenty-one months earlier. I remember chasing up and down a column of flagging men carrying my Bren gun and full pack, urging them to greater effort. It was interesting to me that it was usually the younger men who gave up first: the older ones seemed more determined never to admit defeat. Army training ensured that the levels of tolerance of its recruits were expanded to the limit.

I was by now well adapted to army life and very happy in the company of men. (Little did I then know that, in later years, I was to be equally content surrounded by a family of entirely the opposite sex: where even the male cat we kept had been neutered!)

We were given frequent short periods of leave and, following the death of my mother, my uncle Stanley and his wife, Norah, had extended to my brothers Harry, Fred, David and me, a home base, which we accepted with gratitude. While in the UK we stayed with them for each leave period, enjoyed superlative hospitality and revelled in the joys of simple things like a hot bath, and auntie's home cooking – and she was a superb cook. None could forget her tea trolley loaded with buttered scones, cakes and sandwiches.

Nothing much seemed to have changed in Brecon in spite of the war. The farmer's wife still called at the house on Friday with butter and eggs, regardless of tight rationing. Indeed I remember how annoyed my aunt became when told she could only have a dozen eggs when she normally had two dozen. She was the kindest of persons. Her one failing, if that is the word, was an obsession with housework and cleaning to which she devoted much of her life. Not a day passed without her rising early in order to scrub the spotless tiles on the front door-step and the paving leading to the front gate, to be sure they were clean before the milkman or the postman arrived, and before she might be seen by neighbours. The long tiled floor leading from her front door to the back kitchen was also scrubbed at least twice a week, not once on each occasion but twice, with the maid working one way and my aunt the other. Not a word was spoken as their bottoms brushed as they passed in the middle, giving both confirmation that not a square inch had been missed. The unused attics did not escape attention either. The floorboards were regularly scrubbed on hands and knees until they glistened white. Later, my few possessions that were stored there when I went overseas were summarily disposed of without reference to me, depriving me of scant records of my early days: there was no room for anything untidy. But this was a small price to pay for a home in wartime and immediately afterwards, and all the love and generous hospitality that accompanied it.

Travelling home or back to camp was never easy. Train services were often disrupted by priority transport requirements, such as troop and ammunition movements, and for the ordinary soldier hitchhiking was often the only means of transportation. Thankfully, those with cars or lorries never failed to respond to the upraised thumb, and I experienced great kindness from drivers who went miles out of their way not just to give me a lift, but also to see that I got to my destination safely. Some would go as far as to enquire about my return journey and offer transport, in spite of severe petrol rationing. Such was the spirit of wartime Britain and the support that civilians gave to those in uniform.

It was on one of my leave visits to Brecon that my uncle, whose business embraced funeral services, was telephoned late one night to be advised of the death of an elderly farmer living on a remote holding in the Beacons. My uncle had been unwell and my aunt would not hear of him going out on a filthy night to see the bereaved family and make the necessary undertaking arrangements. They turned to me, and I was despatched to pick up the head funeral carpenter who did the measuring. Having armed himself with his wooden two-foot ruler we found our way, in dreadful weather, to a remote farmhouse in the mountains. I shall never forget the scene that greeted us. The family and neighbours of the deceased were assembled in the farm kitchen, with food stacked on the table and a huge log fire burning in the hearth. Everyone present seemed to be celebrating rather than mourning. I was in uniform, and was immediately given a seat of honour and plied with cider brewed on the farm. The widow was engaged in conversation with an elderly man who sat near the fire. As I listened to their discussion her contribution seemed limited to 'well I never' and his to 'well I never did'. I assumed they were in complete agreement over something! After extending our condolences we were invited upstairs to view the body, but I declined thinking it best to leave such things to a professional. The family insisted. 'Go on' said the widow 'He don't look bad. Bless him! He ought to look good. Haven't we just had a week in Porthcawl?' As my only visit to Porthcawl had been during a storm in winter I was not surprised that it had finished off the old man. This, happily, was my only venture into the undertaking business.

During another leave period I visited my uncle Jack and his wife Gladwys, who were then living in the Lake District. Jack had long been a favourite uncle, always full of fun and delightful company. He was rumoured to have been a wild lad in his younger days and, on one occasion, to have placed a bar of soap in the tea urn at a party for his Sunday-school class. On my visit I found them trying to sell their smallholding, which was in a state of considerable decay. One evening an estate agent called to show a potential buyer around and I was deputed to stand in various parts of the house either to hold up some element of the structure that was in danger of collapse, or to prevent easy assess to an area that was best left unseen.

Back in camp in Northumberland in June 1944, I received my posting orders, and was instructed to report to Liverpool for embarkation. After long delays at Crewe station, where all the English railways seemed to converge, and where trains would be shunted around for hours on end, our train was diverted into a siding and left there for several hours before we were coupled to another proceeding to Liverpool. Hundreds of us assembled on the quayside before we embarked on a liner, converted to carry troops, for an overseas destination, one shrouded in secrecy.

We were part of an extensive convoy of merchant and naval vessels which, as darkness fell, slipped silently out of harbour and sailed due west into the Atlantic. We were escorted by a flotilla of naval vessels – destroyers and corvettes – and it was comforting to see them in the grey distance, keeping guard over us, an impressive sight in the haunting silence. We used to scan the sky at night for indications of where we might be heading and thought from our reading of the stars that we must be on our way to Canada for further training. In the total silence we had to observe, we used to stand on deck, gazing out to sea, wondering what danger might be out there. Those allowed on deck were not permitted to smoke or show any lights. Our shipping losses at the time were horrendous and we had regular lifeboat drills. I could only just swim, and the thought of being plunged into those cold waters at dead of night was not something to dwell on. There was always tension in the air, and that eerie silence, especially when the night was still and there was hardly a ripple on the water: out there somewhere in the darkness there might well have been a U-boat watching and waiting.

We kept the troops busy most of the time performing routine

tasks – endless kit inspections, small arms training and talks in preparation for whatever lay ahead – if only to relieve their boredom, but we officers still found time to read or play bridge for a few hours each day.

After two days we noticed a change in our direction: we were now sailing south. Then one morning we woke to find that we were sailing south-east, then we turned again to the south – so our destination was not Canada after all. Our fears grew. Now our gurus reckoned we must be heading for Gibraltar and Burma, but no, we passed Gibraltar still heading south and a few days later sailed through the boom nets guarding Freetown harbour in Sierra Leone and experienced our first glimpse of tropical Africa.

But this was not the end of our journey and, after discharging some troops and replenishing supplies, we sailed on to Lagos in Nigeria, which turned out to be our destination. As we went ashore the sun bore down with incredible intensity. We were not yet acclimatised to this. Our tropical kit had only been issued to us days before we arrived; such had been the need to keep our destination secret. We now had to contend with the torment of hungry mosquitoes that bit any flesh they could find. Sleeping under mosquito nets seemed suffocating until we got used to them: every movement created discomfort. We were required to wear long sleeves, boots and puttees, and it seemed to us, as we sweated it out, that those who had designed our tropical dress had never experienced any climate south of Dover. But what an adventure this was, every new day a myriad of fresh discoveries, new experiences, sights and sounds. I was entranced by the colourful people and the strange flora and fauna of Africa, so vibrant and all so different from anything I had known or seen before.

Our immediate mission was to recruit and train troops for

the West African Engineers attached to the 81st and 82nd (West African) Divisions already deployed in Burma, and this we proceeded to do for the next nine months. Army recruiting staff visited the villages, many of them in remote areas, and asked the headmen for 'soldiers for King George', and they came forth in their hundreds. The raw recruits then had to be turned into soldiers within less than a year. There were some problems with the diverse tribes, but on the whole these were well managed. The Hausa men from the north were a proud people, taller, more regal and generally better soldiers than either the Yoruba tribesmen from the south-west, or the Ibo from the south-east. Each tribal group was, as far as possible, kept separate to avoid conflict between them. Whatever the British had failed to do in British colonial Africa, they had been highly successful in governing this huge territory so that its peoples could live together in peace. (After Independence in 1960, there was violent civil (tribal) war in which hundreds of thousands died.) I accompanied a recruiting team on one visit to Kaduna in northern Nigeria and it was there, in May 1945, that we heard of the death of Hitler and shortly afterwards celebrated the end of the European campaign. But it was not for us the relief that it was to our forces facing the armies that had surrendered in Europe, for we knew we were destined for Burma and a jungle campaign that looked far from ending.

During my time in Nigeria I was sent up country to establish a weapons training school at Ibadan. I knew little about small arms weaponry – which is probably why I was chosen for this task – the way the army operated never ceased to surprise me. The base camp at Ibadan had already been set up when I arrived, but that was about all. We had to establish firing ranges and prepare all the details for a major programme. Troops soon arrived and training began. This occupied the days fully, and was anything but congenial: it was incredibly hot and at night we sat in our little tents with virtually nothing to do but clean our pressure lamps in turn, as they were extinguished by accumulations of insects attracted to their light.

The army education service provided us with some reading material and I remember reading Tolstoy's 'War and Peace' and 'What Then Must We Do?' There was a surfeit of left-wing literature on offer at the time and little else. I have often reflected on the impact the biased army reading matter, as I experienced it, might have had on our returning soldiers when they came to vote in the election of 1945, when Churchill and the Conservative Party were sent packing to the opposition benches.

Each time we had another intake of recruits trained and ready for Burma I expected to see my name on the posting instructions. But, oddly, this did not happen, and my enquiries led to the astonishing discovery that mine had been removed from the list by order of the chief engineer who, it appeared, could not face the day without his early morning tennis workout with me on clay courts using borrowed rackets. With hindsight it is clear that I have a lot to thank my tennis for. I could rate this as another lucky escape in that the early drafts we sent forward to Burma were quickly immersed in jungle campaigns where West African soldiers played a significant role, often as carriers – whole artillery pieces, dismantled into their several parts, were moved surreptitiously through impenetrable jungle by these men, carrying colossal loads on their heads.

Eventually my name appeared on a draft for Burma and I was promoted captain RE shortly before leaving, a promotion that was probably more to do with my tennis prowess than anything else, although I was not all that good. Perhaps if I had developed a better backhand I might have become a colonel there and then!

When I embarked with my fellow officers and a boatload of Nigerian soldiers in July 1945, we had the feeling that we were on the way to join a forgotten army. It was not until many years later that I read a letter from Winston Churchill to his wife Clementine, which showed we were not entirely forgotten. He wrote:

> 'A third army on the Burmese frontier is fighting in the most unhealthy country in the world under the worst possible conditions...The casualties in Burma in the first six months amounted to 288,000 killed and 40,000 wounded.'

In the event we did not get very far on our journey east. Nearing Gibraltar our ship developed mechanical trouble – a split propeller shaft – and a replacement had to be sent out from England. We spent a week waiting for the part to arrive and be fitted and while we waited we would take the troops for a daily march around the Rock to a small, secluded bay where they would strip off and plunge into the warm water. We probably scared more than a few crabs when my two hundred naked African warriors stormed down the beach and dived into the sea. With little else to do during the day I joined the other officers in long hours mostly playing bridge.

When our ship was seaworthy again we sailed into the Mediterranean heading for the Suez Canal and Bombay. We had little expected the outbreaks of dysentery, pneumonia and malaria that afflicted our troops on the high seas, and our medics had to work overtime coping with these. Never having faced low night temperatures, our men were going down like ninepins. They appeared to have little immunity to the chill of the night air and, sadly, we lost a number of them and some days began with funerals at sea. We hit a cold snap and had to hold the troops below deck much of the time to keep them warm, allowing them up only twice daily for a brief airing. The stench when we opened the holds to let them out was indescribable. Although we did our level best for them it seemed, at times, very reminiscent of what I had heard of the transport of human cargoes at the time of the slave trade.

We eventually disembarked in Bombay and proceeded by train across the width of India to Calcutta and beyond to board a huge floating raft that took us, with our vehicles and other paraphernalia, up the Brahmaputra river to Comilla in Assam. Our vehicles were securely anchored to the raft and our men huddled in groups, keeping as dry as they could under their army waterproofs, in a ceaseless torrential downpour. The river was swollen with dark brown floodwater carrying tons of silt and debris as it made its way to the sea. The force of the current taxed the crews and ferries towing our raft to their utmost as we meandered across and up the river against a raging torrent. At some points the river was well over a mile wide with extensive flooding of the low plains on either side.

When we arrived at Comilla, close to the northern Burmese border, we moved into a tented encampment and it rained incessantly. Comilla has, reputedly, the highest rainfall in the world and my experience certainly confirmed this. It was there that we heard with a mixture of horror and relief of the use of the atomic bomb on Hiroshima and Nagasaki, which led to the Japanese surrender on 10th August 1945. This began a new wave of speculation as to where we might be sent if the fighting to the south was really at an end. We had few sources of reliable information: the troops looked to the officers for news and we had none to give. In monsoon conditions we waited for fresh orders, hoping against hope that we would soon be sent home or that, at the very least, somebody would be able to tell us something.

While I was still trying to keep myself and my tent dry and

my oil lamp clear of insects, I was confronted by Major-General Hugh Stockwell, General Officer Commanding 82nd (West African) Division. He strode into my tent, confirmed my identity, told me who he was and informed me that he and I were leaving by plane early the next day for Rangoon. I was to be ready to depart with him at 8 a.m. I thought my time had come!

CHAPTER SIX

MUTINY AND CHAOS

'Chaos is come again'
Shakespeare.

A s we travelled south in one of the old Dakotas of Burma Command, Stockwell explained to me that he was taking me to assume command of 32nd Nigerian Artisan Works Coy. RE, based in Rangoon. The company, attached to the 82nd (West African) Division, had experienced something of a mutiny. Their commanding officer had been shot, a British NCO had fled in terror of his life and there was to be an Inquiry. It seemed that the troops had demanded to be taken home immediately on hearing of the Japanese surrender. 'King George had plenty ships to bring us here, where are they now?' they demanded to know. I had not previously heard of a mutiny in the modern army and wondered just what lay ahead.

Dakotas were the wartime workhorses of the air transport arm in Burma, robust and generally reliable. (Some of them were still in use when I returned to Burma some twenty years later in very different circumstances.) For transporting war supplies the interior of our plane had been stripped and for our flight to Rangoon we sat with a few other soldiers on loose crates ranged down each side of the fuselage. These planes did not fly high so it was easy to see the canopy of trees that shrouded everything below. There was something sinister about the jungle we gazed down on. Only days earlier there would have been Japanese troops there, perhaps there still were, for it was to take some weeks before news of the surrender could reach all the combatants and they would lay down their arms.

75

When we arrived at our destination, a tented camp site in a field adjacent to Mingaladon airport, the General strode majestically into the first tent, announced to the rebellious troops who he was and ordered them to get on parade. He used his swagger stick to good effect, prodding the men and gesticulating with it much as a conductor directs his orchestra. With me in hot pursuit, he charged into each tent until he had all the men assembled in the middle of the field. Then, ignoring me, he formed the men into ranks and went up and down talking to individual soldiers, 'I'm in command here – I'm a General – see that' – his baton tapped his shoulder badges – and to each man he addressed a string of personal questions 'How many wives you catch?' 'Where you come from?' And so on. After that introduction he started to drill the men himself while I watched in amazement. This was a superb demonstration of leadership. Some of these men had recently mutinied, now they were entirely under his command. Half an hour later he announced that he had brought me along to take charge of the company. Those suspected of murder would be tried and if found guilty would be hanged. If there was any more trouble he would be back. Major Jenkins (the first I had heard of this promotion) would be left in command. And off he went leaving me with an unpredictable challenge, staring at a sea of a few hundred black, inquisitive faces.

Taking my cue from the general I took over the drill he had begun and continued until such time as I felt that my authority had at least been observed and I felt reasonably confident that order had replaced chaos. Then, turning to the African sergeant major I said, 'sergeant major how goes it'. 'OK saar – they like you'. 'Thank Heavens for that,' I thought. Any other outcome might have proved somewhat inconvenient to say the least. That evening I sat in my tent, took off my three pips, sewed on a crown and wrote to my aunt and uncle in Brecon telling them of my promotion. The army postal service was remarkably reliable and I learned later that my letters did get through.

With the company I took over a group of British officers and some British and Nigerian NCOs, who shared my admiration for Stockwell's display of generalship, and we set about our duties. The first task assigned to my new company was the reconstruction of the heavily bombed airstrip at Mingaladon, which was now the main supply airport for Southern Burma. As luck would have it I had been trained to lay what was called Parkinson's steel plank, which was designed to give roads and landing strips a durable covering. The company that had put it down had, unfortunately, not appreciated the importance of using the locking pins – or perhaps they could not find them – which were all that held the strips of planking together. In consequence the metal had coiled up, engulfing the first planes that landed, with disastrous consequences. When we had the pins in place, the new surface stayed locked together and supply planes were soon pouring in. We remained at the airport for some weeks repairing buildings, bridges and roads. (Twenty years later, when I returned to Burma, I found the steel planking still there on the airstrip firmly embedded in turf. I also tracked down a Bailey Bridge we had built further inland, still in daily use.)

We lived entirely in tents with ditches dug around them to take away the floodwater and keep the interiors reasonably dry. The humidity in Burma, especially in the monsoon months, is exceedingly oppressive and decidedly depressing. The mosquitoes were ever present and precautions had to be taken against malaria, and a host of other tropical diseases that plagued our troops, in spite of all our inoculations. Oddly the British coped with the climate and conditions rather better than the Africans whose lives were additionally threatened by many of the diseases we brought to them, such as influenza and the common cold.

Our tasks included the repair of stretches of road which we did by levelling and shaping them manually with laterite – a mixture of mineral sands – and then covering this with sheets of bituminous felt. To seal the joins and make it all waterproof, we would pour petrol or paraffin on the seams, retire to a nearby ditch, upwind of the resultant smoke, and set fire to a stretch of road at a time. The heat sealed the covering very effectively and gave a durable surface. On one occasion, on the road leading north from Rangoon to the airport, we had prepared a stretch for firing and I had just given the order, when around a bend in the road came a fast moving convoy of flagged cars including an open vehicle carrying my C. in C. Admiral Lord Louis Mountbatten and his staff officers. They drove straight into my little conflagration and the Admiral emerged with his usually impeccable white uniform sadly blackened and his facial expression even blacker. 'Who the hell is in charge here?' 'Me sir, please sir' was about all I could manage as I crawled from my ditch. I prefer to forget his words of welcome – they were none too convivial. (I recalled this occasion to him when we met in London years later when we could laugh about it.)

One evening as I sat in my little canvas bath in our camp at Mingaladon airport, where we had been working all day, with my African batman pouring tepid water over me, there was a burst of machine gun fire that ripped through our company tents. It was a miraculous escape for me because the top of my tent caught a few rounds on their way elsewhere. For some days I walked with a stoop. Outside, the whole company hugged the ground as though searching for earthworms. The firing continued sporadically for over an hour, during which time it would have been most unwise to move: this was no time for heroics. Afterwards we discovered that two Indian units, camped on either side of us, had been settling a dispute resulting from the slaughter of a water buffalo, to which one

faction had given the status of a sacred cow. We found a few
dead Indian soldiers in the ditches around our camp the next
morning, but suffered no casualties ourselves.

The former governor of Burma, Sir Reginald Dorman
Smith, returned to Rangoon in October 1945. The popularity of
this move, and of the governor personally, was in some doubt,
and it fell to me to provide part of the guard in the harbour area
when he came ashore. In all his colonial splendour he
disembarked safely and, fortunately, we had no incidents. It
was considered too risky for him to inspect the guard and he
was bundled quickly into an official car and driven away.
Whether his return was politically judicious seemed very
doubtful to me at that time, though I have to admit that my
knowledge of Burmese politics was very limited. The soldier
is, after all, but a pawn in a much bigger game and is rarely
wholly aware of the implications of all he sees. It was not long
before the governor retired, ill health being the official reason
given.

One of my first and most distasteful tasks on taking up my
new command in Rangoon was to arrange the court martial of
the two young African soldiers who had, allegedly, mutinied
and shot an officer prior to my joining the company.
Fortunately for me I was not involved in the trial. One of the
young soldiers was acquitted and the other, to the dismay of the
whole company, was sentenced to be hanged. The doomed
prisoner was detained locally until I received the order for his
execution. This came some ten days before Christmas 1945
when I was instructed to deliver the prisoner to a hangman at
Insein gaol in Rangoon on the 25th These things had to be done
within a prescribed number of days; it was of no consequence
that this day had any special significance. I was just twenty-
five at the time, and although toughened by recent events, this
proved almost too much for me, and I lost a lot of sleep over it,

especially as I had so much sympathy with the young lad of about twenty-two years who was to die. It would have been relatively easy for him to abscond and I almost wished he had. He had claimed that the shooting was an accident. But this was war and I duly took the prisoner, handcuffed to a NCO and delivered him, together with, as instructed, a new blanket for his burial.

On arrival at Insein gaol my blood froze. There could not have been a more forbidding place, with its ancient lichen covered walls capped with spikes and coils of barbed wire. The crazed faces of prisoners gazed at us from padlocked cells as I marched my squad to an enclosure within the perimeter walls, and duly handed over the condemned man, and the blanket, to a Chinese warder-cum-hangman, who, in front of my prisoner, said he would keep the new blanket for himself; he had plenty of old ones for burials. The English sergeant who accompanied me was an older man and seeing how distressed I was, told me to wait, and volunteered to witness the execution himself. This was, I think, the only occasion in my life when I have 'chickened out' and I have no regrets. After the execution we travelled back to a traumatised camp in silence. My conscience was deeply troubled because I felt for the young soldier who had been taken from his home country and pitched into an environment that he could barely have understood. As his commanding officer I thought I had let him down. It is not surprising that I recall this poignant memory every Christmas day.

The days seemed longer than ever as we waited for orders to embark for our return to Africa and home. The Africans had already demonstrated their displeasure at the delay and I slept with my revolver under my pillow. I had assumed that I would be sailing with them, but this was not to be. I had, after all, not been in Burma long and I was to be given another assignment before being allowed to return home.

CHAPTER SEVEN

ON THE ROAD TO MANDALAY

'Come back you British soldier,
Come you back to Mandalay.'

Rudyard Kipling.

W ithin a few weeks of the hanging in Rangoon gaol, the field telephone rang in my tent on Mingaladon airfield. It was Major-General Stockwell on the line. I was to hand over the company to my second-in-command and proceed to Mandalay. This time some elements of a Gold Coast company (26th W.A. Artisan Works) had mutinied, and I was to go there immediately, assume command and restore order. There had been further shootings. 'Go at once and sort things out. And best of luck'.

At dawn the next day I unceremoniously handed over to my second-in-command, said my goodbyes, and set out to drive in my jeep from Rangoon to Mandalay. Apart from the area around Rangoon, which I had explored during my brief stay, the rest, particularly the interior of Burma, was a new world to me. The experience of driving alone along those potholed roads was both fraught and exhilarating. It was hot and dusty and I was all too aware that the area was by no means entirely safe. There were still some Japs around and, although most of them had by now surrendered, I could not be entirely sure. I passed very few military or other vehicles, on mostly deserted roads, apart from the occasional cart drawn by water buffalo or a monk in a saffron robe walking seemingly aimlessly. The roadside was still littered with the debris of war and abandoned vehicles lay everywhere, stripped of tyres and every other reusable part before being dragged clear of the carriageway. At intervals along the road gold-leaf-clad spires of Buddhist shrines shone in the brilliant sunlight. It was a ten-hour drive of some three hundred and fifty miles and I'd have given a lot to have had some company on that lonely journey.

As I drove north I wondered what would await me in Mandalay. I had learned something of Nigerians during my brief stay with them, and had gained a passing knowledge of the language of the Hausa people, but I knew little of the Gold Coast, its people, their tribal structures, languages, culture or customs. After all Nigeria and the Gold Coast are very different countries and I felt decidedly vulnerable and ill-prepared for my new command as I made my way into the unknown.

I stopped a few times to refuel from the jerrycans I carried, and arrived at the campsite in the old Royal Palace grounds in Mandalay in the early evening, to find the troops lolling about in and around their tents. As I parked my jeep I was conscious of many eyes staring at me from the huts and tents that encircled the encampment. I drew a deep breath and adopted precisely the same tactics as the general when he first took me to Rangoon. I had neither his rank and experience nor, as a 26-year-old, his presence, but I pressed on. I strode in shouting orders to the men to get on parade and, having mustered the two hundred or so men, and avoided getting myself shot in the process, I drilled them for half-an-hour before inspecting the ranks and exchanging the customary personal questions about their home villages, their wives and their children. There was no going back now, and I turned and asked the African sergeant major 'How goes it sergeant major?' 'OK sarr, I think they like you'. I was glad to hear this again and just hoped he thought right, or I might not have been around in the morning. But there was no more rebellion and the troublemakers were given fairly light punishment. In mitigation it transpired that the NCOs, who had been attacked, but not killed, had been guilty of some degree of provocation. I thought again of the lad we had hanged in Rangoon and wondered whether in that case too, in spite of the fairness of military courts, there might have been some circumstances that had not been given full weight.

I found my new company comfortably billeted in tents and old-style Burmese houses built of lacquered teak, dotted about in the old Royal Palace grounds where we could walk safely for miles within the majestic formal gardens that once afforded privacy for the kings of ancient Burma. Here and there were vivid splashes of colour from flame trees, cannas and a host of shrubs and trees I had never seen before and could not identify. The remains of some old stone buildings could be seen struggling to survive the iron grasp of jungle. What mystical culture had once occupied this land? And what splendour, intrigue and rituals now lay hidden there? One could only marvel at the ancient awesome splendour of the place. For me it was magical. The heavy stone pillars supporting the gates at each entrance to the grounds particularly intrigued me. I had read of an old and gruesome custom the Burmese had of burying young virgins alive in such pillars to keep out evil spirits and was dying to knock one down to test the truth of this, but never had the nerve. I did, however, read an account of this horrific practice some years later – of the screams of young girls as they were slowly bricked up – and concluded that it probably was true. How I should have loved the time and resources to dig deeply into the intriguing depths of that mysterious place. Outside the palace walls and the lotus-strewn moat, people – monks in their saffron robes, peasants, girls with flowers in their hair and tribesmen from the neighbouring hills, their skin wrinkled by a relentless sun – went about their business as if we did not exist. It was all very surreal.

During the long torrid evenings, we used to recline on the wide balconies of our bungalows drinking, reading or talking of what we did before the war and what we hoped to do after it was all over. Few of us had any firm plans, except those who had been standing by to enter university when the war started and those whose careers had been rudely interrupted. Most of us could still only dream about what might lie ahead. It seemed certain that my options were limited to rejoining the family firm and I was resigned to that.

But the days were not for dreaming and it was essential, while we waited for orders for our repatriation, to keep the troops busy if only to prevent them from thinking too much about returning home before ships could be found to take them. Camp maintenance jobs and repairing damaged bridges in central Burma, some of which we replaced with army Bailey Bridges, were a godsend. We also helped the municipal authorities to fill the many holes in the roads – the area potholed far exceeded the useable surface – and to restore the quality of the water supply. The Royal Engineers were masters of improvisation and our troops with their experience of living in similar conditions at home, were no exception. Much of the work we called on them to do, nevertheless, seemed pretty pointless to them, which made it a trying time for us all. The war was over, our troops wanted to go home – and so did we – we were also aware that our presence in Burma was none too welcome to the local people, but we had to bide our time until ships could be provided to transport us. We did not have long to wait, but each week seemed an eternity.

With the war over, the working day for officers and men was shortened, and while the British officers and NCOs had their own ways of relaxation – we had a clay tennis court within our compound – our troops had only the new-found pleasures of the brothels of Mandalay, and it was not long before the alarm bells were ringing at every sick parade. The medical officer read the riot act and I had to do something. We ordered each platoon to parade in turn on the field behind our tents and when the sergeant major shouted the order 'Platoon drop shorts'; they fell to the ground. We then proceeded down the ranks examining every possible point of contact with our Burmese hosts. Yes, we had a problem. The damage was extensive, and while there was nothing we could do for the local ladies, penicillin for the troops was ordered in bulk and injections began. Although officers had the pleasure of the company of a unit of British nurses living in the compound in huts adjacent to ours, we had no such worries, or at least I was told of none. I had had little to do with females in my life and I remained remote and apprehensive about them. Consequently I took little part in the fraternisation with the neighbours and our medical officer took care of any concerns he may have had in respect of my colleagues.

My immediate superior, the chief engineer, had been posted home shortly before I was and, in his absence, I had been directed to assume his position, which carried the rank of lieutenant-colonel. In the confused situation that prevailed before we left Mandalay this promotion in the field, if that is what it was, was never confirmed officially, but on my return to England it was acknowledged as a temporary rank and I was demobilised in the rank of substantive major. Thus I had moved from gunner RA to acting lieutenant-colonel RE in the space of just over four years – years that had seemed an eternity – but this was wartime, and in war both chaos and normality are ill-defined.

In acknowledgement of all the pleasure accorded by the local girls to our troops and, I trust by our troops to their hosts, when the time came for us to leave Mandalay, it seemed appropriate to make an occasion of our departure. I accordingly organised a full ceremonial march through the main streets of the city to the railway station where we entrained in mid-1946 for our journey to Rangoon. We did not have a brass band to see us off but instead our march was accompanied by the stirring rhythmic beat of African drums.

We were soon aboard an ocean liner and sailing via the Suez Canal for Takoradi in the Gold Coast (now Ghana). Apart from daily inspections of the troops' quarters and writing Daily Orders, I and my fellow officers and NCOs had little to do on board and again I settled down to long days and nights of reading and playing bridge. Most of our men had only a limited knowledge of English, which made it difficult for us to do much for them by way of education, but we did what we could to teach them something of our language.

Our homecoming in Takoradi reminded me in many ways of my earlier arrival in Freetown. The heat and humidity were just as overbearing. The sea was without a ripple as we sailed through the boom protecting the port, and the sounds of Africa could be heard as we entered the outer harbour: a mixture of dockside industrial noise and the music of the jungle, which assumed deafening proportions at night and was still just audible by day.

As we neared the quayside we were met with a scene that greatly disappointed us all. As our liner tied up there was hardly a soul to be seen. The dockers we had glimpsed in the distance had mysteriously disappeared. Where was the homecoming welcome we had all expected? Then, suddenly, the huge doors of the godowns that surrounded the dockside were rolled back and out swarmed what seemed to us the whole population of Takoradi, headed by two military bands. It would be hard to imagine a more colourful sight and, for us, emotional experience. The jubilation of the troops (and their kinsfolk) knew no bounds. Many on board caught glimpses of their loved ones in the crowds below; the cheering was deafening and we lost control completely. What had happened to all that discipline we thought we had instilled? Troops disappeared over the side and we made no attempt to stop them. I stood at the ship's rail with my fellow officers and we just laughed. The best we could do was to pass word around that the men should report to their depot in two days time to hand in their uniforms and collect their blankets. We resigned ourselves to the likelihood that we would see none of them for at least forty-eight hours. I wish I had met and could have thanked the genius who organised that reception for us.

We had only a brief period to wait for our passage home during which time I found myself appointed garrison commander of Takoradi harbour, with two further duties to perform. First there were a number of outstanding courts martial to conduct, mostly for petty crimes. These were dealt with swiftly and I hope most leniently. There was one difficult case I had to try, where a witness had to be called from within a prison. To my dismay he was ushered in shackled to eight other miscreants; the procedures for separating the men were apparently beyond the wit of the custodian of the day, and I questioned my witness while he was still in his allotted place on the chain.

My other task was to take detachments of troops back to their villages and hand them over to their village headmen with suitable expressions of thanks for the service they had rendered to King George. In return they plied me with some weird and dubious concoctions to eat and drink, but these visits to remote settlements were generally exciting, joyful and rewarding. There were less happy moments though, when it fell to me to express sympathy to those who had been widowed as a result of the Burma campaign. How desperately inadequate this seemed.

About two-thirds of the Gold Coast people were then living in traditional villages made of small round huts with conical roofs and walls made of straw, mud and bamboo. Pigs and chickens wandering about in the compounds presented picturesque scenes of order and tranquillity. During the day they were mostly abandoned, with the children in school or working in the fields with their parents. But I noticed that there was always someone on guard in every village we entered. We wondered then what impact the homecoming of so many troops, who had seen a very different world outside their homeland, would have on the old village order.

We eventually received our instructions to return home, said goodbye to our African sappers and boarded our ships. The journey was uneventful, except that the army forwarding agents, Cox and Kings, managed to lose all my kit, which had been sent ahead, including all my notes, records, addresses and photographs. I lost the lot, and no compensation was forthcoming. The sad consequence of this for me was that I had no means of keeping in touch with all those friends and colleagues made during my army service. It was a cruel blow. The loss was partly made good through a few contacts I still had, but I had no easy means of linking up with the Africans who had supported us so well in Burma and for whom I felt genuine affection.

There was considerable political agitation for independence for the Gold Coast after World War II, and Ghana eventually became an independent sovereign state after the British Government passed the Ghana Independence Act in 1957. Some forty years later I had a chance to enquire about my old company when I met Bishop Joseph Dadson, Bishop of Tamale and Sunyani, who was visiting Sir Harold Smedley, a former high commissioner to Ghana who, like me, had retired to Ferring. The Bishop took back to Ghana a photograph of my company and me, taken in 1946, and showed it to some of his army friends. They recognised three of my soldiers from the young men staring at the camera. One of them was acting Head of State, another was commandant of the Military Academy in Ghana and the third was a district army commander. We must have trained them well! The Bishop suggested that I should return to Ghana to speak at the Military Academy, but I have not so far been able to do this.

Our arrival at Liverpool was unceremonious and I remember that it rained heavily all day. We were summarily despatched to a nearby army centre and issued with a standard demobilisation suit and a travel warrant to get ourselves home. It struck me how different this homecoming was from our arrival in Takoradi, where the local people had given us such a stupendous reception. Perhaps homecoming soldiers should expect nothing, but it seemed a dreadful letdown at the time. The only formal recognition of my service came in a letter from the Mayor of Brecon, sent to all returning soldiers, expressing thanks and enclosing a cheque for five pounds. The end of the war marked a watershed in the history of mankind and I appreciated that somebody had bothered to thank me personally for my very small part in it. My three war medals came later by post, accompanied by a list of those to which I was entitled – The Defence and Victory medals and the Burma Star – indicated by ticked boxes. There was nothing more.

It is rare for any war to be justified, but few could question the grounds on which we fought the 2nd World War. In a strange way, for all the horrors and suffering it brought to the millions of its victims, it was, for me personally, a good war. In retrospect, despite the hardships and tedium along the way, I would not have missed those years for anything. My army experience had brought me immeasurable benefit and I felt I had gained in every sense, being transformed from sickly youth

91

into confident manhood in a very short span of time, and felt ready to face whatever lay ahead.

I was sorry to see the end of national conscription when it was abolished some years later, for I feel sure we would have been a far better nation had we retained it in one form or another, giving young men (and women) some of the opportunities I had enjoyed. But for me my military days were over and I was acutely aware that I was one of the lucky ones having, with all my brothers, emerged from the conflict physically unscathed.

Mervyn, self, mother and David - 1940

I join the 1ˢᵗ Brecon Bn. Home Guard – 1941.
Why should Britain tremble?

7D Squad R.A. School of Survey, Larkhill – 1942
Self middle row 2nd from right.
Reggie Underwood, back row extreme right

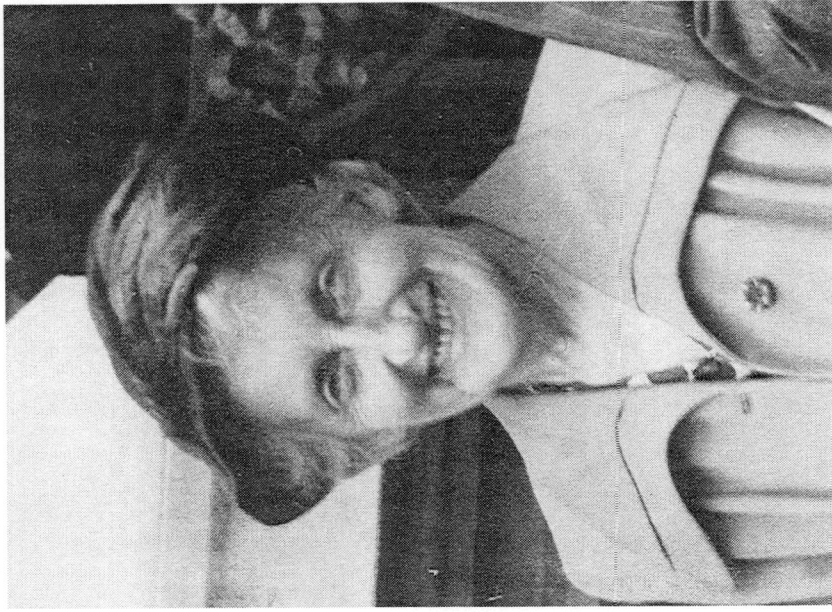

Auntie Norah who gave me a
home after my mother died

Study in African headdress.
Self and colleagues – Kaduna V.E.Day – 1945

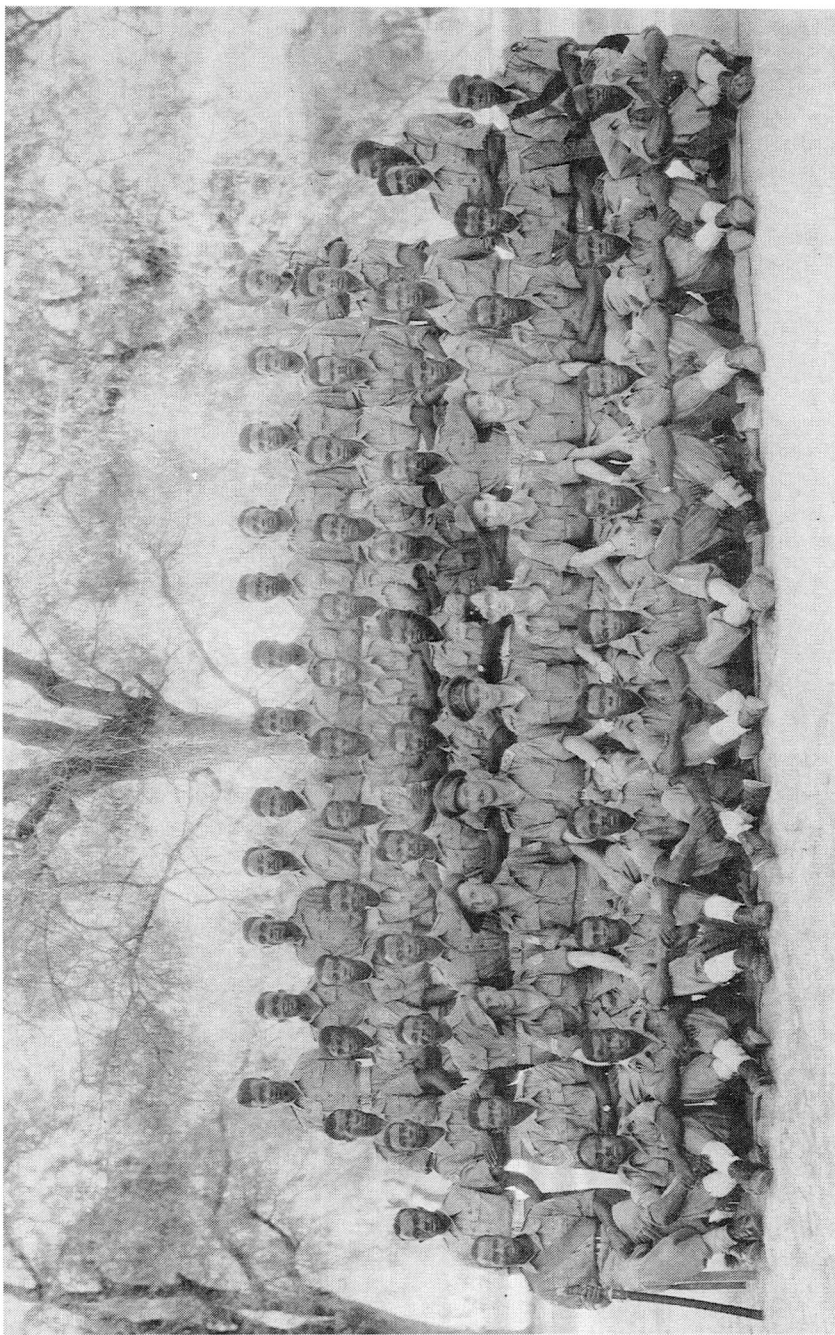

1st Platoon 26 (WA) Artisan Works Co. RE, Mandalay – March 1946
Major Jenkins RE (centre) with some of his warriors

Home and awaiting
demobilization – 1946

So Much To Do
So Little Time

. . . .

Part III

Students And Student Politics

CHAPTER EIGHT

TO STUDY OR CHANGE THE WORLD

'Wearing all that weight of learning
lightly like a flower'

Tennyson.

E arly in the war Prime Minister Winston Churchill had
promised the British people 'nothing but blood, toil,
tears and sweat'. At the end of six years of conflict the
survivors were left in no doubt about the significance of his
words.

Not long after the war ended the United States government,
with admirable generosity, poured aid into the devastated
countries of Europe under what became known as the Marshall
Plan. Paradoxically, at least in its initial stages, this benefited
our wartime adversaries rather more than the British, and while
we struggled to restore some semblance of normality we
watched our old enemies rebuilding their economies with the
help of massive external support.

In the autumn of 1946 I was one of many thousands who
had served in the armed forces returning home to begin life
anew. For many it was a time of great opportunity, and for the
majority it was also one of frightening uncertainty. For those
who had been away for what seemed an eternity so much had
changed, and there were many less fortunate than I who had
little or nothing to return to. Few of our cities had escaped the
nightly bombing and many families had lost someone near to
them. Just about everything was in short supply and food and
clothing were still rationed. Few could escape the adjustments
that had to be made, and I was no exception: we each had to

93

make a new beginning.

I returned to a very different world from the one I had left behind in 1942. My brothers Mervyn, and Leslie, had both married during the early part of the war and, as I had been available in the UK for much of that time, I had been called on to act as 'best man' for each of them. By the time I got home Mervyn and his wife, Valerie, had already occupied our old family home, so I returned to live temporarily with my aunt and uncle in Brecon while I reflected on what I should do next.

I knew that my uncle had set his heart on my returning to carry on the family tradition in the building industry, in partnership with my brother Mervyn. I was not at all sure that that was what I wanted but as things stood, I saw no alternative and had accepted as inevitable that I would eventually join the firm. Accordingly I began making enquiries about further education prospects to prepare me for a career in the construction industry.

At the army demobilisation centre I had learned about grants for ex-servicemen, but with my educational background it seemed unlikely that I would qualify. Nevertheless, I was advised to apply and soon established that, mainly because of my military record, I would be eligible and that a four-year course being offered at Cardiff Technical College in building technology, leading to a National Diploma, would be ideal to prepare me to carry on the family tradition. So off I went to Cardiff to enrol for the autumn term of 1946, and to find somewhere to live.

On leaving the services I reflected on the contrasts and similarities between the first phase of my life and the second. The home environment and the circumscribed life I had led as a child and teenager, in a relatively isolated Welsh valley township, bore few similarities to the life the army had provided. Every day my life as a serviceman had been planned by others in some detail. The services with their rigid structure, regulated almost entirely by rank, offered few choices for the individual. The system worked well because all concerned were obliged to accept the enforced environment. I was soon to discover that civilian life was markedly different and that I would in future have to take much more responsibility for myself than I had ever done in the past. Meals would not be provided on time and in a pre-determined place, and no longer would daily plans be made for me. Those things that my home, and later the army, had provided as a matter of course, were no longer in place and many adjustments had to be made.

Had I been a teenager going up to university for the first time, I doubt whether I would have given any of this much thought, but being older and facing tertiary education, without having had the schooling that most new undergraduates would have had, added to the general apprehension I felt. Leaving the army also meant that, apart from my training grant of £236 p.a. that would be coming from the Ministry of Education, my financial resources had dried up. I had managed to save very little from my army pay and now I had to learn how to survive 'on a shoestring'.

I lived for the next four years in Cardiff, for the first year with a retired couple, who had a most attractive daughter of my age, but she was already engaged and I was not much interested in girls anyway, although I did find her something of a diversion. When she married and her husband moved in, I left. After that I lived for three years in Miskin Street, with a retired and delightful couple, Mr. and Mrs Cooke, who took a great interest in me and my activities and treated me like a son.

There were exciting and difficult times ahead, not least the winter of 1946-7, which turned out to be the harshest of the century, when coal supplies to the power stations threatened to run out, severe power cuts led to a paralysis of British industry, and homes were without heating for several hours each day. These were times when I wished I was back in Burma or Africa, where at least the central heating was universal and guaranteed.

Cardiff Technical College where I enrolled has, since my time there, become part of the University of Wales, but in 1946 it was a separate entity occupying a number of mostly dilapidated buildings scattered around the city. When my course began, I found myself one of a group of sixteen of widely varying ages, mostly ex-servicemen, but some straight from school. As I was still technically in the army until the following January, and had no civilian clothes other than my demob suit, I attended lectures in uniform. I was the most senior in service rank in the class and the others, especially the ex-service contingent, turned to me if anything needed to be negotiated with the college authorities. I little knew that this was to lead to my involvement in student politics to an extent I could never have imagined.

As we settled down to college life, one of the issues causing us concern as mature students was the seemingly petty regime of regulations that had been devised for the protection and safety of earlier and younger generations. We were, on average, at least five years older and found some of the rules irksome and we wanted them changed. When our initial overtures to the college authorities fell on deaf ears, I sought an interview with our newly elected Member of Parliament, George Thomas, (who later became Speaker of the House of Commons and retired as Viscount Tonypandy.) He was then living in Cardiff with his mother, and we met in his family parlour where he listened sympathetically, and later interceded with the college authorities. As a result we achieved some relaxation of the more troublesome restrictions. My colleagues were impressed with this minor achievement and my position as 'leader of the pack' was confirmed.

There then occurred an event that was to change the course of my life. Out of the blue I had an invitation from a staunch Conservative, John Parry Lewis, an officer of Cardiff university students union, to attend a meeting of representatives of the four constituent colleges of the University of Wales. They were seeking a candidate to represent the Welsh universities and colleges as Welsh vice-president on the executive committee of the British National Union of Students (NUS). I had not met John before but he seemed to know about me. I knew nothing of the NUS either, but was soon to learn. Being a member of a technical college I was, in respect of the Welsh universities, something of an outsider. Nevertheless, I went to the meeting – more out of curiosity than anything else – and was flattered when, after being interviewed, I was called back, told I had been selected and offered the nomination. I wondered afterwards if they had any other candidates to consider!

My first task was to find out what the NUS position entailed. From leaflets lying about the college I learned that the National Union of Students of the Universities and Colleges of England, Wales and Northern Ireland had some 236 constituent colleges representing around 105,000 students. Its headquarters staff at 3, Endsleigh Street, London, consisted of twelve full-time officials who were mainly occupied with furthering student interests and particularly their welfare. A variety of services were being provided, ranging from the provision of cheap travel facilities to vacation work camps. I was impressed by the contribution the union appeared to be making on behalf of its members and decided to pursue the matter further. I was later informed by students more politically aware than I, that the NUS was affiliated to the International Union of Students (IUS) which was communist controlled, and that left-wing politics dominated the NUS. As I had minimal interest in politics I attached little significance to this at the time.

I soon found myself embroiled in a mixture of lectures and project work in Cardiff, interspersed with long weekend meetings in London and elsewhere throughout the UK. The NUS executive committee, of which I had become a member by virtue of my Welsh constituency, consisted of ten representatives elected from universities and colleges. Officers were expected to visit colleges to explain NUS policy, and there were service departments we were appointed to oversee. Papers and speeches had to be prepared and delivered. I had little previous experience of anything of this kind and often found the business of the committees to which I was appointed difficult to follow. There seemed to be undue emphasis on matters of international political concern rather than domestic student issues, and I frequently found myself thinking along lines different from my fellow committee members. The president at the time, W. B. Rust, who was some three years older than most of us was most helpful in breaking me in.

Perhaps, not surprisingly, I was ill-prepared to discuss many of the issues on the agenda at that time, such as republicanism in Spain, revolution in Cuba, communism in China and the war in Korea, topics that originated through the connection with the international union. Little information on any such matters had reached me in my tents in Burma or West Africa where the light from my lantern would have been inadequate to read about them anyway. I was bemused to establish the relevance of some of these issues to students in Britain, but I went along with the idea that we had to face up to our wider responsibilities – whatever they were! Most of the time I sat, listened and learned.

NUS council meetings, the main governing bodies of the union, were held three times a year at one or other of the member universities or colleges, and it was usual for about a hundred delegates to attend. At my very first council meeting, held in 1947, I faced a motion aimed to dispense with the office of Welsh vice-president to which I had only just been elected. It seemed that I was under attack before I had even started. In the lively debate that followed it was argued that there was no case for Wales to have a special seat on the executive committee. Scotland had always had a national union of its own (the Scottish NUS would not merge with the NUS until 1971) and Northern Ireland had no special representation, so why should Wales? It fell to me to make an impassioned defence of my seat and I made what, seen in retrospect, was an emotional and highly nationalistic appeal to the delegates, laced with a lot of nonsense about the history of Welsh rugby, the culture of the valleys, daffodils, St. David, colliery bands and male voice choirs. Suffice it to say that I won the vote with a good majority and for the time being at least my seat was secure. I wonder how many delegates thought 'if he can get away with that, he must have something!'

From that time we re-established the Welsh Universities and Colleges Students Council on a more formal basis than hitherto, and I found myself chairing meetings at the four constituent university colleges of Cardiff, Swansea, Bangor and Aberystwyth But being a member of the Welsh Universities and Colleges Representative Council and Welsh vice-president of the National Union of Students, I was already neglecting my studies and spending too much time on student business. At the same time I was enjoying my role as an activist and, with some degree of arrogance, felt confident that I could cope with the extra curricular activities I had taken on.

As I progressed through my second year in Cardiff my course workload began to increase, but this never overly worried me. My childhood experience had equipped me to read and absorb information readily, a facility that came in useful throughout my life. When I had worked with my uncle before the war, measuring building work under the army Schedule of Works system, where every item of work had to be related to a list of prices and a job number, I began to appreciate what a boon a good memory was. After some months I had found that I could do much of my work without reference to the manuals. I was always able to retain appreciable amounts of detail for the period while I was using it, and, conversely, I found it just as easy to forget it all when I no longer needed it. Similarly, in my army days I had memorised much of the army handbook on the Bailey Bridge, which enabled me to carry out reconnaissance and bridge design at night, without referring to the books. This trait, which had proved invaluable before, now became a godsend when I had to spend so much time on student union business, rather than being immersed in my college books. Fortunately, I absorbed enough to pass all my examinations when the time came.

By the start of my second year in Cardiff I must have impressed my tutors sufficiently in at least one discipline, namely builders' quantities, for them to recommend that I be appointed lecturer in the subject at my college. My Ministry of Education grant was proving just enough for me to survive, but I needed the extra money and took the job. Course materials were non-existent, and I faced a major task in preparing a range of construction drawings to use in class. I taught for a year and finally handed in my notice when the pressure of my other commitments became too demanding for me to carry on.

My younger brother David married in June 1948 and again I was called upon to serve as 'best man'. David seemed destined to follow me around, first in the army and now as an undergraduate. After the wedding he and his wife, Elaine, came to live in Cardiff where David had enrolled for an honours degree course in economics. Mainly through them I was able to keep in touch with my family.

CHAPTER NINE

FROM VALLEYS TO RALLIES

'Necessity does the work
of courage'

George Eliot.

In June 1948 I received a telephone call from the NUS president, inviting me to represent the union at the Sokol Festival which was due to commence in Prague on 6th July. He told me this was being organised by the International Union of Students and was to be a major youth and student gathering attended by students from all parts of the world. I assumed he thought me a good choice because I was relatively unknown and had no clear political label. (Years later he told me that he also had me in mind as his potential successor, and thought this exposure to international affairs would give me a higher profile in the union.)

At first I was hesitant about accepting the invitation. The war had left Europe in turmoil and there was a frightening tension between East and West, made worse by the threat of nuclear devastation. One war had ended but we were engulfed in another, the Cold War, which challenged the existing order in the West. Communist ideology and territorial ambitions were gaining ground in many parts of the world. In the words of Winston Churchill, in his famous speech delivered in Fulton, Missouri in March 1946, 'from Stettin in the Baltic to Trieste in the Adriatic an Iron Curtain has descended across the continent'.

A leading article that appeared in *The Times* in September 1999, described the Cold War as 'an epic, military and ideological confrontation that was the dominant event of the

103

second half of the century that hung over the lives of every adult alive today, influencing not only politics but science, culture and even language'.

And the poet and writer, Stephen Spender, wrote in his 1949 journal:

> 'What distresses me is having to reflect that Russia, although certainly not the 'Cause of peace,' is nevertheless, a cause. It has a faith to offer millions of people all over the world, even though communism might destroy the liberty of all except a few political leaders.'

The Sokol Festival was thus taking place against a turbulent background. The Czechoslovak communist coup d'état had just taken place, and Jan Masaryk, the foreign minister, had been found dead in the courtyard beneath his office window a month later. The further advance of communism into Europe was causing considerable concern in the West and reports appearing in the British press pointed to continuing opposition to the coup within Czechoslovakia, and to the persecution of anticommunist student and youth leaders. Nevertheless, I was immediately attracted to the idea of seeing something of what was happening behind the Iron Curtain, and began negotiations for leave from my studies, which involved agreement from the Ministry of Education and my college authorities.

Some of my closest friends tried to dissuade me from going, fearing that it might prove dangerous; while others saw the invitation as a plot to compromise my political neutrality in student eyes. It was undoubtedly a time of danger and intrigue but I believed then, as I do now, that opportunities in life are there to be taken, and I rarely passed one up. When I had the necessary permission I determined to go.

Before leaving the UK I had made some enquiries about the IUS, the sponsors of my invitation, and the context in which it had been formed, and had been faced with conflicting interpretations of its purpose. It appeared to have been established as part of the Soviet Union's grand strategy for subverting the non-communist world through the influence of what had become known as 'front' organisations. On the other hand it was said to be striving to achieve unity between student groups worldwide and was providing services, such as travel facilities and sanatoria which appeared commendable. I decided to keep an open mind on the subject.

I little realised it, but my visit to Prague was to launch me into an environment where the Cold War was being waged with ferocious intensity by young Marxist ideologues, fighting to capture the hearts and minds of young people throughout the world. But my knowledge of the political purpose of the festival and the background to the communist coup, apart from critical press reports in the UK, was limited at the time.

Making the journey by air at the height of the great divide in Europe left me wondering how our troops in the Special Operations Executive must have felt when they were dropped in France behind enemy lines in wartime. I was all too aware that the British government would have had no means of coming to my rescue had that proved necessary. In spite of my recent army experience I felt apprehensive and alone, not just when flying as the only passenger on the flight into Prague, but also on arrival, when I found myself surrounded by thousands of young delegates drawn from over a hundred countries, I was left in no doubt about their political affiliations.

The UK media had reported that, following the setting up of national 'Action Committees' by the new Czechoslovak regime, police had broken up a student demonstration in support of President Benes, that five professors had been summarily dismissed from Charles university, Prague, and that many students were being debarred from their studies. I wondered what chance I would have of finding out anything useful on my own in such a hostile environment.

The main events of the festival were held in a gigantic new stadium of Wembley proportions, and we were entertained over the next few days with dazzling mass displays involving thousands of jubilant young people rejoicing in their 'new-found freedom'. Demonstrations by many beautifully costumed participants, forming sensational patterns as they danced well rehearsed choreography, was as impressive as anything I had ever seen, while stirring music from the bands of the Soviet army and robust singing by army and youth choirs captivated us. All the many colourful indoor and outdoor displays of the 'triumph of communism over capitalism' were brilliantly orchestrated and each led to rapturous applause that echoed and re-echoed around the stadium. Superficially, there appeared to be total unity between the assembled delegates as they manifested their 'love for the Soviet Union', and for everything they fervently believed communism to stand for. I remained extremely sceptical. I had seen pictures of the Hitler Youth in similar mass demonstrations before the war, and I found myself relating the Sokol Festival events to these. I did not respond enthusiastically to assertions that 'the Soviet people are vastly superior to the peoples of any other country' which sounded markedly racist to me. But for all that, the festival was a highly emotional experience that left an indelible imprint on the thousands of young participants, especially those from colonial and other third-world countries, on whom the impact was probably far greater than it was on me. Being the only official delegate from Britain, and one of very few from a non-communist country, I was conscious of the organisers taking a special interest in me and felt ill at ease much of the time.

Interspersed with all the propaganda presented to the young

visitors as 'the new culture of communism', we were invited to attend meetings with various ministers of the new regime, who explained 'the inevitability of the triumph of communism and the great happiness of the Czechoslovak people at being liberated'. Rounds of rapturous applause from the visiting delegates followed each such declaration. Every mention of Stalin – and there were many – was greeted with another prolonged outburst of clapping. While all this adoration struck me as excessive, these young people, especially those from communist countries, did seem genuine in their adulation. But in contrast to their radiant smiles as they registered their love of Stalin and their own leaders, their outrage at any hint of dissent knew no bounds, as I was soon to discover.

At one of the smaller meetings I was invited to attend, I found myself face to face with the new Czechoslovak Prime Minister Antonin Zapotocky. I listened through translators to his account of recent political changes, and to his assertion that all the people were happy and pleased by their 'liberation'. As most of the other delegates felt obliged to offer their congratulations I faced a dilemma. Should I stay silent, or say something? In all conscience I could not offer congratulations, yet I felt that to stay silent would only misrepresent my position. Moreover, students had been surreptitiously whispering to me that all was not as it was being made to appear. One had pushed a note into my pocket pleading with me to tell the world about the repression and arrests of students. Another asked for help to escape the country. I was in no position to establish much for myself, but I sensed very strongly that many students were anything but happy with what had occurred. I took the bull by the horns and asked the prime minister why, if everyone was ecstatic about the changes, had I encountered so many individuals who were decidedly unhappy about the situation and anxious for the world to know the truth? There was a momentary silence as my remark was translated.

Those who understood English were already on their feet and converging on me. The prime minister himself saved the day by leaping to his feet and leaving the room without a further word. I was reprimanded by my fellow delegates and left wondering what would happen to those who had allowed me to attend that meeting, or even to go to Prague in the first place! It would have been prudent to stay silent, but that was not my nature. The incident only increased my apprehension and made me more aware of my isolation. Thinking students must have found conflict between the reality they saw and what they conceived socialism to be and were clearly terrified about the consequences for those who openly dissented and for those who had already disappeared.

When the festival ended I took an early flight home to report to a NUS council. Again I was the only passenger on board the Czechoslovak aeroplane and, on arrival at Heathrow, was delayed by an official who wanted further information about my trip. I had had no contact with the British embassy in Prague during my visit feeling sure they would have regarded me as a young communist. I now had visions of the Security Service building up massive files that would dog me for the rest of my days, and wondered how much of what I had really said and done in Prague would filter through to official records. I went straight from Heathrow to Oxford to report to what turned out to be a crucial meeting.

I was first involved in an executive committee meeting, held the night before the council, at which I reported on my Prague visit. The IUS, fearing that my report might be adverse, had already sent over a powerful team that included their British general secretary, Tom Madden, to present their case. He attended both the late night meeting and the council held the following day. I voiced my reservations about the conduct of the IUS, which had unreservedly supported the coup and had

108

failed to back the elected Czech student leaders. Madden, who was a very capable advocate, put up a strong defence of the actions of the IUS. After much political argument I agreed to a compromise resolution, which condemned both IUS support for the Soviet take-over of Czechoslovakia and the activities of the Action Committees, while preserving a working link with the international student body. Like most compromises the resolution we eventually agreed to put to council was far from ideal from the standpoint of any of the protagonists.

It fell to me to present the resolution to the full council on the following morning. By now it was clear that this was turning into a major crisis in NUS affairs and before I retired I spent some time preparing my notes. If council could not agree a compromise the union could disintegrate. Feelings were running high.

NUS councils present a forbidding audience at any time, and this meeting was no exception. Delegates represented some of the leading young intellectuals of the post-war era including a high proportion of former officers in the armed services – some of relatively senior rank. The level of debate at councils was invariably of a high order and my report was listened to intently. In his book *Students and The Cold War*, published in 1996, Dr. Kotek, a Belgian research student recorded:

> 'But the most telling speech came from Stanley Jenkins, whose report was heard in tense silence. Jenkins' temperament was cool and distant, and he never gave the impression of wanting to dominate or even convince his audience, but he was somebody to whom one listened with respect. His description of his experiences in Czechoslovakia was striking. He gave examples of the extreme tension and fear that had gripped Czech students – some had not dared to talk about politics in public, others were desperate to flee the country. He presented a damning picture of the new Czechoslovakia and of the Action

109

Committees, which, he had been told, would remain in control until there was political stability in the country.'

I spoke for over an hour and from the ensuing vote, which endorsed the compromise motion, it seems that I won over most of the centre ground as well as those of the political Left, the communists excluded. There was pressure from many NUS constituent colleges to condemn the IUS and to have no further links with them. At the opposite end of the political spectrum IUS supporters were seeking to achieve support for their position. At least for the time being, the immediate crisis that had threatened student unity appeared to be over. My stand, which had my predecessor's support, for constructive opposition within the international body was now established, and was to be the basis for NUS policy for the next two years.

At the time of the Sokol Festival, when the Iron Curtain was tightly drawn, the student movement provided one of few chinks through which the British people could penetrate it. My visit had given me my first glimpse of the communist world and the true nature of the IUS, and I had been able to convey something of what I found to my colleagues attending the Oxford council and through the press to the British people. This was before the days of widespread television coverage, although there was extensive radio and press reporting of our affairs. Where the leadership in the universities and colleges was in the hands of non-communists, the essence of my report had filtered back to thousands of British students and to many student groups abroad who had sent fraternal delegates to our meeting. After the Oxford council I returned to Cardiff and my studies to make up for lost time.

This foray into international student affairs had, as Rust envisaged, proved a unique occasion for me to make myself known to council delegates and establish my non-communist credentials. At the same time, ironically, my support for the

110

compromise resolution, although it had won the approval of council, had begun to cast doubts in the minds of several of my more right-wing supporters about my personal political allegiances. There was always a suspicion that someone who was prepared to countenance working in any way within a communist controlled body might just be a fellow-traveller or what later came to be known as a 'submarine'.

As it happened, although my uncle had strong ties to the Conservative party, my parents had never shown any party affiliations that I can recall, and there were no issues from my childhood days that had led me to any particular philosophy: in the jargon of the time, I would have been considered a singularly a-political individual. It was this 'neutrality' that made me broadly acceptable to most of the diverse groupings of students in post-war Britain, as represented in the NUS. Later I was to chair national committees comprising representatives of student factions having leanings towards (a) Conservatives, (b) Labour (c) Liberals (d) Catholics and other Christian groups, not to mention the atheists. Steering a course through that lot taught me a great deal that was to prove invaluable in later life. At the Sokol Festival my hosts presumably began by accepting me, at best as one of them, and at worst, not unduly hostile. After the Oxford council I was clearly identified as implacably anticommunist.

To balance my budget I had replied to a college advertisement that led to my taking a temporary job in the summer vacation of 1948 as an assistant surveyor at Stevenage – one of the first new towns to be built after the war. Although the NUS paid for my various trips for the union, I was always hard up, and still tied to that wretched demob. suit. My aunt in Brecon thought my parting gift from the army had had its day and insisted on my getting a new suit, tailor-made by my uncle's tailor in Cardiff, for which she paid. This suit was to last me for the next three years and assured me of something presentable to wear for the many high level meetings I was to have in Europe and elsewhere, until I started to earn enough to buy another.

On leaving my temporary job at Stevenage, I made straight for Paris with a small delegation to take part in a council of the International Union of Students. This was my first appearance at an IUS council and it proved a highly emotional occasion. I still did not know a great deal about the organisation, its purpose or origins, but it soon became clear to me that the communists controlled every aspect of the proceedings and were contriving in every possible way to achieve unanimous resolutions on a range of international issues. They were always praising the achievements of communism and denigrating the West and, in particular, British colonialism came in for repeated attacks.

I was now aware that the IUS, lavishly funded by the communist countries and especially the Soviet Union, had begun its quest for world domination of the student movement shortly after the war by establishing an office in Prague, which was not at that time under Soviet control. It was a matter of policy for 'front' organisations to conceal the link with their political masters and, wherever possible, to establish their main bases outside the communist bloc countries. They also made sure that leading western figureheads were appointed to prominent office. The IUS, having achieved this with an office in Prague and a British general secretary, was pursuing its task on behalf of the Soviet Union in deadly earnest.

At the Paris council I first saw the lengths to which the organisers were prepared to go to ensure that the main resolutions of their meetings were presented so as to express nothing but total unity: communists were never happy with opposition votes and even abstentions were unacceptable. To this end they had developed some shrewd techniques to achieve their objectives. The most common was to make nominal concessions, e.g. to agree to insert words such as 'some delegates disagreed' or 'some delegates thought', but to leave the content undisturbed and claim that the resolution was passed unanimously, knowing that few would read the small print or the full text. Communist jargon was baffling to me and there was a whole new vocabulary to contend with. To the Marxist, 'democracy', 'unity', 'justice' and 'colonialism' had different meanings from those familiar to me and I found this political world of 'double-speak', as it came to be known, mind-boggling. My war experience had made me appreciate the need, as they put it, to 'purge the globe of nazism and fascism' but I was not so sure about 'ridding the world of all vestiges of capitalism'. Perhaps I felt personally threatened!

When it came to the Paris council vote on the main resolution that was cleverly worded to achieve unanimity, our delegation divided, leaving me of all the delegates voting, as one of very few, and the only member of the British delegation, to abstain. None voted against. It was not a comfortable position to be in, and the mood of the council towards me was positively hostile. Immediately after the vote Eastern European delegates took the podium to remind the British delegates of the sacrifices made by the Soviet Union during the war – the loss of twenty-seven million Soviet lives, and so much more. None could deny the emotional force of statements like that. If anyone had asked me at that time to explain or defend my abstention I would have had some difficulty. But instinctively I knew that behind the facade of unity the communists were anxious to present, their real purpose was being concealed. Even at that time Stalin was reportedly a tyrant whose crimes transcended those of Hitler, but hard evidence was not readily available, and to mention such allegations in an IUS meeting would have invited a lynching party. Soviet propaganda had identified fascism as the great enemy of peace and those who opposed communism were *ipso facto* fascists, a label they now uncompromisingly attached to me. Looking back, I realise now that my opposition was based largely on gut feeling and instinct rather than any logic or argument I could bring to bear at the time. I was learning fast, but still had some way to go.

Communist conferences were carried forward on a wave of adulation of Stalin and the Soviet Union, and emotionalism, and I was acutely aware of the pressures this exerted on individual delegates. But I was surprised that close and politically reliable colleagues who were with me in Paris were sometimes carried away by the occasion, though I know that some lived to regret their susceptibility to the intense political, and especially emotional, pressure.

We were soon made aware that emphasis for the IUS in Britain was to be on what they called 'the fight against colonialism'. To the Cominform, (The Soviet Information Bureau, charged with the various communist programmes to subvert the West) and to the IUS, (which was an instrument of the Cominform) countries like India, Burma and those of Latin America were all considered colonial areas. A Colonial Bureau had been established within the Prague HQ when the IUS was first formed and, ironically in 1950, in pursuit of the 'front' technique, the IUS appointed me as chairman of the British committee of the Bureau! What a miscalculation that proved to be! Perhaps they thought that contact with colonial students in the UK would convert me to their cause.

My committee comprised representatives of all the colonial groups in our colleges and when we met, we were mainly concerned with practical help for students from our dependencies and I kept politics out of it as much as I could,

114

but in many respects they were inseparable from the problems our colonial peoples faced. We were hosts to them in Britain and they were mostly too polite and well-mannered to make an issue of their colonial status, while desperately anxious to make the best use of the educational opportunities being made available to them.

The IUS attacks against British colonialism, with a total disregard for what we in the West interpreted as Soviet colonialism elsewhere, were to lead to frequent clashes at subsequent international meetings. In support of their attacks on us, communist delegates who opposed us were generally well briefed by their masters. We were confronted with volumes of statistics alleging, for example, the imbalance between expenditure on white and native children's education in our colonial dependencies, or the percentages of national wealth devoted to social or military requirements. No weight was ever given on the credit side. We had to admit that, in the British dependencies, all was not as we would have liked, and none of us felt entirely happy with the arguments we deployed in defence of our policies; they often sounded unconvincing if not pathetic. We could never escape the fact that colonialism was something of an Achilles heel.

I could only judge the issue from my own experience of British overseas administrations, limited though this was, and could not believe that life in British colonies was half as bad as our adversaries made out. We tried to point out that Britain had already begun to transfer power peacefully to many formerly dependent people who, significantly, had chosen to remain within the Commonwealth of Nations. Such claims were treated with derision. I was later to live in Cyprus, Singapore and Malaya, and I, and vast numbers of residents of those countries, had nothing but the highest regard for those who had administered and developed the institutions we left behind. At

115

least, during the time of British rule, most of our colonies had lived in peace under the rule of law. Compared with what I later saw of other colonial administrations, we British had little to feel ashamed of and much to be proud about.

Communists were established masters of propaganda. What Hitler and Goebbels had practised in Germany, they had learned well. But this cost money and vast amounts of it were being channelled into the offices of 'front' organisations all over the world and used to influence people in many lands. The IUS Press and Information Department ensured that its news and article services flooded every target area they could reach. Their magazine *World Student News* printed 10,000 copies of an English edition and about 2,000 copies in a dozen or more other languages. It was a significant and largely successful operation.

From the outset of the Cold War the Cominform had established links between the powerful youth (WFDY) and student (IUS) communist 'front' organisations. Near the head of both stood Alexander Shelepin, a protégé of Stalin, and head of the influential Russian youth movement, the Komsomol, which was heavily subsidised by the Soviet government. He was a vice-president of both. When he finished his task with the youth and student organisations he went on to hold high office under Stalin and Khruschev, including Head of the Soviet State Security Service, the KGB (1958-1961), Head of the Soviet Trades Union Movement and a member of the Supreme Praesidium of the Soviet Union (1961-1975). In his 'student' days I sometimes shared the vice-president's office with him in Prague, and was to cross swords with him on many occasions. We had several backstage encounters during major conferences, when I wrestled, with the aid of interpreters, to understand his convoluted arguments seeking to reach agreement on the wording of resolutions to be put to IUS meetings. It often seemed that the only accord we could ever accept was an agreement to disagree, a formula I frequently used in despair. There was rarely any convergence of ideas.

A high proportion of the young delegates attending communist meetings in Eastern Europe just after the war, had been officers in the armed services of their countries, and others were mature students who had deferred their studies until the war was over. There was always doubt about the student status of some of the leading activists in the IUS. For example the first full-time president, Joseph Grohman, remained in office from the beginning of 1946 until 1951, and Alexander Shelepin held office until after the death of Stalin in March 1953, while still prominent in the leadership of the Soviet Union and a number of Soviet organisations, somehow escaping the consequences of his close association with his disgraced and deceased idol.

Shelepin made two visits to London in my years with the NUS. On one of these we toured British universities and shared a platform. I was always at pains to explain NUS policy, which was highly critical of the IUS pro-soviet line, while he defended the opposite corner. Mostly, on home ground, I had audiences supporting me, but he commanded majority support at some of the meetings. At the London School of Economics he won the day hands down and I was booed off stage. It is noteworthy that, in April 1965, when he visited the UK as a guest of Prime Minister Harold Wilson, he announced that he had never been to Britain before, yet I have a photograph of him standing with me on the steps of the NUS office in London in 1950. The *Daily Mail* astutely evaluated this man, when it published a headline which read 'Keep this man out of Britain'.

On the same tour we found ourselves sitting on a train with his interpreter and an elderly lady who paid quiet attention to our discussion. I had just finished answering some question about party political influence on the British press when the lady demanded to correct the record: she did not think I had given my guest a fair account. It was just my luck, for I later discovered that she was Lady Astor, a leading figure in the Liberal Party and the first woman to sit in the House of Commons. If Shelepin had thought, as he probably did, that I was not representative of British students, that intervention must have confirmed his view.

As I travelled around Europe attending various conferences, I never ceased to be amazed at the importance accorded to student and youth leaders, particularly in Eastern Europe. It was, of course, these groups that were most likely to provide the next generation of national leaders, and the communists were well aware of this. They would also have been considered of significance in that they not only comprised the bulk of young intellectuals but also those who had had first hand experience of war and were thus, perhaps, more susceptible to new ideas and to change. They were certainly amenable to overtures about peace and reconciliation between nations, and that became the main thrust of Soviet propaganda.

This heightened regard for students was exemplified in France by our being entertained at the Elysée Palace, during the course of a meeting in Paris, by the French President Auriol. On that occasion I found myself sitting next to him in a magnificent dining chamber. The first course was a huge plate of oysters. Having never tasted them before (or since) I sat looking at them for some time wondering how or where to begin, while the president scoffed his plateful. He then turned to me and said that if I did not like seafood he did. He promptly seized my plate and devoured another dozen.

Ralph Blumenau, who was NUS vice-president in charge of

our international affairs, came from a family that had escaped from Germany at the beginning of Hitler's campaign against the Jews. I thought him one of the most perceptive of student leaders of that time, and politically mature beyond his years. He commented on the Eastern European student leaders in an article he wrote in 1948, for a student magazine of the day, *Student Focus*:

> 'These are not students playing politics: these are politicians. The head of the Romanian delegation is the secretary to Anna Pauker, Romania's Foreign Minister; members of the Polish, Soviet and Czech delegations play a more important part in political life than in England – can you imagine such a council being received at Buckingham Palace or even at 10, Downing Street?'

The young communist students we came into contact with were far more politically aware than their counter-parts in the West. I had entered the world of undergraduate politics with little knowledge of the subject and oblivious to most of what had gone before on the international student scene. I was totally unaware of the intense interest being shown at the time by many in government, as evidenced by documents made public under the Thirty-year Rule, which show that the British and American governments were deeply concerned about many aspects of the subversive effect of the 'front' organisations on youth and students in the West. They had frequently discussed the threat and debated whether, for example, visas should be granted for communist student leaders to attend meetings in the UK, or whether advice should be given about British undergraduates participating in meetings in Eastern Europe. Although I personally did not encounter any hostility from our own authorities, we were aware that leaders of the NUS were regarded in the Foreign Office as young communists. Not surprisingly we had no support from officialdom in any of the Eastern European exploits described in later chapters, until the very end of my term of office, when there was some recognition of what we were trying to do. Ralph Blumenau did eventually succeed in getting some background papers from the Foreign Office on which he drew for a major speech I was to make in Prague, but it had taken a long time to change the Foreign Office attitude. At the most critical time for us in our fight to counter communist subversion, it seemed to me that we were fighting a battle on behalf of the West and getting no help whatsoever, even when we requested it, and I resented what I saw as the negative attitude adopted towards us.

The American administration seemed even less anxious to be associated with their young emissaries than the British were, and did not become involved until much later. After my time in the student movement, when the Americans became convinced of the danger of communist infiltration of western society through youth and student organisations, the CIA intervened in a big way and poured money into a wide range of anti or non-communist organisations. In the end their involvement proved the downfall of some of the very organisations, such as the World Assembly of Youth, that had been set up to counter the communist threat. It was a sorry ending. But before that there was a period in which we struggled almost alone in a rearguard action within the IUS itself.

Some of the early notes of warning about the real purpose of the IUS had emanated from an American student vice-president, Bill Ellis, long before I became involved, but I did not know of this at the time. He had, for example, raised early doubts about whether Dr. Tom Madden, the British IUS secretary, was really representative of British students and youth. Unfortunately his warnings went unheeded.

It helped the communists that many western students unions were tied by constitutions that restricted their activities to

120

matters that 'affected students as such', a clause that virtually precluded their participation in political activities. The British NUS constitution was of that kind. Interpretation of the clause had always proved difficult, and in IUS circles such neutrality was unsustainable and indefensible. Did war affect students as such? This was the kind of question hurled back at us, and we had no ready answer. In all our political debates behind the Iron Curtain we were at a disadvantage because of this restriction. But at home this had frequently saved the national union from division and I used to refer to it as a 'counter-self-destruct' device. In meetings in Eastern Europe we tried first to observe this a-political convention, but as it prevented us from presenting counter-arguments to communist accusations against us, we tended at later meetings to disregard it altogether.

Another handicap we faced in the West, apart from the limitations our own constitution imposed, was that we had to observe an established convention that banned all reference to the political affiliations of delegates attending our meetings. This proved an obstacle in that one could not legitimately draw attention to the fact that a speaker was of any known political persuasion and, in particular, that speakers sent to our councils as fraternal delegates from Eastern Europe were almost certainly communists, and that their contributions to our debates should be seen in that light. We had in the NUS membership at that time a number of small teachers' training and domestic science colleges whose union deliberations were most unlikely to have embraced political issues. Thus it fell to the activists to brief such delegates regarding political overtones, behind the scenes.

As time wore on I became torn between the growing intensity of my NUS involvement and my studies, and had just resigned myself to concentrating on the latter when I received a

121

surprise invitation.

CHAPTER TEN

ON TOUR AND FLYING THE FLAG

'Wit is but truth made amusing'

Bulwer Lytton.

In January 1949, in my third year at Cardiff, I received an invitation from the NUS president to join a three-man undergraduate debating team to tour India, Pakistan and Ceylon (now Sri Lanka). I was flattered to be asked but concerned that to accept would mean that I would be away from Cardiff for about three months of what might prove to be my final year. I had already applied for a grant for a fourth year, leading to a Higher National Diploma, but this had yet to be approved. Moreover I had had no previous experience of university debating. John Parry Lewis, who had introduced me into NUS affairs in the first place, wrote to persuade me not to go. He saw the whole thing as a communist plot to get me out of the country and thereby lessen my chances of election as NUS president in the following year! I was in two minds about going, but after discussing the invitation with my college principal, he agreed, as did the Ministry of Education, to grant me the necessary leave of absence. Thus on 23rd January 1949 I departed by KLM airways for Karachi, in company with two other undergraduates, one our team leader, Colin Jackson, from Oxford university, representing England, who was already an experienced Oxford union debater and had previously led a British team to the USA and another to South Africa. He had served with the Royal Fusiliers. The other team member was Alexander McLellan, reading English at Glasgow university, representing Scotland, who had served in a Rajput Regiment of Indian Artillery. He was a debating novice like myself. His Scottish accent was to fascinate his audiences on the subcontinent and occasionally I would draw a laugh at his

123

expense by offering to translate him into English. At the conclusion of our debates in India, to the delight of our audiences, he would usually round off with a few words in classical Hindi, delivered, as the press recorded, 'with a strong Scottish burr'. My Welsh lilt, deliberately accentuated on these occasions, was perhaps easier for them to comprehend. I remember listening to the sound tracks of Indian films on my earlier visit to India during the war and thinking how similar the Urdu intonation is to that of the Welsh speaker.

Our tour took place against the background of the independence granted to India and Pakistan in 1947. The partition of the country into two states had resulted in a mass migration of Moslems to Pakistan and Hindus to India and, when we first arrived in West Pakistan, the upheaval this had caused was still in evidence. As we travelled by train from Karachi to Lahore we were told that, only a few days earlier, a train on the same track had been attacked by Hindus who had slain hundreds of Moslem refugees seeking safety in their new homeland. We heard, and in the press read, similar stories of Moslem attacks on Hindus and, while we could do little to confirm these reports for ourselves, we had no reason to doubt them. Some three-quarters of a million people were reported to have died as a direct consequence of Partition.

Before setting out from England we had surmised that the British Council, which was sponsoring the tour, was doing so mainly in order to test public reaction to a British presence in the subcontinent. They need not have worried; the friendly reception we received throughout the tour was overwhelming, indeed the hospitality could not have been surpassed. Wherever we went staff and students in their hundreds turned out to meet us and hear our debates. We were greeted on station platforms when we arrived, whether by day or night and wined and dined by many state governors and premiers, including the governors of Madras, and Dhaka, and the chancellors and vice-chancellors of many universities. When we journeyed by train word went ahead to ensure that we would be well provided for. We were asked what food we liked, so that it could be prepared on the train and, at each arrival, we were garlanded with flowers. I was never sure when it was polite to cast these off, and a dozen or so can be cumbersome to wear all day in the heat. The impression we gained, wherever we went, was that our hosts wanted the British back, if not in government, at least as friends, tourists and advisers.

When we embarked on our trip it was my understanding that the British Council would be meeting all our expenses, and it was not until we were well into India that Colin Jackson, our team leader and impresario, revealed that the British Council was only committed to paying our fares out and back. We had set out with many introductions from the British Royal Overseas League, and these were to provide us with an entree at many points, but there was no provision for financing our other travels. Colin lived on optimism and with his unlimited charm and enterprise it did not take him long to negotiate further cash advances from British Council representatives that covered our travelling expenses, as well as hospitality from financiers and industrialists. One outstanding example of this generosity provided for our stay in Bombay where we were invited by a member of the Tata family, owners of the Taj Mahal Hotel, to stay there for as long as we wished as his personal guests. We never saw our benefactor again, but we took up his offer and enjoyed three days living in imperial splendour at the Taj.

In just under three months we travelled, by road, rail and air, from Karachi, on the west coast of Pakistan, to Calcutta on the east coast of India, then west to Bombay before going north to Dehra Dun, Bagdogra, Siliguri, Darjeeling and Mussoorie in

125

the Himalayas. We stopped off at numerous places for debates including Lahore, Amritsar, Jullundur, Delhi, Lucknow, Allahabad, Benares, Poona and Nagpur. Thereafter our travels continued into East Pakistan, to Dhaka and Andhra Waltair, before we headed south for more debates in Madras, Chidambaram, Annamalai and Trivandrum, with other stops along the way. We then headed south to Ceylon and, after visiting colleges in Colombo, where we were entertained by the Prime Minister, Mr. Senanayake, and Kandy where, perched high on howdahs we rode on elephants through tropical jungle, we returned by way of central India, stopping off at Bangalore, Hyderabad, Agra and Aligarh.

It was a strenuous and demanding itinerary, but we were young, fit and ready for anything, and what an incredible adventure it proved to be. With similar armed service backgrounds, we three debaters got on exceedingly well together, and thoroughly enjoyed every minute of it.

It would be impossible to pick out all the highlights from a tour that covered so much ground and included such colour and variety. Some of the sights and sounds were unforgettable. Who could fail to be impressed by the grandeur of the Golden Temple at Amritsar, the solitary beauty of the Taj Mahal, the gigantic scale of the Himalayas, the splendour of the palaces of the Maharajas, or the devotion of the followers of India's many religious sects as they attended their temples or bathed in the waters of the Ganges. What memories! And we shall never forget the deep and sincere kindness shown to us wherever we went.

As we travelled the length and breadth of the subcontinent we enjoyed an amazingly diverse range of experiences, some more appreciated than others. We enjoyed being taken on the river for a delightful picnic in Dhaka with the state governor in his launch, while in Bombay a more dubious pleasure was afforded by students who insisted on taking us to see the famous burial grounds for Parsees where bodies are placed on high platforms for birds to devour the flesh: such morbid tastes.

We had to cover great distances to attend all the debates and visits we had arranged, or had been arranged for us, and we made many internal flights with Air India on the old aeroplanes they then had in use, many of which seemed past their safe operational dates. We marvelled that they could still get off the ground. We also travelled for days and nights on trains hauled by ancient locomotives that hissed, clanked and groaned their way over tracks badly in need of maintenance, but they got us there in the end.

Our tour took place during the time of prohibition in India and as we had little idea as to where the demarcation lines had been drawn, before taking a drink of anything alcoholic, we had first to establish which side of the line we were on. We knew the penalties of being caught with alcohol in prohibited areas and were prepared. Whenever we thought we were crossing a line we poured any alcohol we had into our orange squash bottles and hoped for the best. But we were caught napping one day when a police team boarded our train unexpectedly and began to search the compartments. I retired to the toilet, decanted our gin into an orange squash bottle and re-emerged to find Colin offering the prohibition police a soft drink from one of my previously fortified containers. They thoroughly enjoyed the English orange juice and went off in good spirits! As one of them departed he turned to me and, with the customary rocking of the head from side to side, said 'I like very much the English orange'. I cannot be sure whether his eye winked or not.

I cannot think why, for none of us cared much for alcohol,

127

but we once applied for a liquor quota, only to discover that this invoked the whole gamut of Indian bureaucracy: they just love paperwork, rubber stamps and multiple copies, practices learned from the British. We were obliged to fill out application forms in quadruplicate, and have them rubber stamped several times. One set of forms required us to state the religions of ancestors going back several generations, so we thought of all the religions we could, and ascribed these to our forebears. My father appeared as a Moslem, my mother as a Buddhist, my grandfather as a Calvinist and my great grandfather as a Mormon. Nobody even read the forms and, after much rubber-stamping, we got our meagre quota.

In all our debates, in order to overcome any issue of 'them versus us', we always contrived to have one member of our team speaking on each side. We had sent ahead a list of suggested topics for debate, but our hosts, who were most anxious to give a good showing, were apprehensive about choosing any of our well-rehearsed subjects that might put them at a disadvantage. Perhaps it was we who should have worried for they produced many fine debaters. To turn the tables on us where they could, they would spring a surprise subject on us, usually on the day of the debate. We even arrived on the platform for some not knowing what theme had been chosen and, before an audience of hundreds, we heard the topic announced in a welcoming speech. On one such occasion in Bombay, where we had perhaps the largest audience of our tour – probably well over two thousand, including many representatives of the Diplomatic Corps for whom the first 20 rows of seating had been reserved – the chancellor announced, with no prior warning, that the subject of the debate would be 'That India should be a secular state' and that 'Mr. Jenkins from the visiting team will open the debate for the motion'. As this was not a subject on our list, and not one we had debated previously, I quickly conferred with my colleagues as to what 'secular' meant precisely. Sadly I had not resolved my dilemma when, to avoid too much embarrassment, I launched into my usual banter about each other's nationalities, the weather, our love of India and anything else that came to mind, including a range of well-worn anecdotes and jokes from earlier encounters on the tour. Eventually the referee graciously drew my attention to the fact that I had exceeded my allotted time, to which I replied 'Oh what a pity! I was just about to address the main question' and sat down, to a burst of laughter and applause. Whether we won or lost the motion was of little consequence to us, though we generally tried to put enough content into our speeches to make them sound plausible. I used to remark on the seriousness of their chosen subjects and, to get a laugh, would inform the listeners, that, in the UK, we rarely debated anything more serious than 'This House prefers to be bottled rather than canned' or 'This House prefers its tea without milk'.

Jackson, a seasoned and accomplished speaker taught us a lot about debating techniques. He would have the audiences rolling in the aisles after a few humorous opening remarks. During one debate in Calcutta, where we had over a thousand sitting cross-legged on the lawns of the campus, Jackson seized on a point an impassioned Indian lady speaker had made about the need for harmony between nations and peace throughout the world. Unfortunately for her she let slip some phrase about 'the world shrinking' and Jackson was onto it in a flash. Expressing astonishment and concern and looking anxiously about him for signs of cracks in the earth's surface, he suggested that if the shrinking process was as serious as we had been led to believe, we ought perhaps to be making our way to the safety of the Himalayas! He could be disarmingly flattering and deflating with remarks such as 'The opposition speaker made a powerful case and I can honestly say that he was far and away the best advocate on our side'. He would describe an opposition speaker as 'the atom bomb of the debate' and then express regret that 'he had exploded on the wrong side'. Nobody got away with a loose statement. We felt sorry for the lady who concluded her peroration with the words 'We are a great people in a great State'. She lived to regret it. As did the student he awarded a 'full blue for a half wit'. In defence of her case for the motion 'the future lies with the East', one undergraduate used the argument 'The sun rises in the east'. Colin lost no time in pointing out that this occurred twelve hours after it had set in the west. I remember a point from Jackson's advice to us on debating techniques – 'Listen carefully to what the other side say, flatter them and then pick on some triviality and turn it against them'. He used this ploy ruthlessly, and to great effect. Our hosts loved it all, thinking it typically British, while we tried to keep a balance between frivolity and seriousness.

The interest shown in our tour was such that we had the doubtful pleasure of seeing our debate speeches quoted in full in the morning papers. We would scan the pages and groan as we read our sordid jokes as they appeared in cold type! This advance notice of the content of our debates, presented in this way to the next team to oppose us, presented a problem. We had no speechwriters to support us and my repertoire, supplemented by a little book of jokes I bought on a station platform, was soon exhausted. We fell back on well-worn chestnuts, pitting English, Welsh and Scottish against each other – without of course, letting the Irish, who were not represented, off the hook. There were complications when we crossed from India to Pakistan requiring a rapid reappraisal of some of our humour. Indeed most of our anecdotes needed to be revamped at every border crossing. Remarks in India such as 'our Pakistani hosts were the kindest and most considerate people', were suitably revised.

The Times Educational Supplement of 30th April 1949 in a report on our tour noted that:

> 'The motion, 'The future belongs to Asia', was always carried, whatever the nationality of the proposer. A remarkable measure of agreement was achieved on the proposal that all university examinations should be abolished'

That was perhaps understandable!

A few of our debates were at Moslem ladies' colleges. It was weird to debate with young ladies enveloped in white veils and hoods resembling row upon row of miniature 'tents'. A ripple or flutter in the fabric was the only indication that a joke had struck home, while a really telling story would cause the sea of 'tents' to rise and fall like hot air balloons about to ascend or crash. After we got home the principal of one of the ladies' colleges wrote to me expressing concern that we might give publicity to photographs we had taken at her college. One of the more orthodox parents had asked for an assurance that all the pictures would be destroyed.

One of a number of radio broadcasts we made during the tour turned out to be a question and answer session when, for forty minutes, we had to answer callers' questions on every aspect of life in Britain: our omniscience was fully tested. I was asked about the press in India and I remember commenting on newspaper advertisements in a morning paper: 'Owner of tractor wishes to contact owner of thresher, object matrimony, please send photograph of machine'. And another: 'For sale, first class pedigree bloodhound, excellently trained, will eat anything and especially fond of children'. We knew, as every British politician knows, that the more one talks the fewer difficult questions one has to answer. I can only hope that no record of that broadcast exists in the archives of Radio India.

The exaggerated importance attached to our visit was similar to the prestige accorded to students I had experienced in Eastern Europe. This was exemplified by the events on a memorable day, 4th April 1949, spent in New Delhi, when we had breakfast with the Indian Prime Minister, Pandit Nehru, at his home, and talked about his days at Oxford, his former links with the All India Students Congress, the state of student unions in India and the threat of left-wing infiltration. Nationalist leaders had made extensive use of students to ferment unrest and anti-British feeling during their struggle for independence and this was a difficult and serious heritage for the new rulers who had sown seeds where they did not now wish to reap. Independence had brought a realisation that the basis of their student organisations must be changed to fit the new role that students would be required and expected to play, and the prime minister was already taking an active interest in moves that were afoot to create a new representative structure of student unions. Sadly, our time with him was all too short and we were unable to pursue these matters in any depth

Our breakfast meeting was followed by an afternoon call at Viceroy House to meet Admiral Lord Louis Mountbatten, the last Viceroy of India and the first governor-general of the new Dominion. Mountbatten had not left India immediately after Partition, having been asked by Nehru and Rajagopalachari, following the assassination of Mahatma Gandhi, to stay as long as possible after the transition of power so as to provide continuity and stability. We found Mountbatten having his pedicure: he lay in the centre of a great hall stretched out on a low divan with beautiful Indian maidens tending his feet as we spoke.

On the same day we had tea in government house with His Excellency the Governor General, Rajagopalachari, the first Indian incumbent of that post, and that night, dinner with the vice-chancellor and his staff at the university. The following day we called on General Nye, the British high commissioner, and the day after that we flew back to Karachi for another debate, a call on the minister of education, lunch with the British high commissioner, tea with the governor-general and dinner with the university vice-chancellor. Each day brought another round of visits and one or two debates.

We never knew what to expect at our next port of call. When we arrived in Mysore at sunrise we were still dressing when the train pulled into the platform. I was in my pyjamas and shaving when students and staff who had turned out to meet and garland us with flowers invaded the train. As most of them seemed to be wearing pyjamas anyway, they scarcely noticed my attire. We were taken to a hotel where, we were told, Beverley Nichols stayed when he began writing his book 'Verdict on India'. Our host who had read the book – in which Nichols advocated the partition of India and wrote, 'a united India is a myth which will cause endless strife', and other of his writings in which he referred to India in derogatory terms – commented that he thought the room in our hotel where Nichols once stayed still needed disinfecting! In Mysore we were entertained by the maharajah who took us big game hunting. We did not actually shoot anything, or have any real prospect of doing so, but it was great fun to ride on elephants with a retinue of beaters.

In both Trivandrum and Bangalore we were officially state guests. The printed programmes for our visits show that we were required by the local army commanders to inspect guards of honour on arrival. With our recent army backgrounds we coped with these ceremonies without difficulty, though we felt undeserving of such honours. Our programme for each visit was usually worked out in advance of our arrival, but we generally found time for a game of tennis or a swim, even if it had to be before the sun was up. I remember that at Trivandrum we took a dip in the sea, at a very early hour, from what must be one of the most beautiful beaches in the world. Seeing a group of women washing clothes in a stream that discharged into the sea near where we bathed, Jackson was quick to revive another joke that he used to good effect at our next debate, when he referred to a *dhobi* as a woman who breaks up rocks with a shirt.

On one of two visits we paid to Calcutta we arrived very late from Bombay, because of a strike by Air India staff. Jackson went off to confirm our onward air bookings and McLellan went to the university to enquire when the debate would actually be held, only to find the students assembling on the university lawns expecting it to begin. In the absence of my colleagues I had taken to my bath at the rear of our hotel suite and, when McLellan returned to the hotel looking for me, he knocked on my door, but failed to rouse me. I had probably fallen asleep. He found Jackson, and they rushed to the campus and the contest began. Naturally my absence was noted and reported in the press, but I knew nothing of the debate until the event was over. When Jackson and McLellan returned to the hotel they found me enjoying a cool beer, bathed, and waiting for them. The event for which I had flown from Bombay had taken place without me.

I mention this incident because I was to hear more of it a few months later at an international student gathering in Sofia, Bulgaria, where I was accused, in one of the many personal attacks I was later to face, of having spent my time in India 'organising reactionary students to struggle against the forces of progress and democratisation' or some such communist nonsense. But more of this in my later account of the Sofia council.

I shall not forget an occasion when we were in a taxi in Calcutta and our driver ran down a small boy and drove on. We were horrified and insisted that he should stop. We picked up the child, who was about eight years old, and appeared to have broken a leg, and asked the driver to take us to the nearest hospital. We seemed to drive for miles at hair-raising speed through streets crammed with oxen, stray cows, carts, dogs and people, before we came to a hospital where dozens of patients lay outside on the grass waiting for medical attention. We carried our victim into the hospital and reported the accident. Presumably, because we were foreigners, they listened sympathetically, while explaining that there was nothing they could do. They had many such cases. We had to leave the lad there and hope that he would eventually be treated. Fortunately we had no health problems ourselves, which was perhaps just as well for one doctor's nameplate I saw was for a Dr. J. S. Singh MD (Madras) Failed!

Another taxi ride I remember well – and it is difficult to forget any taxi ride in India – was when we went north from Dehra Dun in the Himalayas to attend a debate in a marquee at Siliguri. We had been advised not to go because of student protest riots over some college problems, but decided to take the risk. The monsoon rains, which obscured all visibility, made our ride through the mountains seem even more precarious than it actually was, and we considered ourselves lucky to reach our destination. Near the end of our debate, just as McLellan was reaching his Hindi peroration, the wind came up unexpectedly and caught the marquee, sending it skywards. In the ensuing chaos we were bundled back into a taxi by the authorities, who feared further student riots, and driven back to Dehra Dun at breakneck speed by a driver who seemed hell-bent on our destruction.

We had made the journey to Dehra Dun by a little train that

chugged its way through the foothills of the Himalayas, on a narrow gauge railway, so snake-like that it seemed to advance a few hundred yards only to loop back on itself time and time again as it negotiated the steep gradients. I had always been fascinated by trains and could have gone on and on gazing through railway carriage windows, and engine smoke, watching the ever-changing panorama. Our travels took us through desert plains, mountain ranges and lush valleys offering fascinating vistas of the countryside and people, some wearing vividly coloured traditional dress, while others tended their crops, aided by teams of oxen, water buffalo, and mules. Time seemed to have passed them by.

We found both Indian and Pakistani students much more politically orientated than undergraduates in the UK. They had become politicised through their long history of support for the non-violent and non-co-operation movement led by Mahatma Gandhi and their colonial past must have contributed to their political awareness. Some universities had as many student unions as they had political parties, and student strikes in support of workers, for the abolition of certain tests and examinations, were commonplace. They even struck if examination papers were not to their liking! Students in Hyderabad, disappointed with their degree examination results and wanting recognition for their role in some recent police action, had demanded reward in the form of special 'passes'. When they did not succeed they had voted to 'starve to death'. Students at Dhaka were still posing a real threat to the stability of their government and were on strike, during our visit, in support of better wages for university servants. Others at Karachi struck on the second day of an examination because they thought the standard set on the first day was too high. Appealing though this latter idea was, I had little hope of introducing it in Cardiff!

I had my camera at the ready most of the time as we travelled around the subcontinent, and I took many photographs, as did my companions. McLellan was an experienced photographer and I often sought his advice about exposure and focus. On one occasion, as so often happened when we stopped our taxi or car in any city, beggars besieged us, with their hands outstretched for alms. A wizened old woman thrust her palm into our cab and I asked my colleagues 'What shall I give her?' 'Try f22 at 100th', said McLellan.

At the end of our travels we calculated that we had covered 25,000 miles in 12 weeks and taken part in 27 debates attended by over 30,000 students. We had visited 21 universities and 15 other colleges, and made 9 broadcasts. We had also fitted in visits to factories and libraries and I had demonstrated my prowess at table tennis at a number of colleges! Our hosts had also fielded an all-India junior tennis champion to give me a game.

Our tour had extensive press coverage and I brought home dozens of press cuttings and photographs. Some debates we won and some we lost. We had argued for causes we often disagreed with, but we had never argued with much force in favour of or against anything. I have a feeling that I did not put my all into my argument for the motion, debated in Karachi, 'In the opinion of this House the only salvation for humanity lies in a world state'. Nor did I enthuse overmuch when putting the motion in New Delhi that 'The future lies with the East'.

We flew home on 9th April 1949, via Basra, Cairo and Rome, with a deep affection for the countries we had visited and for the many who had looked after us so well. After reporting on the tour to a NUS council at Bangor in North Wales, I returned to Cardiff to write thank you letters for the hospitality we had received on our tour, to give interviews to

the press and make a few broadcasts on local radio. From one
script I prepared for a broadcast I made from Cardiff, I see that
I said:

> 'Almost everyone we spoke to in India would like to
> see some formula for India's continuance in the
> Commonwealth, but with independence in the sense that
> she would no longer be under the domination of any
> foreign power – which means Britain. The Administration
> is struggling, in the absence of British administrators who
> left at the time of Partition but we saw everywhere
> evidence that the people are tackling their enormous
> problems earnestly and are making good progress.
> Everywhere we went and everything we saw and heard
> convinced us that British prestige in these countries has
> never stood higher than it does today.'

And in an article I wrote for the NUS journal *Student
Chronicle* on my return, I was amused, in later years, to read
the following.

> 'We lost count of the number of colleges, libraries and
> hospitals we visited, and the number of questions we
> answered in YMCAs, YMIAs, colleges, convents, boys'
> and girls' schools. I shall never forget three consecutive
> questions in one of the ladies' colleges; they were: "What
> do girls in Britain do in their spare time?" "Do children
> under three have free issues of cod-liver oil?" And
> "Would you abolish the House of Lords?" I can remember
> that we denied any knowledge of what girls do in their
> spare time; we abolished cod-liver oil, and kept the House
> of Lords. I hope we said the right thing.'

These broadcasts and articles led to invitations to speak at
colleges and other venues but these had to wait while I caught
up with my studies, but I did accept a number later on.

When the dust had settled, we three debaters met in London
to prepare our report for the British Council. For our sponsors

138

it might have seemed a deft, low-key public relations exercise – had it gone wrong it could perhaps have been written off as a 'student misadventure', – but it did not, and we could fairly describe it in our report as a public relations triumph. Without any doubt we created a bond with all those students and university staff we met that would have lasting benefit for both Governments and for the British Council. We must also have had some effect on the thinking of students with regard to the value of non-political student unions and for moderate and constructive attitudes towards politics and authority. We were certainly able to satisfy any doubts our sponsors may have entertained about the warmth of the reception accorded to us.

For our part we had gained personally from acquiring greater knowledge of the countries we visited and of the aspirations and thinking of the younger generation and future leaders of the subcontinent. We returned home with the highest regard for their intelligence, social and political skills. Their style of debating was markedly different from ours but, from studying them, our own skills emerged enhanced. We had also been able to identify a very genuine empathy between the students we met and students in the UK, and although this was perhaps only to be expected after the long British association, it was gratifying to know that this had been relatively undamaged by the traumatic move to independence.

After preparing our report we went our separate ways. Colin became a Labour MP. We never met again, but I did renew my acquaintance with Alex McLellan fifty years later, when I arranged to meet him on a holiday visit to Loch Rannoch in Scotland. Fifty years had taken nothing away from the many happy memories of our fascinating debating tour.

On my return to college I found myself three months behind with my work, but in my absence a few friends had kept adequate lecture notes for me, directing my attention to all those areas I needed to address in order to catch up. They were incredibly supportive, and their notes were placed at my disposal. In a few weeks I felt fairly confident that I had recovered the lost ground, which was just as well for I faced end of term examinations within weeks of my return. Fortunately, the results showed no material loss for having absented myself for so long,

To put this episode of my life into context, I remember returning home anxious to recount my travels to my aunt and uncle, neither of whom had ever travelled far from Brecon and who had never been on an aeroplane. Instead they settled down to watch a programme on their first ever television set and my story had to be filed for me to relate on a later occasion.

CHAPTER ELEVEN

POLITICAL GAMES

'Heaven's best aid is wasted upon men
Who to themselves are false'

Wordsworth.

Throughout 1949 the intensity of my NUS work increased. Almost every weekend I found myself travelling by train from Cardiff to London for lengthy meetings which often lasted late into the night followed by a long train journey back to Cardiff in the early hours of Monday to begin lectures on the same day. I was already involved in the work of the NUS executive, international and finance committees and a number of sub-committees. I had also become involved with other external bodies such as the World Assembly of Youth, where I worked closely with Guthrie Moir, its British president, who became a strong supporter in my battles with the extreme Left, and with International Student Service which, in collaboration with the NUS Grants and Welfare Department, headed by Martin Ennals, was making a notable contribution to student welfare.

It was on one of many late night journeys when I was returning from London to Cardiff, after a busy weekend of meetings, and just as we entered the Severn tunnel, that an elderly lady, my sole companion in the train compartment, surprised me with the remark 'Young man, I hope you don't mind my speaking to you, but you have such an interesting aura' What could I say? She went on to say 'I am an experienced medium and I find you a most interesting subject'. I still did not know what to make of this and there was no easy escape route in a tunnel. 'Would you be surprised' she continued 'if I told you that you were about to undertake a

141

great change in your life. Something will happen to you of great importance. I cannot say what it is, but you are destined to hold high office'. By this time we were well into the tunnel and I was convinced that I had run into a real 'nutter'. She insisted that some significant event lay just around the corner. I was glad to emerge from the tunnel and see her leave the train at Newport. But I often reflected on her prediction as the next few months unfolded. In the student context, events were to show that she had keen powers of perception.

The next landmark event for me was a NUS council held at Exeter university in July 1949. At this meeting there was extensive lobbying for candidates for the presidency. Under the terms of the NUS constitution Bill Rust had to stand down after having served two years: his student days were over. I was approached to stand by a number of delegates – mostly those whose politics were right of centre – but I was reluctant to run. There had never before been a national president from one of the technical colleges, and I felt fairly new to the game. There was, too, the distinct prospect of a majority of any new executive being politically well to the left of centre. For some years communists and left-wingers had held considerable influence within the NUS executive; and I wondered if life would be tenable for me, if the team elected with me turned out to be politically divorced from my thinking. And would I command sufficient support if I stood on so negative a platform as simply anti-communist? I had no political party affiliation of my own but, paradoxically, in the event this actually strengthened my position. As so often happens in politics it is the negatives rather than the positives that count! I was left with the nagging suspicion that, should I not run for the presidency, I might spend the rest of my life regretting that I had backed away from a major challenge.

The question of whether or not I should stand was resolved

while I was in a bus queue talking to John McNab, a former naval officer who was president of Queen Mary College London students union, and right of centre in his politics. We discussed the forthcoming elections, the danger of increased communist influence in the universities if they produced another left-wing executive and, in the end, we struck a deal. I agreed to seek election as president if he would stand as vice-president. I thought John had a good chance of being elected and felt reassured to think that, if I made it, I would have at least one staunch ally on the executive. And so it came to pass. NUS elections were conducted on a single transferable vote system and, with a field of five candidates, there was no need for a second count for John and I both had convincing majorities. While all the communists would almost certainly have voted against me, many in the middle ground must have supported me. The compromise resolution that followed my Sokol Festival report to the Oxford NUS council, when I had gone along with the decision to continue to try to make the IUS work, i.e. to work constructively from within the organisation to try to reform it, must have won me a number of marginal votes. I learned afterwards that the presidents of some of our major university student unions and the leaders of other important groupings had given me their support, in particular a number of national student leaders including Jim Driscoll of Cardiff university (Young Conservatives); Jacques Davies (Young Catholics); John Watkinson (Sheffield); Stan Josephs (Manchester); Fred Jarvis (Oxford NALSO, the Labour Party affiliate); Fred Gee (University College, London); Willoughby (Bristol) and Frank Panton (Nottingham).

I was glad to have had a substantially non-communist committee elected with me and in the year ahead John McNab proved a tower of strength. At least on our home ground we were making inroads into areas formerly, if not entirely dominated, at least heavily influenced, by the extreme Left.

It was at the Exeter council that I was reminded that I was still making the change from soldier to student. I was, out of habit, inclined to use military terms without realising it and when I reported that I had sent a 'signal', meaning a telegram, to Prague, my use of the word 'signal' prompted a line of undergraduates at the back of the hall to stand in unison and give a demonstration of semaphore!

My uncle Stanley had expressed interest in my student exploits from time to time and I had invited him to attend the Exeter meeting. Just as I rose to speak in one of the debates I saw him being ushered in at the back of the hall. After the meeting he drove me home for the weekend. He said little on the journey but on arrival he said to my aunt 'You should have heard him girl. He got to his feet and it came out like diarrhoea – for nearly an hour.' I just hoped he was not referring to either the content or the quality of my contribution to the debate.

The NUS presidency brought me a flood of invitations to receptions, student union meetings, dinners, university balls, and the like. Although these involved a lot of travelling and speech making most were extremely enjoyable. It was often difficult to choose between those one should not support and those one would really like to attend. Fortunately I had taken some ballroom dancing classes in my youth and was reasonably well prepared for the ladies' college formal dances, at one of which I was invited by the principal to lead off with the highly embarrassed president of their students union. Thankfully, it was one of the more conventional dances I could cope with, and no honour was lost.

On each of my returns from Eastern Europe I would visit some of our constituent colleges, taking part in debates on our relations with the international student community, presenting NUS to potential and new affiliates, and generally flying the

144

flag. And I had a number of invitations from embassies in the capital. I remember attending a reception at the Netherlands embassy to meet Queen Juliana. As I bowed and shook hands she also leaned forward, our heads cracked together and I almost knocked her out. It was embarrassing for me, but she thought it highly amusing. She had a genuine interest in student affairs and asked me a number of questions about the NUS. I was once invited to a reception at No.10 Downing Street by Clement Attlee, the prime minister – the first sign that the NUS might be gaining respectability – but had to decline because of an IUS meeting in Budapest, which for me had priority. But I did manage to attend a formal reception later at Lancaster House, as part of the 1951 Festival of Britain celebrations at which I met both Mr and Mrs. Attlee. On another occasion the Indian Students Union in Britain invited me to a dinner attended by Earl and Countess Mountbatten and Sree Krishna Menon, high commissioner for India. That evening I had to propose the toast to The President of the Republic of India. Afterwards, over coffee, Mountbatten spoke to me, and I reminded him of my attempted arson on his convoy in Burma in 1946 and of our talks in New Delhi in 1949. He remembered both and commented that it was perhaps imprudent for a company commander to attempt the incineration of his commander-in-chief.

My predecessors in the NUS had already laid the foundations for many valued student services, such as vacation work camps and travel facilities, long before I took office and it fell to me to consolidate and develop some of their good work. One of the innovations of my time was the holding of an annual students Arts Festival, which offered a platform for college stage and musical productions. I opened one of these in Liverpool university in 1950. In subsequent years these festivals grew in appeal and with support and sponsorship were to make a useful contribution to the development of young artistic talents.

Student Rag Weeks, which took place annually, were one of the high spots of the undergraduate year in my time. When Fred Gee – a close colleague and ardent supporter of mine – was president of University College London students union, he was involved in a prank that must rank high in the annals of rag week exploits. A group of undergraduates moved into Piccadilly Circus in the middle of the morning and set up a workman's canvas tent in the centre of the roadway, stopping all the traffic, ostensibly to repair a gas main. They sat there for several hours before they were 'exposed'.

During the summer vacation one of my closest student colleagues, Ralph Blumenau, who was reading history at Oxford, invited me to join him on a holiday in Spain. I had never been there before and badly needed a break. This was not long after the Spanish civil war had ended in victory for General Franco – a victory followed by brutal purges of those who had opposed him. Spain was now a fascist dictatorship and Franco the last of the fascist leaders to remain in power in Europe. After the war he came to be seen in the West as something of a bulwark against communism and was partially rehabilitated. Nevertheless, I wondered how my visit to a fascist state would be interpreted in Eastern Europe, but thought going worth the risk. I remember setting off to the Iberian Peninsula with exactly £20 in my pocket to cover the fortnight – my student grant left me with little to spare – but in spite of the budgetary constraints we travelled extensively by train and road to visit some of the great Spanish museums and art galleries and places of historic interest. We saw the works of the well-known Spanish painters at the Prado in Madrid and the spectacular treasures of Seville and Toledo. Blumenau's knowledge and love of history and his interest in everything we saw was infectious and greatly added to my enjoyment. I remember being impressed by the cleanliness and comfort of the air-conditioned trains, and by the golden sands of the Costa Blanca. Perhaps this is what attracted me to buy a chalet there in later years. So many such ambitions, secretly stored in my subconscious, came to be realised, but many years later.

I was still pursuing my studies, making visits to colleges up and down the country and chairing committees in London and elsewhere. But, as time went on, my term as NUS president engaged me more and more with the IUS and international student politics, to the exclusion of almost everything else. In August 1949, I found myself again in Eastern Europe – this time in Budapest – to participate in a World Festival of Youth and Students, which had been combined with an event, styled as the 'World Student Games'. The press estimated the attendance at 100,000, which was probably not far wide of the mark. For reasons never explained to me, though it was not hard to divine the purpose of the festival organisers, I was delayed for almost a week in Prague before being allowed a visa to enter Hungary. When I eventually arrived I found the work of the Games Control Commission, of which I was supposed to be a member, almost completed, and the games due to commence. The organisers had obviously preferred to keep me out of the way until all the important decisions had been made. Stalin was tightening his grip on Eastern Europe – all had to conform. After lodging a protest, I took my place on the commission, only a few hours before the main party of British participants arrived.

Here I was in another Eastern European capital city that I had not previously visited, tied to meetings that confined me to staying indoors for most of the time. The city was alive with activities in which young people from many lands participated. There were open-air events in all the parks and mass dancing in the squares, carnivals and excursions. There was so much I wanted to see but no time for tourism. Our hosts did, however, provide a few opportunities for us to see something of the sights and as we were driven around we caught glimpses of St. Stephen's Basilica and the many gothic spires, cupolas and steeples which punctuate the skyline and I remember a most enjoyable boat trip down the river Danube that divides the two parts of the old cities, Buda and Pest. One of the young communist activists from India, Vimla Bakaya, had beautiful hair groomed in a long pigtail which, as we sailed on the Danube, I was challenged by my fellow students to cut off with scissors. I resisted the temptation but was reminded of this incident some years later when the lady was arrested in Bombay in connection with a bomb-making plot. In those days my companions were decidedly revolutionary.

As for most athletic meetings in Eastern Europe at that time, the British universities sent only a handful of competitors compared with the host countries, each of which sent hundreds. For the Budapest games Scotland entered six swimmers and the rest of the UK had only one or two entries in a smattering of events. In the 1948 Olympics there had been no Soviet participants and the Americans had taken most of the honours. At the games in Budapest in August 1949 the tables were turned – the USA was not represented and the USSR took almost all the honours, although the Eastern European countries, particularly the East Germans, gave them a good run in many disciplines. In addition to the athletes, there were many hundreds of non-competing political activists attending, subsidised to be there simply to boost the propaganda thrust of the Soviet machine.

There were difficulties for me from the start. There had already been heated arguments about which countries should be allowed to compete in the games. Those labelled 'fascist' – a term interpreted by the organisers entirely from a communist

148

standpoint – were, of course, excluded. At the opening ceremony in the Ujpest stadium, after the hoisting of national flags, the release of thousands of pigeons, a flight of planes dropping flowers, and speeches of greeting from the leaders of the main delegations, there was to be a parade of competitors, to show the young people of the world 'the superiority of the Soviet system'.

The first conflict arose when we dug our toes in regarding a proposal to include in the programme the laying of a wreath on the Soviet war memorial and no other. The dispute was eventually resolved to the satisfaction of the majority who went along with the proposed ceremony, leaving me and most of my colleagues refusing to take part, though some on the political fringes of our delegation did. We soon came under attack. The festival organisers declared that:

> 'I had exposed myself.' (A problem with translation I trust!). 'The Red Army liberated more than half of Europe. Anyone who does not honour this memory should re-examine his conscience and his desire for peace'.

This was a typical piece of communist political analysis. I said in reply:

> 'We respect the Soviet army but cannot honour it especially. We would not have objected to laying a wreath on the tomb of the Hungarian soldiers or of the Unknown Soldier, but not on the Soviet soldiers' tomb and no other, which is obviously a partisan and political act.'

For all the good such statements did I might just as well have saved my breath, for nothing we said or did could breach the Iron Curtain.

The next political crisis came when I was called from my

149

bed one morning to discuss with the organisers the possibility of boosting the impact of the opening ceremony by adding an extra fifty or so from the main British delegation, i.e. not competitors, but drawn from the left-wing hangers-on. The organisers considered – quite rightly – that as contingents in the parade would be arranged in French alphabetical order, Britain (Angleterre) would be at the head, and a mere handful of British sportsmen would look insignificant leading the parade. They also sought my agreement to non-competitors from other countries taking part in the parade of athletes. This would have opened the door to the participation *en-masse* of those from the Free German Youth (communists from West Germany), unrepresentative Americans, 'Free Greek' partisans and so on. My answer on both points was a categorical 'No'. The organisers went ahead nonetheless, and added a number of contingents to the parade that had no right to be there, merely to enhance the propaganda value of the event.

In order to uphold the non-political nature of the games in accordance with Olympic principles which we were supposed to observe, we had endless battles behind the scenes about taking down the hundreds of photographs of Stalin, Lenin and Hungarian communist leaders posted throughout the city. But to suggest anything of the sort in Eastern Europe at that time was like calling the Archbishop of Canterbury a heathen at a meeting of the Holy Synod. On balance I would have felt decidedly safer doing the latter than the former.

The festival organisers saw to it that whenever we wanted to register objection to the political bias being shown, we incurred the risk of isolating the British and presenting them as aloof, disruptive and opposed to 'peace' and the 'new-found unanimity' between nations. To abstain or oppose was never easy, and we found ourselves in such a position time and time again. The local press coverage of all these events was, of course, heavily biased in favour of the communist countries, and it soon became clear that whatever we did or said would either be distorted, misrepresented or ignored. Coverage of the sporting events was always in terms such as: 'Bulgaria secures another victory for the Peoples' Democracies', or, 'the Glorious Soviet Union defeats all-comers'.

The organisers were ever anxious to demonstrate the superiority of Soviet competitors and every event was seen as a means to that end. If there were no non-communist entrants, some had to be found. So short were we of British competitors that, at one point, I was almost cajoled into filling a vacancy on a British bobsleigh team to replace an injured competitor. The team had been cobbled together at the eleventh hour. I had never been aboard a bobsleigh in my life and, having seen the speed at which they travelled, I successfully pleaded vertigo, angina, rheumatism and poor eyesight.

As a member of the control commission I found myself having to arbitrate in a number of disputes. One in particular, over wrestling, was to stick in my mind. A competitor had reputedly broken his opponent's collarbone, tied him in a knot and thrown him out of the ring. The question was whether this counted as a 'technical fall'. I knew nothing about the rules of wrestling, and whether it was the wrong type of knot that had been used and didn't count, or something else. There did not seem to be any point of political principle at stake, on which I might have had a view, so I decided to support the jury who had awarded the contest to a non-Soviet competitor. Having seen the muscles of the competitors I was loath to pick a fight with any of them. However, next day the press accused me of 'blatant political discrimination'. There was no way to avoid the politics.

One of several lavish receptions we attended was given by

the Hungarian Secretary of State for Foreign Affairs, after which we were taken by an official of the communist party on a tour of a museum displaying 'the fruits of the struggle of the people's democracy over the forces of reaction'. I remember on that occasion responding to some ridiculous diatribe about 'the liberation of the people and their new-found democracy', with a patently un-diplomatic remark, about how frequently those now styled as 'enemies of the people' changed places with those who now stood as their accusers. I suggested they looked more closely at history. I was almost devoured on that occasion. When it was all over it was good to get home. We felt bound, however, to acknowledge that the games had provided the communist camp with a major propaganda success.

CHAPTER TWELVE

ARCH-FASCIST, IMPERIALIST BEAST

'Fascism is a religion; the twentieth century will
be known in history as the century of Fascism.'

Benito Mussolini.

The next major international student event I attended
was a meeting of the IUS council held in Sofia from
15th to 25th September 1949. Our delegation included Bill Rust,
Ralph Blumenau, and our enterprising travel director, Harry
Baum, as well as a number of delegates from our constituent
colleges. As usual, young communist and fellow-traveller
hangers-on, who far outnumbered the official delegation,
accompanied us. (With hindsight, it is interesting to speculate
as to who paid their travel and other expenses.) Their presence
at these functions was always embarrassing to us. Whatever we
said as the official delegation they were at pains to repudiate,
and while we were often denied access to the platform they
were generally given preferential treatment.

We travelled out by train across Europe, taking almost two
days to reach our destination. The many controls at each
European border personified unfriendliness and often took
hours to negotiate. Passports and visas had to be checked;
declarations made about currencies and our compartments and
baggage were frequently searched. On the way we linked up
with delegations joining our train at Prague, Budapest and
other cities along the way. We were surprised to be greeted on
the station platform in Sofia early in the morning by a number
of government ministers: such was the importance attached to
these events.

Our Bulgarian hosts who were anxious to show their visitors

153

the achievements of the Soviet system had arranged an intensive programme for us. They lost no opportunity to impress us, but the result was not always what they had hoped for. One day we were taken in coaches from Sofia to visit an agrarian commune where they were manufacturing equipment that, we were told, was to revolutionise the country's agriculture. We found ourselves in a field full of what looked to us like rusting tractors that appeared to have been dumped: it seemed unlikely that any of them would work. Small hope for the future of the agrarian revolution, we thought. What we saw of the Bulgarian countryside and the conditions under which the peasantry appeared to live made quite the opposite impression from what our hosts had sought to achieve. We were stunned by the abject poverty we saw in many of the villages through which we passed. I had seen poverty in places like Calcutta, but this seemed worse, if only because it was in Europe. We formed much the same impression of the countryside and economy of Hungary during our travels there. It seemed strange to see oxen rather than tractors working fields so close to home.

The Sofia council began with a major row about the credentials of the Yugoslav delegates. This was inevitable considering the tensions between Moscow and Belgrade at the time and we had fully expected it. It was rumoured that Yugoslav delegates had arrived in Sofia, and been arrested and deported. We demanded to know the facts but got nowhere. Fortunately, to the consternation of our hosts, the arrival of the Yugoslav students had been witnessed by members of the Scottish Students Union delegation who had seen them being escorted to aircraft taking them out of the country. The Yugoslavs had asked the Scots to intervene on their behalf and, eventually, under pressure from the Scots and us, the IUS president felt obliged to make a statement. He alleged that the expelled Yugoslavs had tried to contact 'known Titoist agents' in Sofia and had been expelled. The Scottish delegation led by its president, Gordon Pirie, and the Danish and Swedish delegations gave us every support in trying to keep the question open, but we were very much in the minority and were shouted down. There was something very unnerving about being behind the Iron Curtain and being, as we were, greatly outnumbered by zealots and dogmatists.

The opening speech to the meeting by the IUS president was predictably highly political and amounted to an out-and-out attack on the United States of America and 'her western stooges'. We sat through long periods of chanting and adulation of Stalin whenever his name was mentioned. The manipulation of the event was grotesque. There was protracted applause for speakers from the Soviet Union, from Republican Spain, Korea, Malaya and others and delegates from our own colonies, or former colonies, were invariably put up to speak against us. We came under attack from an Indian delegate for refusing to take part in the wreath laying ceremony at the Soviet war memorial in Budapest. We had dealt with this at the time, but such situations were constantly contrived to wound us, and they did.

My absence from an earlier debate in Calcutta was raised by one of the communists. We had learned after we left India that there had been riots in Calcutta around the time of our visit and some students had been killed. I was now accused of having been instrumental in their deaths. It was somewhat difficult for me, and would have appeared a trifle unbelievable, to explain in that forum that, far from slaughtering Indian students on the streets of Calcutta, I was actually luxuriating in a bath in my hotel. Clearly, I had to come up with something better than that, if I was to be believed. When this matter was introduced at the Sofia council I went to the platform when eventually allowed – and we frequently were not allowed to make our points – and demanded to know the dates of the incident to which my accusers referred. We had difficulty at first in establishing the facts. Had I been given access to my passport I could have shown that I was not even in Calcutta at the time the incident took place. To clear my name I asked for the return of my passport – they had been taken from us on arrival in Eastern Europe – but this was refused, 'there were administrative problems'. Hence my alibi could not be proved and delegates from countries around the world censured me. The communist press subsequently gave considerable prominence to the 'past crimes of the leader of the British delegation' and to my 'implausible alibi'. Our inability to counter the Calcutta charges adequately, because they would not give us access to our passports, drew on us, and on me in particular, the wrath of hundreds of very militant and angry delegates gathered in Sofia. IUS publicity was now being specifically targeted to separate the 'majority of British students' from 'their reactionary and unrepresentative leadership'.

Even more was made of this incident later, when Alexander Shelepin wrote an article for the IUS magazine *World Student News*, published world-wide in more than one hundred languages, entitled 'The Mask Is Off' in which he referred to me as 'The arch-fascist, imperialist beast'. Coming from a future Head of the KGB, I rated this a compliment; he was obviously none too fond of me and I'm sure this did much to clear my records with MI5 and make me acceptable to the British Establishment; but it was all most unpleasant at the time. Perhaps it's just as well that I've never courted popularity!

On our return to the UK our report to the next NUS council was received with less incredulity than hitherto, but there were still many delegates who found it difficult to believe all we told them about our experiences behind the 'Curtain'. And as I had anticipated, it proved none too easy for me to explain my absence from a major debate while in my bath in Calcutta!

In the course of my three years involvement with the IUS I paid a number of visits to Eastern Europe. On one occasion I waited for Shelepin in Prague for two days while, as I heard later, he delayed in Moscow for Stalin's agreement to the text of a resolution he was bringing to our meeting. This insight into the inner workings of the communist machine was probably unique to me and I was able to inform my colleagues in the NUS and they, in turn, passed word around their colleges. Whenever Shelepin and I did sit down to examine the texts of these resolutions we could never agree and they would go forward, leaving me and my colleagues to face the mob he would orchestrate on the floor of the council or congress.

I spent hours walking the streets of Prague alone. I found it a fascinating place. It has a charm of its own which contrasts with its heavy classical architecture. It is often described as 'the city of a thousand spires'. The Hradcany Castle approached by narrow cobblestone streets, towers over the city where I used to walk alone at night – apart from the company of my 'watchers' – members of the surveillance team assigned to me. The paranoia about spies and spying prevalent in the eastern bloc countries at the time demanded that all foreigners be regarded with suspicion, and leaders such as myself merited twenty-four hour surveillance. The Charles Bridge, which spans the river Vltava, built in the 14th Century, with its rows of stone statues adorning either side, was much too narrow for traffic even then, and one night I stood alone on the bridge with my 'escorts' loitering at either end. They were constant reminders that this was indeed a police state. The tramcars clanked their way around the city until late into the night and the taverns never seemed to close. I grew to love the dark brown beers, often brewed in caverns under the premises where we sat and drank during the evenings with other students.

On these convivial occasions most contingents managed to exhibit some talent to entertain the other delegates but the British always showed up badly, not for their drinking, which they managed very well, but in the singing and entertainment departments. For one thing there never seemed enough of us together at any one time who knew the words of any particular song. We might start something but we invariably faded after the first few lines. Consequently, we always tended to give a dismal representation of our culture. I suppose we might have managed a rendering of 'Rule Britannia' or at least the first verse of 'God Save the Queen', but that might not have been seen in the best light! On our return to the UK we decided to remedy this situation as best we could and the NUS produced a book of student songs, which was published, reviving many of the old favourites – 'Ging Gang Gwli', 'I Aint Gonna Grieve', 'Dahn The Plug 'ole' and many others. But I do not recall that the publication improved our cultural performances to any significant degree.

On one occasion when I was in Prague waiting for delegates to arrive from around the world so that some meeting could begin, I decided to look up two Czechoslovak ladies who taught English, to whom I had been given an introduction from a relative of theirs in England. I wanted to converse in English with some local people, but was aware that in doing so I could be putting them at risk. However, I decided to try to outwit my custodians and I travelled to the address I had been given by tram, leaping on and off, and even tried to lose my 'shadows' by darting through hotel blocks and taking lifts. When I thought I had shaken them off I received a warm welcome from the delightful ladies with whom I enjoyed an interesting conversation and an English tea. However, I learned afterwards that I had not been as clever as I had thought, and that the ladies had subsequently been arrested and interrogated. We had talked about nothing remotely political for they were obviously aware of the dangers. I remember feeling guilty about having put them at risk and thinking what an appallingly repressive atmosphere they lived in.

I found this repression and the ideological pressures frightening. While we student leaders were all somewhere on the political learning curve, for those trapped behind the Iron Curtain it seemed there was no room for further learning. The dogma of Marxism said it all. The Cold War followed immediately after the 2nd World War during which the Soviet Union had been one of our staunchest allies. Not surprisingly in the immediate aftermath of the war many ex-servicemen, like myself, were especially receptive to the idea that young people should continue to try to work things out together rather than risk another conflagration. Initially I found it hard to believe that the Soviet leaders were as evil as some would have had us believe, but how wrong I was in that naive assumption. What was really going on in what later became known as 'the evil empire', while Stalinist youth were applauding his name to the echo at our meetings in Eastern Europe, did not become entirely clear to the world until many years later when Stalin was denounced, after his death, by Khruschev and others. Only then did the harsh reality of the political purges and the deaths of tens of thousands in the Russian gulags become public knowledge.

160

CHAPTER THIRTEEN

ENSNARED OVER YUGOSLAVIA

'In this life we want nothing but facts,
Nothing but facts.'

Dickens.

The next crisis for the NUS, and for me, arose as a consequence of the clash between the Soviet leader, Joseph Stalin and Marshall Tito, when the latter had asserted his right to a greater degree of independence from Soviet domination than Stalin was prepared to allow to any of the countries of the communist bloc. Stalin interpreted Tito's claims as a threat to the hegemony of the Soviet Empire and had decreed that his regime be brought to book. This led to a Cominform decision to isolate the Yugoslavs and expel them from all the 'front' organisations. Instructions went out from Moscow to that effect and, in February 1950, the matter came to a head for us in the NUS, when the IUS executive committee met in our offices in London. Bill Rust was still a vice-president of the international body and he attended, as did I, as president of the NUS. We also had two British observers present one of whom, Ralph Blumenau, took shorthand notes and later published a detailed account of the proceedings.

For me the Yugoslav question highlighted, better than anything I had hitherto experienced, the true nature of communist 'front' organisations. The Foreign Office could, and I think should, have done more to enlighten us, but we now know that within the FO there was reluctance to apply any pressure on British youth and student organisations for fear that this might prove counter-productive. The history of left-wing influence within the NUS may well have justified their concern.

By the time of the IUS meeting in London, political sentiment in the British colleges had already begun to change and there was far less unquestioning support for the IUS than even a year earlier. More students had accompanied our delegations to Eastern Europe as we attended various councils, congresses and other communist sponsored events, and had returned disillusioned by what they had seen at first hand. This change of sentiment had filtered through our councils to the student body and, by the time of the critical debate in London over the Yugoslav issue, the majority view was that we should leave the IUS, if the Yugoslav issue was not settled to our satisfaction.

The London meeting opened in an atmosphere of considerable tension. The IUS chairman, Grohman, began by reading out an indictment of the Yugoslavs. Ralph Blumenau recorded an early exchange between Grohman and myself, which arose when the Yugoslavs were refused admission to the meeting:

> Jenkins: 'Is it true that the council is one of the governing bodies of the IUS?
>
> Grohman: 'Yes'.
>
> Jenkins: 'Is it also true that the discussion now taking place concerns an organisation that is still a member of the IUS?'
>
> Grohman: 'Yes.'
>
> Jenkins: 'Is it not therefore true that the constitution will be infringed if the discussion continues without the Yugoslavs being present?'

Grohman heatedly retorted that he was not prepared to be interrogated in this way 'as though before the Un-American Activities Committee'. He had heard enough and could have no more of it. Apparently it was acceptable to treat the Yugoslavs in this way, but not the IUS president.

The two delegates who had arrived from Belgrade were eventually admitted to the meeting but this was no guarantee that they would be allowed a fair hearing. Grohman began their interrogation. Is it not true that 4,000 students were in gaol in Yugoslavia? He was told this was 'a fiction'.

The rest of the debate though deadly serious became pure farce. Delegate after delegate roundly attacked the Yugoslav representatives. The Polish representative asserted that 18,000 people were being detained in concentration camps. This too was denied. The Yugoslav delegates were accused of many other violations of students' rights by the Belgrade regime and they denied them all. The British representatives were appalled by the tenor of this interrogation and attacked the chairman for his conduct. Grohman was white with rage, while the Russians – they included the influential Alexander Shelepin – remained impassive, and seemed intent to let others do their dirty work for them. I tried in vain to point out that there was no evidence to back the allegations being levelled at the accused and proposed that a delegation should be sent to Yugoslavia to establish the facts, but the meeting was in no mood to waste time on this issue, and a vote was taken to expel the Yugoslavs. Mine, the British vote, was the only one against.

The Yugoslav national union of students was thus expelled from the international student movement and Comintern action followed worldwide to expel the Yugoslavs from all of the 'front' organisations. Once the decision had been taken in Moscow, that was that. The NUS reaction was predictable and it decided to suspend its membership of the IUS while it sent its own team to Belgrade to investigate what it could for itself. An invitation to the IUS to join this delegation was summarily rejected.

We then selected a delegation of three NUS representatives, and, on 6th April 1950, I set off for Yugoslavia, travelling by boat and train, via Ostende, Basle, Milan, Venice and Trieste, in company with Bill Rust, my predecessor, and Alan Johnson (president of Leeds university students union), with a mandate to investigate and report. We had also recruited as interpreter an exceptionally brilliant student from the London School of Economics, Val Sherman, who spoke fluent Serbo-Croat and a number of other languages.

On arrival we began by making clear to the government and university officials who received us that we would not be led by the nose. We would determine where we wanted to go and to whom we wanted to talk. Our hosts seemed only too happy to give us a free run and, as I remember it, they met every request we made. We confirmed that many students and professors had been detained, as the IUS had alleged, and we found and talked with some of them, held prisoner in isolated caves on the Adriatic coast. In one cave we found 650 prisoners living like cattle, sleeping on boards with 18 inches allowed for each individual. They had an exercise yard of a mere 1,000 square feet. They were required to work on road construction projects, but we found no evidence of physical mistreatment. They were mostly being detained for no reason other than that they supported the pro-Stalinist faction. Tito had considered them a threat and had put them away for the time being. While we naturally condemned this, to us it seemed little different from what the communists themselves did, and were doing, to all those who opposed them. We cross-checked the reports and anecdotes related to us by prisoners, wherever we could. We asked for, and were granted, a meeting with Marshall Tito, but this was unexpectedly cancelled and instead we met one of his deputies. We had discussions with the

Rectors of Belgrade and Zagreb universities and with many student groups. After visiting Ljubljana, Sarajavo, Belgrade and Zagreb, we returned to London to write our report. This task fell mainly to Rust and when we had agreed the content and it was published, it hit the headlines of the British press.

Our report acknowledged the difficulty of studying life or political action in a country where the language, traditions and social and political patterns were so different from our own and, in so short a time. We concluded that everything on the political front in Yugoslavia would certainly not meet with approval in the West and there was much we must condemn. But we could see insufficient justification for the international student organisation to expel the Yugoslav national student body. We came to the conclusion that 90% of the information given in the various IUS reports on which the expulsion had been based was untrue. In any event, the number of non-communist students suffering persecution of one kind or another in the Soviet Union and Eastern Europe far outweighed anything we had been able to detect in Yugoslavia.

As we knew Val Sherman as a marxist, and as he was with us only as an interpreter, and not as a member of our delegation, we tended to exclude him from our discussions, though we were most appreciative of his help. (He was later to turn his back on communism and emerged in the 1980s as head of Prime Minister Margaret Thatcher's Political Policy Unit in Downing Street and received a knighthood at the end of his tour of duty.)

Following publication of our report, the IUS immediately began to discredit it and to attack the NUS worldwide. An influential communist Eastern European newspaper reported that:

> 'The 'non-political' president of the NUS Mr. Jenkins,
> wants to bring students together, not by supporting them,

165

but by tourism. Mr. Jenkins is a passionate tourist. But, rather oddly, he prefers to tour concentration camps. The most recent camps he has visited are those of fascist Yugoslavia; for one has to understand that this non-political Mr. Jenkins is a fanatical advocate of Tito and the Titoist youth organisation that has been expelled from the IUS. In his report on his visit to these death camps, he expressed approval of the factories of death where only 'orchestras' had been presented to him. In Poland millions of people were burnt in the crematoria of Auschwitz and Majdanek, to the sound of military music. No further commentary on his report is needed.'

This was typical of the way in which the communist press reported events, but it was marginally consoling to think that if their reaction was any measure of the impact we had made, we seemed to have scored a point or two. The vitriol continued to be focused on me as leader of the British NUS and news magazines such as the IUS journal *World Student News* continued for some months to lambaste me as 'imperialist', 'reactionary', 'an agent of Tito' and goodness knows what else. As with all propaganda, the bigger the lie and the louder and more frequently it can be asserted, the more likely it is to be believed, but by now British students were more alive to the ways of the communist propagandist and these personal attacks were beginning to prove counter-productive.

Following the Yugoslav expulsion the debate about NUS membership of the IUS continued with renewed intensity in all the politically active British colleges, and involved a much higher proportion of the student population than hitherto. The British press also continued to give the subject much more attention than had been customary. Had there been television in those days, our activities would almost certainly have had wide coverage.

Although international affairs took up much of my time, it

had little effect on the day-to-day work of the NUS and its headquarters' staff, who continued to organise vacation camps, travel, an annual arts and drama festival and to negotiate better living conditions and grants for its members. Each year some hundreds of students participated in a wide range of travel and vacation programmes sponsored by the organisation.

I was usually required to contribute items each month to the NUS journal *Student News* and I retained some copies. From an issue of the time, I see that I was still a staunch advocate of maintaining links with the IUS for the practical benefits it could bring our members and, in spite of all that had happened, I wrote:

> 'The NUS council meeting in Manchester unanimously adopted a declaration on the International Union of Students, which included these words: 'this council reaffirms its belief that the International Union of Students is an organisation in which the students of the world can and should work for the attainment of better understanding, international co-operation, goodwill and peace, which are so necessary to all students, particularly at the present time...We also believe that international understanding can best be attained by personal contact, discussion, and genuine and sincere attempt to resolve the differences which keep students of the world apart and so limit opportunities for students to meet and reach agreement.'

This was a fair reflection of my thinking at the time. With hindsight, and in light of the Yugoslav debacle, we must be given credit for idealism, if not good sense. This declaration of the council was carried unanimously, so at least I felt in tune with my constituency, whatever differences I had with left-wing members of my committee regarding our international policy.

Running concurrently with our student activities was the

167

Cominform 'Peace Campaign', perhaps their most successful propaganda coup, to which they gave great prominence. The communists cleverly stole 'peace' for themselves: they 'stood for peace'. They argued that if one was against the Soviet Union one was against peace. This clever monopoly, or, what *The Times* called 'hijacking of a good cause', as their exclusive preserve, was to present a serious problem for us in the student movement. There was one occasion in 1950, when Bill Rust and I were invited by the IUS to visit Moscow. I had never been there and it seemed a golden opportunity. We arrived in Prague by air, but my visa for Russia was withheld. Bill got his and found himself in Moscow attending a well-publicised mass meeting of the World Peace Movement. He was called to the rostrum, before all the cameras, to sign the 'Peace Pledge' on behalf of British students. It proved a difficult decision for him. Failure to sign would have established him (and by proxy British students) as against peace. On the other hand, to sign was to endorse the policies of the Soviet Union. In the event he chose to sign while entering reservations. Sadly the world saw only the signature and, on Bill's return to the UK, the NUS council censured him for his action. I was spared this and returned from Prague to the UK. In retrospect I feel confident that I would not have signed, whatever the consequences, but I am writing this nearly fifty years after the event.

I took my Higher National Diploma finals in Cardiff in July 1950, when I also took examinations that led to my becoming a Licentiate of the Institute of Builders. I added a string of City & Guild's building qualifications while I was about it but I cannot say I had my heart in any of this. But with no alternative career in prospect I felt I needed a fallback position.

CHAPTER FOURTEEN

TRAITORS TO YOUR OWN PEOPLE!

'Though this be madness, yet there's
method in 't.'

Shakespeare.

I was re-elected for a second term as NUS president in July 1950, with a large majority. The union had already agreed that on completion of my studies at Cardiff, and subject to re-election, I should become a salaried officer and be paid £236 per annum, the equivalent of the student grant I had been receiving. Up to that time no student union in the UK had a full-time elected officer who was paid. Thus I became the first, and took up my duties on 1st August 1950. (It is now commonplace for the larger unions to have at least one full-time paid student officer; some have two or more.)

On taking up my appointment I moved from Cardiff to London and lodged near the NUS offices at their hostel in Endsleigh Street, WC1. The union had a small staff working under an excellent secretary, Douglas Meyer, but they all had their duties and I soon discovered that there was no slack to provide me with other than minimum support. My schedule throughout my first year as president while still a student had been tough enough and I had hoped that my second term would have been less so. But this was not to be. Each visit I made to Eastern Europe led to intensified attacks from IUS supporters in students unions at home and I had many invitations from non-communist unions to speak at colleges up and down the country. I seemed to be under constant siege.

One of my first and most pleasurable duties in my second term was to act as 'best man' for a student colleague, John

Watkinson, who had been a staunch ally in my political battles and was later to become president of the union at Sheffield university. I was by now becoming something of a specialist in these marital duties having been 'best man' for four of my brothers, and was convinced that this was a case of my being 'always the best man and never the groom'.

We did not appreciate its significance at the time, but the 2nd IUS congress held in Prague in August 1950, our next face to face encounter with our Eastern European adversaries was to become a turning point on the student front in the Cold War. Tensions between the Soviet Union and the West had been building up over the years and the war in Korea – a major confrontation between Soviet and United Nations forces – was exacerbating the situation with every day that passed. There were a number of flashpoints around the world that looked increasingly threatening, and it was not surprising that in the months leading up to the congress, governments throughout the West had been expressing concern about the participation of so many of their young people in an event they identified as a tool of communist subversion.

Most of the western national students unions had by now disaffiliated from the IUS, leaving only the British, the Danes and the Swedes, but it was certain that huge numbers from communist controlled and extreme left-wing groups from the West would be attracted (and subsidised) and would attend. Western governments took the view that there was nothing much that could be done to stop this, but (as British government papers since released have shown) 'a keen eye was to be kept on the event'. The billing of the meeting as 'A congress of the youth and students of the world – for peace, national independence and a democratic education', did little to allay the fears of non-communist governments as to the intentions of the sponsors. Unlike IUS councils, where

170

participants usually numbered about a hundred, congresses generally involved around a thousand.

As the event approached, officials at the Soviet embassy in London must have become worried that the official NUS delegation might prove an embarrassment and, on 1st August 1950, I was invited to meet a senior Soviet envoy, Modin, at a restaurant in the city. I asked Ralph Blumenau to accompany me. It was clear that the object of the exercise was to find out more about our attitudes to enable the authorities in Moscow, or Prague, to determine whether or not the NUS should be allowed to participate. (It transpired many years later that Modin was a KGB officer who worked in London as case officer on some notorious British spy cases, including Blake, and Burgess and Maclean. I am thankful that I did not agree to see him alone! We were almost certain to have been under surveillance by MI5.) It seems we gave little away for our delegation was subsequently granted visas.

The official NUS delegation I led in Prague was twenty-five strong, but in addition, there were nearly a hundred unofficial left-wing delegates, mainly communists, who were invited by the IUS to ensure that our official delegation would be adequately counter-balanced by their supporters. For the journey to Prague my brother, Harry, had loaned me his little open-topped MG sports car, and John McNab came with me to share the driving. We took a route across France, Belgium and Germany to Czechoslovakia. Although such a journey would be commonplace today, it was quite an adventure then, and my brother's car was already something of an antique. We had notified the Czech. embassy in London that we would be travelling by road, and were not altogether surprised to be met at the frontier by two large black escort cars filled with sinister looking civilians wearing sombre black raincoats. They were to escort us everywhere, until we reached the frontier on our way home two weeks later. Once over the frontier and behind the Iron Curtain we had a distinct feeling of unease.

Some 550 delegates, 160 observers, 444 visitors and 18 fraternal delegates – totalling 1172 students from 78 countries – took part in the congress. Although our delegation was bound by policy mandates on the main issues, our numbers included a minority of communists nominated by their colleges and fellow-travellers – too many loose canons for comfort – and I was to have my hands full adhering to the official line of the majority. As it turned out, whatever the official delegation said was countered and contradicted at every turn by communist or Student Labour Federation (left-wing socialist) delegates speaking, as they claimed, 'with the true voice of British students'.

Rust and I had arranged a meeting at the Foreign Office in London before we left, partly to allay their fears, and also to ensure that no obstacles would be placed in the way of our delegation. We suggested to the officials we saw that we might need help to counter Soviet propaganda and, later, they were responsive to an approach made by Blumenau for statistics that he put to good use in our main presentation to congress. Our meeting with FCO officials led, incidentally, to a somewhat embarrassing situation for us in Prague where, shortly after we arrived, a first secretary from the British mission assailed us in the lobby of our hotel, in full view of everyone, to invite us to play cricket at the embassy! The Communist *Daily Worker,* in its headlines in England the following day, reported this as an 'attempt to subvert the British delegation with tea and cricket at the embassy'.

Whenever I moved to my car, parked outside the congress hall, there was frenzied activity as my 'shadows' passed signals to each other and rushed to their vehicles. I was not allowed to move without my escorts. By way of light relief, McNab and I drove around Prague watching them follow us. We sometimes played games with them, darting around corners and braking sharply, only to see them charging on, slamming on their brakes and reversing hurriedly to pick up the scent. On one occasion I took the wrong road and they overtook me, and abandoning their secretiveness, waved to me to follow.

A few colleagues and I attended a tense meeting of the IUS council the night before the main congress opened: these were relatively small gatherings of around seventy members. We were soon embroiled in heated arguments about the credentials of participants and other procedural wrangles. It was customary for only the communist student groups in each country to be accredited: the rest were dismissed as 'fascist' or 'unrepresentative'. The Scottish Union of Students and the Scandinavians invariably supported us in our attempts to admit others, but the solidarity of the eastern bloc was absolute. As expected the Yugoslav issue was placed on the agenda and again we felt obliged to make a stand on their behalf, but to no avail.

The Czechoslovak press reported the opening of the congress in grand style. Messages of support were said to have been received from every corner of the globe, and the local tabloids were full of pictures of 'representative students' from many lands assembled for a great demonstration of 'communist unity'. There was no room for dissension here. One Czech. newspaper reported that:

> 'The presence of leading figures of science and culture from many countries, and the support of the mass international organisations of workers, women, youth, teachers and journalists, made it clear that the congress was an event of significance for all sections of peace lovers in all countries.'

In elections for a committee to organise the congress,

conducted prior to its opening, I was elected to the praesidium and Fred Jarvis to the steering committee. The united front had to be seen to be intact.

An event of the magnitude of an IUS congress, staged with no expense spared, would have left impression enough on the hundreds who attended, without the drama that was to ensue.

On the opening day only ardent communist supporters were called upon to make speeches and the local press reported every word. For my fellow delegates and me events reached a climax on the second day, when we came under attack from many delegations. We sat at a long table near the centre of the floor and watched with apprehension as many demonstrations were staged around our position. At the height of these our chairs were jostled ominously and there were times when some of us felt in real physical danger. The British Student Labour Federation (SLF) delegates joined in the attacks against us and at one point an ambulance that was being presented to the Korean delegation was ceremoniously driven through the centre of the congress hall narrowly missing me as it made its way to the rostrum. Some of our female delegates took out their knitting and carried on as though oblivious to the uproar as we waited for the time when we could make our contribution to the debate. Speaker after speaker attacked the British as 'fascist colonialists' and 'enemies of peace'. But far from intimidating us, the speeches and demonstrations only hardened our resolve to stick it out.

As the congress progressed, the international political background – the communist revolution in China, the war in Korea, the anti-colonialist struggle – was introduced into every stage of the proceedings with dramatic effect. With every passing hour the event looked less and less like anything to do with students.

We had been shown the text of the main resolution that the congress would be invited to adopt, and intended to reply in uncompromising terms. Blumenau had drafted our statement and the delegation had approved the text at late night sittings. Throughout the bedlam I waited my turn to take the rostrum. There was a hushed and expectant silence as I made my way to the platform. I had a long report to present and began by giving details of UK budget figures for education and on work we had undertaken for our members in the UK. Then I came to our relations with the IUS and our views on their political bias. I began by telling the meeting that the IUS was no longer representative and that 'of the 246 constituent colleges of the British NUS only 9 had this year paid any subscription to the IUS'. I drew attention to the way in which the organisation had violated its own statutes to expel the Yugoslavs, and accused the IUS of one-sidedness. Why did it only criticise the western camp? Was the socialist camp not also to be condemned, considering it spent a higher percentage of national income on military expenditure than the West? I provided statistics. The book written by Dr. Kotek records that:

> 'Jenkins was constantly interrupted by boos and shouts of indignation. He had to wait for long periods, until the boos and hisses had come to an end, but wait he did: he thought it important they should hear what we had to say'.

> 'Jenkins went on to point out that: The Partisans of Peace and the IUS are not against every war. They are not against war in Korea. They are not against war in China. They are not against war in Vietnam. They are not against war in any part of the world, provided it is a war fought for communist aims. If East Germany were to attack West Germany tomorrow, just as North Korea attacked South Korea yesterday, we can be sure that the Partisans of Peace and IUS would support such a war'.

When the translators caught up, and there was always a short wait for this to happen, the storm broke. While our delegation sat impassively – some of the lady members

175

continued with their knitting – two members of the British Student Labour Federation, who had prepared for this moment, rushed to the platform to denounce me amid tumultuous cheers. One of them, Miss Knevitt, from the British Peace Movement, was given a bunch of flowers as she left the platform, and both were chaired triumphantly round and round the tables where we sat. Massive searchlights in the stadium were focused on us as the cameras hummed. In the midst of the uproar a Rumanian delegate rushed to the podium to declare that he had not come to listen to imperialist propaganda and proposed that the congress should censure our entire statement. A young Austrian communist called on us 'to return to the path of peace and democracy'. A Malay delegate wondered why I had said nothing about the 'imperialist war in Malaya'. Another described me as 'a great defender of Yugoslav fascists'. 'Heroes' from many countries were chaired around the hall to prolonged chanting of slogans such as 'Ko-re-a! Ko-re-a!' 'Hands-off-Malaya!' and 'Stalin, Stalin, Stalin'. Members of a large delegation of Korean youth and soldiers, led by a Korean Lt. colonel, and reportedly 'straight from the fighting front', were given an exuberant welcome, and carried around the hall by members of the other delegations. Ours was the focus of all these demonstrations and they lasted, sometimes for forty-five minutes and more. We sat through it all as impassively as we could. The object of the focussed and vitriolic personal attacks on me, as leader of the British delegation, was clearly to divide our ranks, but our opponents did not succeed.

The congress secretariat had asked for copies of all statements to be handed in twenty-four hours before they were delivered 'to assist the translators'. It now became obvious that there was another purpose. The Soviet leader Shelepin, in the chair, had prepared himself to answer our submission point by point. Abandoning any pretence at impartiality, he launched into a bitter and lengthy attack, from which the following extract well illustrates the tone.

> 'Only an ignorant person like you, Mr. Jenkins, could assert that the IUS was guilty of preparing a war. Yes, Mr. Jenkins, to our regret we must upset you. We educate the Soviet youth to love the Soviet army; and our children, our youth the whole of our people love the Soviet Army which, headed during the war by Comrade Stalin, saved from Fascist slavery, the whole world, including your country, Britain, Mr. Jenkins. You, Mr. Jenkins and Mr. Rust, are traitors to your own people. You help to get Britain transformed into the 49th State of America. When you slander the Soviet Union, you act as the enemy not only of the Soviet people, but of the British people as well.'

Thirty minutes of standing ovation and chants of 'Stalin, Stalin, Stalin' followed his speech, in yet another boisterous demonstration that seemed endless to us as we sat there in silence. Blumenau and others have since written that they feared for my safety.

An Austrian delegate then rushed to the rostrum to make a statement:

> 'I wish to appeal to the NUS delegation. The British NUS has definitely reached the crossroads; either they shall go honestly with us on the way to democracy and peace, or they shall find themselves suddenly among the scum of the earth'

The Rumanian delegates proposed a vote of censure on me 'for making a speech in defence of imperialism' and this was put to the congress by Shelepin and carried by a large majority. The following day this vote was widely reported in the British press, in particular by the communist *Daily Worker*.

When the tension in the congress hall was at its height an official summoned me to a meeting outside. I was apprehensive when led away along a series of corridors and down a flight of steps to a room in what seemed a largely deserted basement of the building. I began to wonder if I would see the light of day again. I was all too aware of the ability of these regimes to dispose of individuals without trace. I was ushered into a large room in which sat a dozen or more men, all dressed in their dark suits. To my astonishment, they told me that reports had been received of my breaking the local speed limits. Did I know what the rules were? After polite warnings about their driving regulations, I was allowed to return to the delegation in the main hall. This could well have been a device to defuse the situation, or perhaps a means of showing me to a new team of 'shadows', so that they could carry on with their task. It was an eerie experience. My colleagues in the hall had been more than a little concerned until I reappeared, and afterwards became very protective and ensured that I had a companion with me at all times. Other members of our delegation also suffered harassment, some were strip-searched and their rooms turned over under the pretext of checking security. Some had their cameras and photographs confiscated.

When I returned to the hall the hubbub had subsided and it was the turn of the Danish observer, Stig Anderson, to speak. His contribution was mild in content compared to mine, but the congress was in no mood to listen to any more speakers who did not support the party line. The signal was given from the chair and the uproar began again. The shouting, hissing and booing exceeded even that given in response to my speech. Following this, the order must have gone out to quell the riot, for the Scottish Union of Students' statement that followed was heard in comparative silence. The cue always came from the chair.

Kotek, in his account of these events, referred to my:

'Heroism and courage in making a stand throughout the

debates which became legendary in student circles'.

While I may have been in a perilous situation, I was never without the loyal and able support of many colleagues.

A few days later Professor J. D. Bernal from the UK, and other dignitaries from the Congress of the Partisans for Peace, the communist dominated World Peace Movement, attended the congress. They arrived carrying gladioli and other flowers of peace and paraded around the hall to rapturous cheers and applause. The psychological pressure was intense. Our own delegation almost split over support for the so-called 'peace resolution' introduced for the congress to endorse. On the face of it the text was marginally acceptable, but I saw it as part and parcel of the same communist propaganda and I voted against it on behalf of our delegation. On these occasions when there was often no time to confer, the decision fell to me. Whenever I could I consulted John McNab and Ralph Blumenau who sat next to me but, as on this occasion, this was not always possible. My opposition vote aroused some divisions within our delegation. The idea of not supporting a resolution on peace was anathema to the vast majority of the delegates assembled from around the globe and I was roundly condemned by the meeting as 'an enemy of peace', but the majority of my delegation supported the stand I had taken.

As the congress proceeded it became more and more obvious that it was part of 'communist front' strategy, and therefore IUS policy, to keep the British NUS as a constituent member come what may. There were a number of pointers to this, such as their willingness to keep one of us as a vice-president. The vice-presidents included representatives from all corners of the earth, but I saw little of the others apart from Shelepin, it was enough that their names and countries should appear in the propaganda; they would, in any event, have been

179

unlikely, if not unable, to do other than support the Soviet line.

During another debate on day three when the Congress was indulging in a lengthy demonstration in support of Stalin, I pushed my way to the rostrum and informed the chairman, Shelepin, that he should stop the demonstration immediately or I would be obliged to withdraw our delegation. To my surprise he called the meeting to order and there were no further demonstrations that day.

After five days the congress concluded with a fanfare of parades, flowers, and yet more speeches condemning the 'imperialists' and praising the 'glorious Soviet Union'. The participants then dispersed, but I stayed on with a small delegation for an IUS council meeting at which four vice-presidents were elected: Shelepin (USSR), Yang Chen (China) Guervaria (Cuba) and myself. I was again in good company! I accepted the post temporarily, pending a policy decision on our remaining affiliated to the IUS. If the NUS had decided to stay in, it would have been advantageous for us to have an inner seat, but in the turmoil of the moment there was little time for mature reflection.

As John and I drove home from Prague we were again escorted the full 130 miles along the road via Pilsen leading into the American zone of Germany, by the cars assigned to us when we arrived. On reaching the frontier I parked my car and, before reporting to the customs post, went back to the leading escort car and opened the door. The occupants cringed as though they feared a grenade being tossed amongst them. Only when I thanked them for escorting us did they relax and in English one of them said something to the effect that they admired us for coming. Little did they know how apprehensive we had been.

Throughout our stay in Prague, members of the delegation and I had been telephoned daily by newspaper reporters in London and Paris. But after a few words the lines from London were usually cut off. However, a few calls from leading British and French reporters in Paris were connected and I was able to give reports on some of the proceedings. We were in no doubt that all these conversations were being intercepted. Such was the international interest in these rarely accessed meetings behind the Iron Curtain, that we had extraordinary coverage wherever the press was free to publish, but not a word of dissent from within the congress got into the papers of Eastern Europe. Even so, any shrewd reader must have concluded from the virulent attacks reported on us that we were not proving either co-operative or compliant.

A by-product of this extensive press coverage was that we won many supporters in the West, not least the staff of the American embassy in Prague, who approached me before I left and invited me to call at some of their military bases en route home through occupied Germany. Travelling via Austria to Berne we stopped off at one American camp where we were invited to indulge ourselves in the luxuries of their army PX stores. For years after the war such things were a revelation to us. Sadly, we had little money to spend, but we took advantage of the hospitality offered to us and were amazed to find how much interest our escapades in Prague had engendered in their eyes. Not long afterwards I was invited to tour American universities with the president of the US national student organisation, but, to my considerable regret, other commitments prevented me from accepting.

Further on our way John McNab and I took time to follow up an invitation extended to us in the UK before we had left for Prague, when we had been asked by representatives of the Moral Rearmament Movement (MRA) to visit their

Headquarters in Caux in Switzerland. MRA activists in the UK had been trying for some time to establish close links with British youth and student leaders. Hitherto I had been invited to a number of their meetings and functions in London. We were curious if not particularly attracted to their cause and decided to look in at Caux, arriving in the second week of September 1950.

The Caux HQ turned out to be a vast chateau bequeathed by some devoted benefactor. The MRA Movement was decidedly anticommunist and had attracted a number of internationally important personalities, some of whom worked at Caux, promoting 'their religion of absolutes', absolute honesty, absolute love and so on. We had no quarrel with any of that, and we found their ideas and the presentation of them interesting. This seemed to us a constructive alternative ideology to communism, but we were less sanguine about the methods they employed. Their well-equipped theatre, and plays especially written to present their gospel, were most impressive, as was their hospitality, but we cringed a bit when senior German and Japanese military commanders took the stage to apologise for their war crimes and beg forgiveness. Much of this was nauseating to us. (It was many years later that I first felt even the slightest inclination to forgive, much less to forget.) As I listened to the Japanese apologists I could not forget the servicemen who had been interned in Changi gaol in Singapore whom I had known, or those who had suffered on the Burma-Thai railway. But there were those at Caux who had had similar experiences, who seemed unreservedly ready to forgive and forget. Perhaps I should have envied them.

It was no coincidence that, on discovering that I played tennis, our hosts at Caux produced no less than Bunny Austin, an MRA supporter, and former British Davis Cup player, to be my personal host. He also shared my room. We had heard tales of the homosexual tendencies of some MRA followers and John and I were both on our guard! After forty-eight hours we were on our way home, unconverted in every sense.

All in all, John and I found the ideological pressure of Caux distasteful and unwelcome, in spite of our high regard for what the movement was trying to do to counter communism. We found them using the same mass persuasion techniques, which we had just left behind in Prague – but in the anti-communist sense – and being used just as effectively. We did not feel attracted to any of it and were anxious to return home and discover what the reaction of our constituent colleges would be to our endeavours in Prague.

The journey home had given us a welcome break and time to prepare for our next task, namely, to report to the next NUS council in Liverpool. As we drove across Europe we took it in turns to drive or make notes for our various reports, speeches, broadcasts and articles for the papers.

I gave a number of interviews to the press on my return and was encouraged to find that, in our absence, we had been given good and supportive coverage in spite of the difficulties of getting information through the Iron Curtain. A number of returning delegates had already written accounts for regional and national papers and the following is a typical example of what we found:

> 'The British and other non-communist delegates had to endure prolonged provocation and insults....many of these incidents were directed against the president of the NUS, whose courageous stand against the politically biased nature of the congress and its Executive report dubbed him a man of great moral courage and high principle.'

After all the abuse it was heartening to read items like this.

A correspondent of *The Times,* who had warned of the dangers of intimidation of members of our delegation, received an assurance from Lord Vansittart that he would be prepared to raise in Parliament any question of this that might arise.

There was, by now, a heightened interest in international student affairs in our college unions at home. One of the casualties of this was Mr. Julian Amery, the MP for Preston North, whose visit to speak at Birmingham university was cancelled 'because the union wanted to encourage 100% attendance at a meeting to debate relations with the IUS.'

Information that became available later showed that the scale of Soviet subsidy for its major events was far higher than anyone thought at the time. For example, we learned that some 29,000 foreign participants took part in the Prague Congress and that the cost of this one event was of the order of US $1 million. These were massive investments in propaganda, intended to subvert the western democracies: one can only speculate as to how close they came to succeeding. Whatever interpretation the IUS placed on investment in students, it clearly was not their intention to lavish such sums so that they could enjoy themselves. World communism saw students – the young intellectuals – as a key target. If enough of them, especially their leaders, could have been won over, who knows how the Cold War might have ended?

In retrospect, it is strange that over a number of years we should have accepted without question funding by the IUS of most of the cost of our participation in their affairs. Rarely did we pay our own way entirely, though we usually paid our travel costs and indeed could not have afforded to do other than accept a degree of support. I regret that we allowed ourselves to become indebted in this way, but I cannot recall that we were ever conscious of any obligation, and it certainly did not affect our attitudes or conduct.

For British students, the Prague congress marked a turning point. To many, even those on the political left, who had not come face to face with communists before, the machinations of the congress had been a profound shock. Having seen the purpose of the IUS more clearly, a substantial majority of our delegation was firmly convinced that our membership was being exploited to present to the world a totally bogus united front of students supporting communist objectives. On our return we prepared a report for our colleges in which we put forward the majority recommendation that we should immediately disaffiliate. We may have lacked evidence to convince British students before the congress, but there was no lack of it now.

CHAPTER FIFTEEN

A ROAD I COULD NOT TAKE

'Two roads diverged in a wood,
I took the one less travelled by.
And that has made all the difference.'

'The Road Not Taken' by Robert Frost.

The events in Prague at the 2nd IUS Congress in the summer of 1950 had aroused considerable interest in the West and the media was well represented at the NUS council held in November at Liverpool university. There were 162 delegates present and 130 observers from the student world, including Olaf Palme, president of the Swedish national union of students, (later to become prime minister of his country), a staunch ally who had supported the British delegations on several occasions in Eastern Europe; a representative of the Yugoslav students; and a few of the leading officers from the IUS, including Grohman the president and Tom Madden the secretary-general. We learned afterwards that four other IUS leaders had been refused visas and had been turned back at Heathrow. To chair such a meeting of university and college delegates was frightening enough without all the visitors, plus a strong team from the national press. I recall that, before making my opening speech, I retired to the bathroom and threw up my lunch.

Kotek, in his record of the Liverpool council wrote:

'Liverpool witnessed one of the most memorable episodes in the whole history of the NUS. At first the outcome seemed a foregone conclusion. The delegates had received a bulky 44-page report in which fifteen out of the eighteen NUS delegates to Prague proposed disaffiliation from the IUS, while recommending that the NUS should take part in its practical activities.'

I felt optimistic when the early vote approving our activities in Prague by 104 votes to 27 indicated that the disaffiliation recommendation would go through. Another vote condemning the activities of the left-wing SLF was a further indication of the way the delegates were thinking. But everything went awry when it came to the crucial vote. Bill Rust presented the motion. He was a good speaker and much respected as a former president. The case for the opposition, to remain within the IUS, was presented by Alan Johnson from Leeds university, one of three who had presented a minority report on their return from Prague. When I put the motion to council the result was close, with 81 votes for staying within the IUS and 79 against, with 4 abstentions.

A call-vote was then demanded, under which each organisation had one vote for every 50 paid-up members. The London School of Economics bloc vote played a significant part in the outcome. In spite of being under communist influence, their union, which had a student membership of 3,000, had actually rejected disaffiliation by only 2 votes, but this gave them a block vote of 60, the whole of which had now to be cast against disaffiliation.

The NUS executive proposal was, in consequence, rejected by 767 votes to 622, with 44 abstentions, in spite of what my delegation and I had considered incontestable evidence in favour of disaffiliation. The skill of our adversaries in organising the opposition could only be admired and my personal position now seemed untenable. We had struggled over three years to retain links around the world through the international student movement and had remained idealistic about so many things, but we had become utterly convinced that to continue to lend our name in any way to the IUS and its work, which we now saw clearly as the furtherance of international communism, was wrong and harmful to British interests. Furthermore, any practical benefits our members might have derived from continuing the link seemed of little significance. We had taken a representative team to Prague, they had seen for themselves, and had returned home recommending disaffiliation by a large majority. The council, as a result of communist cash and organisation, had defeated us on a technicality.

I had not previously given this scenario much thought because I sensed that the recommendation of the delegation would have been supported by at least three quarters of the student population and, as the first vote had shown, by those attending the Liverpool council. This was no time for hesitation and I immediately told council it had taken a road I could not take, tendered my resignation, took off my chain of office and left the platform. There was a stunned silence as each member of the executive committee followed me, leaving only Frank Cummins (communist) and Edith Collett (more an idealist than anything else) sitting on the platform in solitary splendour. (They were joint signatories, with Alan Johnson, of the minority report.)

The majority of delegates present were non-communist and had by their earlier vote shown that they did not agree with the bloc-vote decision. They now realised that their union faced the threat of communist control. The resulting chaos on the floor was brought under control when a senior treasurer took the chair while delegates sought to salvage the situation.

I was then involved in frantic discussions in the body of the hall that eventually led to the idea of holding a national referendum on IUS membership. In spite of the risks, this seemed the best course open to us, and the council voted by 98 votes to 40 with 14 abstentions, to organise one. I was asked to resume office until the result was known and agreed. I was, however, anxious that the vote should be taken on the IUS question and not as a vote of confidence in me and, to ensure this, I announced that I would resign after the referendum, whatever the result. I felt this was the honourable thing to do in the circumstances. It was, nonetheless, not an easy decision. I had no idea at the time what career I might follow, and it seemed doubtful whether anything would compare with the excitement and challenge of the preceding three years. Following the council vote all the committee and I returned to the platform with the exception of Fred Jarvis who declined.

Kotek recorded in his book that:

> 'The decision of the NUS not to disaffiliate was taken very badly by the British authorities.'

They must have been concerned that, in spite of all our efforts, communists now had such a stranglehold on the British student movement that it would take a great deal to counter it.

Reflecting on my actions that day I believe my resignation did much to alert council delegates to the threat their union faced and that it contributed in no small measure to the outcome of the referendum that followed, but for me it was a devastating blow.

CHAPTER SIXTEEN

DERAILING THE TRAIN
'Tis easier far to lose than to resign'

Lyttleton.

<hr>

My next task was to prepare for the national referendum on future NUS relations with the IUS that would finally test the balance of British student opinion. From my perspective what mattered now was the college votes and the extent to which communists could influence them. I knew from the voting at the Liverpool council that I had a fight on my hands and, although the task appeared formidable, I was reasonably confident of success. The stand the majority of the delegation had taken, following the Prague congress, had met with widespread approval throughout the West and we had received encouraging messages of support from student groups in many western countries. Reports of the Liverpool council decisions regarding continued membership of the IUS that appeared in the British press, suggested that outsiders found the rejection of the majority recommendation of the Prague delegation totally baffling. It was clear that most British students were equally confused.

I knew that the voting in a referendum would be different from that at NUS council meetings, where at least twenty-five per cent of the delegates were either communists or fellow-travellers. This was not the situation in the vast majority of colleges where the extent of left-wing political influence was very varied. The left-wingers were generally the most active in union affairs and they had held a position of some influence on the national executive for a number of years. They frequently succeeded in mandating their delegates to council, thereby frustrating the will of the majority. British students were not

191

easily drawn into politics and, although the immediate post-war generation was older than the intake in normal times, there was still a tendency for doubters 'to sit on the fence'. Many feared that the primary role of the NUS, namely, to provide services for its members, would be swamped by the political machinations of the international body that turned everything into a Cold War issue, however hard we tried to steer them away from politics. The majority, however, remained oblivious to any danger, wanted to concentrate on their studies and were content to leave these matters to others. To a large extent the Marxists depended for their success on student apathy: they had a common agenda and the rest did not. As in the trades unions and elsewhere, it was general practice for them to turn up at meetings and stay to the end, hoping to vote and carry the day when others had left and they had a majority.

During the campaign period I received invitations to visit and speak at meetings in Europe, but declined them all. I was thoroughly exhausted by this time and there was still much to be done at home. It was not until I received a warm invitation from an old friend, Pierre Trouvat, president of the French National Union of Students, to attend one of their meetings in Grenoble that I agreed to go. The visit turned out to be a hugely social occasion. French students know how to enjoy themselves and Pierre proved a magnificent, if over-indulgent, host. I was also taken to Paris to see the nightlife and I have one lasting memory of this. I had clearly enjoyed too much hospitality, and when seeking another place I found myself backstage at some nightclub in a room full of young ladies scantily clad, or not clad at all. I remember beating a hasty retreat with girls in hot pursuit.

We learned, many years later, that the British communists received a clandestine subsidy of $15,000 from the IUS for the referendum campaign. This money found its way into propaganda distributed within the colleges, and paid for visits by speakers to influence student opinion. The NUS did not have such resources but I personally visited dozens of colleges and campaigned through the length and breadth of the country, as did a number of my colleagues. Except where colleges had active non-communist leaders, I often faced meetings packed with leftists rounded up to barrack and oppose.

In various conversations I had in Eastern Europe throughout 1949-1950, particularly with leaders of the Scandinavian student organisations, with whom we always worked closely, there had been talk of forming a non-political international student body. Any such organisation would inevitably have been a direct rival to the IUS and, while we were still members of that organisation, and the policy of the NUS had been to make the IUS work, but in a less political way, I had been obliged to resist any move to establish an alternative.

After the Prague congress, however, we assumed that the IUS link would soon be severed irrevocably and Olaf Palme, the Swedish student leader, and I had lengthy talks in the isolation of the corridor of a train travelling through Eastern Europe. We agreed to work towards holding a conference in Stockholm, as soon as possible, to explore with leaders of other western unions, the idea of forming a new student international. Palme agreed to organise it, and I to take the chair. We invited the IUS to send a representative, but they refused.

Most of my colleagues and I had by now seen how utterly impossible it was to work within the IUS and we were ready to seek an alternative method of pursuing our international aims. But we still had our members to convince about the merit of holding this conference, which marked a significant change of policy. And I recognised that I would have to eat many of my own words to bring it about, having previously championed the case for constructive opposition within the enemy camp.

The deal I had struck with Palme on that train was to lead, within a few months, to the first International Student Conference, held in Stockholm in the spring of 1951. The NUS agreed to participate provided that it was no more than an exploratory exercise. In spite of our new awareness of what communism was really like, we recognised that most of the young people in the West remained idealistic and anxious not to exacerbate the divide that on the global stage was already posing a serious threat to peace.

The Swedish Government was pessimistic about the conference succeeding, and correspondence between the American embassy in Stockholm and the State Department in Washington has since shown that to them 'the situation looked very bad – and certainly incomprehensible.' They must have been surprised when 68 delegates from 21 national unions attended, representing approximately 2 million students.

This was my first visit to Scandinavia and, in spite of having little spare time from the conference proceedings, I was taken on a few sightseeing tours and entertained by my hosts, Palme and the Swedish National Union of Students. I had also worked closely with the Danish student union leaders on a number of occasions, and they asked me to visit Denmark on my way home. Unfortunately, I was unable to do this but I returned the invitation to their president, Stig. Anderson, and, later, he accompanied me to my hometown, Brecon, during a visit to the UK.

Because the conference took place during the period when the referendum was being organised in the UK, my position as chairman was ambivalent in that my union had not then

194

decided where it stood on the issue. The Swedes had agreed not to rush things and talked in terms of a loose system of co-operation: they too recognised that many unions were not ready to join forces in what would have been seen as a reinforcing of the gulf between those already aligned on both sides of the Cold War. Thus at Stockholm most of the participants felt they could only explore the ground and await developments, particularly the result of the UK referendum. I took satisfaction from knowing that the West was, at long last, starting to get its act together. (For years I retained a recording of the whole of the proceedings of the Stockholm Conference made on one of the early wire tape recorders but, later, when I went abroad, it fell victim to my aunt in Brecon on one of her clearing-out campaigns.)

It was not an easy meeting for me to manage. In spite of the unanimity of view on the need for co-operation between the non-communist unions, there was considerable difference of opinion as to what form this should take. But, by the end, the extent of support for an international service organisation had been established and the ground prepared for a future conference.

When it came, the result of the British referendum vote was very close and, to my great relief, resulted in a majority in support of the position I had taken. Nearly a third of the 105,000 members of the NUS cast their votes: 18,000 for disaffiliation and 15,000 for continued membership of the IUS. Although still a close-run thing, it marked a watershed in student international relations and I felt that we had won the day. For those of us who had tried, first to make the international student body work, and then to stop the communist tide which seemed to be advancing inexorably, it was comforting that the referendum had vindicated our stance. If anyone had won the battle it was we, not the communists.

We had come a long way from the day, three years earlier, when I first joined the NUS executive committee, dominated as it then was by the political left. We can only speculate as to the consequences for the West if the opposition had been allowed more time to infiltrate our youth and student organisations.

Acting on the referendum result, the next NUS council, held in Southampton in March 1951, voted, by 114 to 38 with 14 abstentions to disaffiliate from the international body. We had stemmed a tide that through 1946 to 1949 seemed virtually unstoppable. As a sop to those who wanted to retain the international student connection it was also decided to claim 'the status of autonomous associated membership' so as to enable our members to continue to benefit from the practical services offered, limited though they were. But this had little significance or relevance. In the event, when the IUS council next met in Bucharest, they rejected the NUS application for any form of associate or fraternal membership.

At the Southampton council I handed over to my elected successor, John Thompson, a robust anti-communist, who had worked harmoniously with me on the executive for over a year. I felt that I was leaving the union in good hands and on course. Council gave me a warm ovation as I left the platform for the last time, as l had promised I would.

In spite of these traumatic events, when the IUS council met in Warsaw in November 1951, Thompson was elected a vice-president to replace me. The NUS was still wavering and the communists were not giving up, but their dominance was no longer a serious issue.

It was not until the NUS council held in October 1952, when Fred Jarvis was elected president, that the NUS finally broke off all contact with the IUS. At that election, for the first time since 1930, an executive that included no communists at all took office. The majority (7 out of 9 seats) passed into the hands of the National Labour Students Organisation (NALSO) which was affiliated to the British Labour Party. By the end of 1952 the IUS no longer had any representative national union affiliates west of the Iron Curtain. As far as the student movement was concerned the Cominform had hit the buffers. I like to think that my colleagues and I played some part in stopping the onward rush of the train and that my successors finally pushed it off the rails altogether.

It was left to the 2nd International Student Conference, held in Edinburgh in 1953, to further the work we had begun in Stockholm. They set up the Co-ordinating Secretariat of Student Unions (COSEC) with an office in Leyden in the Netherlands, which was in essence a new 'students international', though decidedly different in concept from its predecessors. A Swede was the first secretary-general, after him attempts were made to persuade Palme to take the job; but he had other plans. In the event, John Thompson, from the British NUS, took the post. COSEC existed until February 1967, when it was revealed in the USA that the American CIA had funded it for a number of years. That was the end of that so far as the student movement was concerned, but our main purpose had been achieved, even though the total collapse of the whole edifice of European communism that had posed such a threat to the West for four decades did not come until the tearing down of the Berlin Wall in 1989.

It is of interest, in retrospect, that one of the first vice-presidents of the IUS, Dr. Holman, was summoned before the American Universities Un-American Activities Committee in March 1952 and charged with un-American activities. The essence of the case against him was his earlier association with the IUS. Dr. Kotek records the cross-examination of Holman in his book, to which I have referred frequently. Holman was not, in the event, convicted.

From this point I retired from the student scene, apart from one exception. The NUS had just embarked on a new venture that John Thompson had asked me to continue to oversee, namely, a bookshop I had been instrumental in setting up, with the idea of cornering the student book market for the benefit of our members. After a time I withdrew, and shortly after that a new manager recommended closure of the business and it ceased to trade within a year. Perhaps it was altogether too specialised and too ambitious a project for the younger undergraduates, who took the helm. Certainly they were unlucky in their choice of manager and some of the other service departments we had established also either closed down or underwent change.

The opening of public records in the UK under the Thirty-year Rule has since revealed that Harold Wilson, the British prime minister, corresponded with the American secretary of state (Dean Atcheson) about my possible appointment as the first secretary-general of COSEC in 1952. The Americans thought that, because of my previous exposure in communist confrontation, and representing a colonial power, I was too marked a personality, and they preferred a Scandinavian. In the event I would not have been available, in that the course of my life had already taken another turn.

Best Man at David's wedding – Bwlch 1948
Back row: L to R: Fred, Mervyn, Harry, Leslie… Front: David and self

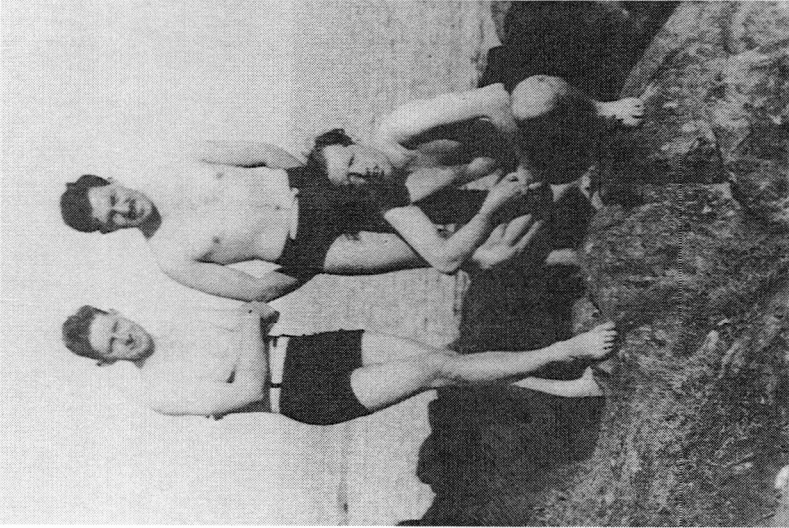

The debating team relax
at tennis – Kavalam 1949

British universities debating team
Kavalam, India 1949. L to R
Self, Alex McLellan, Colin Jackson

Taking a camel ride
at Agra Fort – 1949

Exhausted sightseers – self and Jackson
after a visit to the Taj Mahal – 1949

A meeting with Pandit Nehru in New Delhi.
L to R McLellan, Nehru and self.

British Debating Team take tea with the first Indian
Governor-General of India – April 1949, New Delhi

Rust and Johnson address Tito's prisoners held captive
on the Adriatic Coast, Yugoslavia – May 1950.

Prague IUS Congress – 1950
McNab and self prepare for battle

IUS Congress, Prague – August 1950.
Stalin mania.

Liverpool NUS Council – November 1950.
I resign the Presidency.
L to R: McNab, Thompson, self, Jarvis, Johnson

So Much To Do
So Little Time

· · · · · · · ·

Part IV

Diplomatic Adventures

CHAPTER SEVENTEEN

WHERE DO I GO FROM HERE

'Self-trust is the first secret of success'

Emerson.

On leaving the student world, I began to ponder about my future: I had previously been too busy to give it much thought. A number of factors had led me to question whether I wanted to return to the family business. I had a suspicion that I would not be too comfortable working with my uncle. I had already found him somewhat inflexible in his approach to my new college ideas for the construction industry, and he appeared to have few ambitions for the development of the business. The science and technology of building construction was advancing rapidly and he did not take readily to change. When on leave from college he would sometimes ask me to visit a building site and give the men instructions and, on one occasion, I designed some reinforced concrete lintels, only to find that he had later told the men to make them almost twice as big: none of his structures was ever likely to collapse! He was a generous and kindly man, we never had a cross word, were good friends, and I respected him greatly, but we were of different generations and outlook and I felt it would have been frustrating to work under him in the family firm.

He had spent much of his life in public service and local government and while he relished much of it, I know that he found some aspects less than congenial. He was a man of high principles and I remember how outraged he was when the Brecon Borough Council first decided to pay councillors their expenses and allowances. I do not think he claimed

199

reimbursement of a penny. He took the view that to pay councillors would inevitably corrupt the system, and that any public service must be entirely voluntary if it was to ensure the participation of individuals with the right motivation. I had some sympathy with that view and had little desire to be involved in local government either.

I also had reservations about living the rest of my days in the town where I had grown up. By now I had seen a lot of the world and feared that Brecon was likely to remain the place I had known – an isolated backwater, dominated by conflicting religious pressures and social barriers. This may have been a harsh judgement, and the future certainly did not turn out that way, as I was to discover during my visits to Brecon in later years. But when I was young, few would have disputed that my evaluation of the outlook was reasonable. Perhaps all small towns and villages were the same, but none of this did other than persuade me to look further afield for an alternative career at the end of my days, first in the army, and then with the National Union of Students, days that had entirely changed me and my perceptions of the world.

The extensive national press coverage, especially of our exploits in Eastern Europe, had led to an approach by a Labour MP, and another from a Liberal party MP, sounding me out regarding my interest in a political career. My uncle in Brecon, who was a leading light in the local Conservative party, had also suggested that he might put my name forward for a forthcoming parliamentary vacancy in his constituency. (I had clearly been successful in keeping my party political sympathies to myself!) It was flattering even to be considered, but I was tired of politics and not happy to link myself exclusively with any one party. For four exhausting years I had led the kind of life I imagined a politician to live, and had found it uncompromising and stressful, though I doubt if members of the House of Commons have ever experienced anything like those assemblies I endured in Prague or Sofia, or the ordeal of being outnumbered by thousands of militant ideologues. I had also begun to sense that one would have to be 'flexible' in matters of principle if one was to succeed in politics, and this did not rest easily with my Victorian upbringing. While I had greatly enjoyed most of my student experiences, I was tired of the rigmarole of committee work and procedural arguments, the points of order and the long night sessions – that is not to say that I had not myself used procedural devices such as 'the previous question' to good effect on a number of occasions. However, by the end of my student days I had reached the conclusion that politics was not the career for me.

Some weeks before I handed over the NUS presidency, I had received a telephone call from Sir Ivison MacAdam, the director-general of the Royal Institute of International Affairs, Chatham House and the very first president of NUS when the Union was inaugurated in 1922. He told me that he had been following my activities through press and radio and had something he wanted to discuss. I went to his office and was surprised when he informed me that he was thinking of retiring and that the vacancy would shortly be advertised. 'Would I be interested to apply for the position?' This was a career beyond my ambitions at the time, and I expressed some doubt as to whether I could really be considered a serious contender. He said he thought so, and urged me to apply. To my surprise I was eventually placed on a short-list of two and, in due course, appeared before a distinguished panel that included some senior members of the Foreign Office. In spite of support from the retiring director-general I was not chosen; instead they appointed a candidate who had had some years of cabinet office experience. I thought little more of this until I chanced to meet one of the committee from Chatham House, who suggested that I should apply directly for the Foreign Office. With tongue in cheek I did, and, having survived the rigorous entry hurdles, found myself accepted for a career in HM Diplomatic Service.

There were several things that attracted me to this. I wanted to travel and work abroad, especially in sunny climes. I also knew that the Cold War was by no means over and would not be until the threat of communism had, at least, been contained. A job that promised to let me play some role in this, however small, appealed to me. The FO also offered a wide range of career opportunities within itself in that a diplomat may be called upon to serve as a trade commissioner in one post, a political officer in another or an information officer or consul elsewhere. This highly regarded profession called for ability to mix with people at all levels, to be capable of learning languages and to handle a variety of tasks. Apart from that, the starting salary was at least four times that which I had been paid as a student leader, and on which I had barely existed for the previous five years

By this time I had moved with two friends, John McNab and Fred Gee, into a small flat off Baker Street. I remember sitting with Gee, on the pavement of the Mall in London in June 1953, to witness the coronation parade while we discussed our futures. But all else was forgotten as we cheered the royal family in their state carriages processing towards the Abbey. The colonies had given us many headaches in our student days; now we marvelled at the spectacle they afforded on that majestic occasion. The elephant bands of the Indian army and the colonial contingents were singularly colourful and impressive. The nation's loyalty to the royal family was very evident on that historic day, enhanced as a memory by the announcement of the conquest of Everest by Edmund Hillary.

As a student leader my horizons had been immeasurably widened; I had travelled extensively and learned much about politics, administration, and people. The theme of 'So much to do, so little time', that had been the hallmark of stages one and two of my days, had continued unabated through stage three. A new life now lay ahead and I faced fresh fields to conquer.

CHAPTER EIGHTEEN

FROM STUDENT ACTIVIST TO DIPLOMAT

'A diplomat is a man who always remembers
a woman's birthday, but never her age.'

Robert Frost.

W hile I was waiting to start my new career it was suggested that I might usefully spend a few months in France brushing up my sparse knowledge of French. I leapt at the opportunity and made my plans. Since my visit to the Moral Rearmament (MRA) centre in Caux, on my return from the student congress in Prague, the London branch of the organisation had kept in touch with me. They were persistent evangelists for their cause and, on learning that I was thinking of going to Paris, suggested that I should stay with one of their colleagues who lived there. This seemed a good idea if only because it solved my immediate accommodation problem. I thought I had made an excellent choice when I discovered that the family I lodged with included a gorgeous teenage daughter, and when she agreed to take me on sightseeing tours I soon learned to appreciate being freed of my student union responsibilities. But I had resolved not to take any girl seriously until I was established in a job and capable of providing for her and our relationship remained platonic. Nevertheless, I have to confess that she did prove a major distraction from my language studies.

At the time I had few friends in Paris outside the MRA circle and found myself being involved in a number of meetings where their activists were trying to arrest the spread of communism on the continent. I was persuaded to accompany one of their teams attending meetings of the World Federation of Trades Unions, a 'communist front' organisation – one in Milan, and another in Rome. I thought I had left all this behind when I parted from the NUS, but here I was in the thick of it again, albeit as a mere spectator. I was intrigued to see the same subversion techniques being deployed in the trades unions, much as we had found them in the student movement. The methods employed to control meetings and the language were identical, as were the demonstrations in adulation of Stalin and communist leaders of the day, and in condemnation of the 'imperialists'. It was all there – the same old chanting of slogans and the endless speeches vilifying everybody and everything that did not subscribe to their ideology. Yet these were older delegates and not student leaders. I was constantly seeking new insights into their thinking and found it surprising that intelligent people allowed their pursuit of Marxist dogma to stifle rational intellectual thought processes and blind them to anything that conflicted with that doctrine. Like the young communists I had met in Eastern Europe, they appeared totally blinkered and devoted to their new 'religion'. It was some time later that the tide turned against communism in the trade union field.

I had no great aptitude for languages and had made little progress with my studies when I was suddenly recalled to London and told I was to be posted to Germany. I began to panic and enrolled to take German lessons, only to learn soon afterwards that I was to proceed to Singapore. In the event, due to some administrative hitch, my departure was delayed for some months and it was not until October 1953 that I departed by air to take up my first overseas appointment. My recent escapades in Eastern Europe appeared to rule me out for any posting in that theatre where my experience might have proved useful – but, on reflection, I would probably have been declared persona-non-grata in any case. I had long been attracted to SE Asia and could hardly wait to begin my next adventure.

My basic research in preparation for my new posting told me that Singapore lay very close to the equator, that it was densely populated with some two million of mixed races, mostly Malays, Chinese and Indians, and that the island became a British Crown Colony in 1867. A mass of office papers I was invited to study informed me that its prosperity was founded on its strategic position as a trading port and as a British naval base. I also learned for the first time the meaning of the word 'isohet' – a line on a climatic map connecting places with equal rainfall, and discovered to my surprise that my hometown Brecon and Singapore had exactly the same annual rainfall, though both fell short of Comilla in Assam where I had had my first encounter with monsoon conditions.

Armed with a few vital statistics and having read a potted history of the adventures of Stamford Raffles, the founder of the colony, and recent telegrams from the post, I set forth on my new assignment. The journey by air found me sitting alongside a young lecturer moving to Singapore to join the staff of the university, who was later to provide me with numerous introductions to the faculties, that led to many pleasant hours in the company of new friends. I had already lived for a short time in British colonies in West Africa, but Singapore, although another colony, was to offer me, as a young diplomat, a very different existence from anything I had experienced hitherto.

In those days the British commissioner-general for SE Asia, from his HQ in Singapore, carried out a representational role with a minimum of reference back to London. When I first arrived there the incumbent, whose staff I joined, was Malcolm MacDonald, a former cabinet minister and son of former Prime Minister, Ramsay MacDonald.

My first appointment, with the rank of second secretary in the office of the commissioner-general, was as assistant to the regional information officer where the focus of my work was mainly liaison with the press. I succeeded an officer who had worked under General Templer in his campaign to win the hearts and minds of the people of Malaya during the Emergency, which was just drawing to a close. The focus of our attention was the advance of communism throughout the area, but I found far less 'communist front' activity in Asia than I had experienced in Europe. Not only was the situation entirely different – the social structures did not lend themselves readily to manipulation in the same way – but the flood of communist propaganda pouring into every country in the region was relentless, and journalists were hungry for information to counter it. I spent the next two years working with representatives of the press based in many of the countries of SE Asia. They were a lively, intelligent and interesting group of people and I greatly enjoyed their company. I seemed to live on aeroplanes, flying in and out of Hong Kong and Malaya, visiting countries led by Prince Norodom in Cambodia, Sukarno in Indonesia, and a succession of leaders in Thailand. The intentions of Ho Chi Minh in Vietnam were uppermost in our minds as reports of secretive troop redeployments trickled through to us and sounded a note of warning of impending trouble in that area.

Being a Foreign Office (later Foreign and Commonwealth Office) employee bore some resemblance to being in the Army in that I again felt part of an influential organisation that provided a considerable degree of support for its staff, with medical care, housing, and transport, and a sense of security born of being a member of the diplomatic corps. There was, however, one problem that I faced in regard to my career, in that contemporaries who had joined the office directly on leaving the armed forces – and there were a large number of them – had already established almost five years seniority over me when I joined. On demobilisation I had spent four years in Cardiff plus an extra year as full-time president of the NUS. But in that time some of my new colleagues had clocked up one or two overseas postings and others had the advantage of having been able to pursue a full-time language course. For the next twenty-eight years of my service this group was poised just above me. The 'Whitehall system' was, perhaps, always over-concerned with seniority rather than ability, though I think this changed somewhat in the days after Mrs. Thatcher became prime minister. Unfortunately, by that time I had moved on. Also, because I had taken a break between leaving the Army and joining the Foreign Office, none of my war service counted for pension entitlement, whereas those who had gone straight from the armed services into the office had all their war years reckoned. My NUS time counted for nothing.

Not only was this an interesting time to be living in Singapore, it was also fascinating to be working in the office of the colonial power. It was virtually certain that Singapore would soon be granted independence, and there were many preparations to be made. There was little doubt as to which of the Singapore political parties would win the first local elections, and some feared that the People's Action Party, headed by Lee Kwan Yew, might turn out to be politically too far to the left for comfort. In the event such fears proved ill-founded and Singapore became a beacon of success in many respects. Communism was, nevertheless, bearing down on the region from China and the Soviet Union, and there was much talk of the 'domino effect' if there were any further communist advances. Much of SE Asia appeared to be at risk.

Once I settled down I revelled in a new life in the sunshine of Singapore. Freed from the trauma and responsibility of my days as a student leader, I began to relax and enjoy life. I soon acquired a motorboat, many new friends and was enjoying weekend trips to offshore islands. The picnics on solitary beaches of silver sand while sitting under clumps of palm trees, the delicious curry lunches prepared by my houseboy and eaten while listening to waves breaking on the shoreline, and the solitary hours for reading, provided memories I shall always treasure.

I had no previous experience of small boats and, as I was returning late one evening from one of my many trips, the tide ran out, as it was very prone to do, rather sooner than anticipated – or had I delayed too long on a paradise island with the girl friend of the time? The water was so shallow when the tide dropped that I found myself aground on a jagged coral reef some miles offshore, in pitch darkness with no lights and had to wait several hours, until the tide turned, before I could make it to the shore. Not surprisingly, no one believed my explanation of events that night!

On another occasion I was returning to Singapore from an offshore island picnic when my outboard motor broke down in the busy main shipping channel leading into Singapore harbour. It would not restart, and as night fell I began to drift in the open sea towards Indonesia. I had no lights or emergency equipment and was scared stiff. It was dark before I got the motor running again, but at a much-reduced speed. With minimal power from my crippled engine I aimed for a small offshore island just visible in the distance, and prayed. I was about to drift past my target when I managed somehow to get the outboard to perform better and reached land. Repairs were made and I got back to Singapore at dawn. We, for I had a girl friend with me, found ourselves on the wrong side of the island and had run aground in a mangrove swamp, some yards from the shore. We climbed out of the boat, into mud up to our knees, and waded to the nearest road to hitch a lift. Mangrove swamp has a foul pervading smell and we did not make pleasant travelling companions for the lady who kindly picked us up. We also had some explaining to do back in the office.

The social round within the diplomatic corps was exhausting, even for me as a fit young man. Although we finished in the office at about 4 p.m., we barely had time to get home, shower and change before the first cocktail party of the evening. Another, and then a dinner party, often followed this. This was the pattern on at least two or three nights each week, and I had difficulty in finding the time for all I wanted to do.

A feature of Singapore entertaining was the understanding between servants to share their employer's china, cutlery, etc. as required. One had to be tactful not to admire a silver or cut-glass bowl appearing on your host's dining table in case it came from your own household! No family was ever short of the necessary china, glass or cutlery, the servants saw to that. Everything 'borrowed' in this way was invariably returned without it being mentioned to the owners and nothing to my knowledge was ever lost or damaged.

Because of my previous connection with the World Assembly of Youth, I found myself involved with the visit of a delegation from that organisation to Singapore in August 1954. I especially remember a magnificent Chinese banquet organised for the visitors by Mr. Tan Lark Sye, Chairman of the Council of Nanyang University when we sat at circular tables spread across the green padang and were waited on by hordes of servants. The twelve courses included shark-fins with sliced chicken, roasted suckling pig, fried bean curd in crab gravy and Malayan fruits. I retained the menu as a souvenir.

Bridge was a popular game with many in the office and a

group of enthusiasts soon got their stranglehold on me. In particular I had met a middle-aged American lady who was a cards fanatic and found myself trapped into playing bridge most evenings. Before long we were competing in tournaments and in no time at all I found that arrangements were being made for me to play all through the coming weeks and my diary was becoming choked with commitments. There was so much else I wanted to do in my leisure hours that I resolved to break the chain by giving up playing altogether, and I have scarcely played a hand since.

I had started taking Malay lessons in company with a friend on the staff of the university, and this too was also eating into my time. We went on to take examinations at the first two levels and enjoyed using our basic knowledge where we could. Though the language was not really required in a country where most spoke English, it proved of value in the more remote parts of the Malay Federation where we spent many weekends, picnicking, swimming and visiting friends.

It was on one of these visits, when I was accompanied by a young lecturer from Singapore university, a science graduate, that I witnessed levitation. Near the roadside at some remote spot we saw a group of people, mostly Indians, watching something intently. We stopped and joined them and saw a young Indian girl lie down on a bearer made of palm fronds, while another Indian played a wind instrument as the girl, as stiff as a corpse, rose slowly from her bed until she was suspended by some inexplicable force about four feet from the ground. We could not believe our eyes and went forward to investigate for ourselves. We found no evidence of physical support and were completely satisfied that this must be levitation. The girl was then lowered, by some invisible hand, to the ground, got up and walked away smiling. If we had not seen this for ourselves in broad daylight we would certainly not have believed it, and I have never seen it done since.

I was but a junior officer at the time and anything I thought or said was unlikely to have much force with my superiors, but I did have my say from time to time, if only within the informality of our tennis playing circles. While I found myself mostly in agreement with the lines we were expected to follow, I was sometimes at loggerheads with certain policies our government was pursuing. There was always an inevitable moral dilemma facing us in our work. The job required absolute loyalty, but the conscience occasionally rebelled. For many of us a difficulty arose wherever it was deemed expedient to prop up a corrupt regime that was buttressing our strategic stance against the main enemy, communism, because, on balance, this was in our best interest. But some of the regimes in SE Asia at that time, to which we often turned a blind eye, were decidedly undemocratic and their excesses unacceptable, providing meat and drink to our main adversary who exploited their imperfections, to win over those who suffered at their hands. It was always arguable that, had we not encouraged and supported some of the leaders in the region, others who might have pursued more ethical policies would have replaced them. On the other hand, even less acceptable leaders could have taken their place. Worse still, disorder and instability may have paved the way for communist revolution. The answers, if there were any, were never clear, and I admired enormously the diligence of my colleagues who carefully sifted all available evidence in order to offer the best possible advice – which was not, of course, always taken – to those back home on whom the responsibility for the formulation of policy rested.

The FCO is often blamed for policies for which it is by no means responsible. In the field, it seemed to me that decisions taken by politicians at home were not always taken by those best able to judge. Their criteria, which included a large measure of domestic politics, were all too frequently at variance with those of us on the spot. I remember in particular listening to a radio debate on one of my home visits, between so-called experts on a country, where I had been resident for some time. I was appalled at their apparent lack of knowledge. Had they uttered such nonsense in the presence of my Head of Mission abroad, they would probably have been packed off home.

On one of many visits to Hong Kong, which I found the most fascinating place in the region, and one that I contrived to visit whenever I could, I added some leave due to me and spent a fabulous week exploring the island. I booked my return to Singapore on a small merchant ship. While waiting for her to sail, there was a broadcast typhoon warning and all passengers were summoned to board their vessels in the harbour without delay. The wind struck with alarming speed and force. I hastened back to my ship and had warning of what was to come when I saw palm trees being uprooted and hurled into the sky. I was never a good sailor – indeed I used to say that I could get seasick getting into my bath – so I was not at all looking forward to the journey. On receiving a further hurricane warning, all vessels were ordered out of the harbour for fear of collisions and we sailed in great haste into the roughest sea I have ever experienced. An Indonesian steward insisted on lashing me to my bunk with twisted sheets, and there I lay for three days of unadulterated misery as we headed for Manila. The ship was tossed like a cork, rising what seemed hundreds of feet and then crashing down on the other side of a wave. Then up it went again. I swallowed all my seasickness pills in the first twenty-four hours and spent much of my time praying 'for those in peril on the sea'. On arrival I was met by a friend from the American embassy who had kindly arranged a full programme for the day, lots of sightseeing and excellent food. In the event I slumped in the back of his car with my eyes tightly shut. Whenever I opened them I could only see that terrifying wall of water still going up and down. It proved to be a day that did little for Anglo-American relations.

The journey from Manila took me to Bali where I spent two delightful days. Armed with an introduction to a recluse painter living in the hills to the east of the island, I hired a taxi and went to see him. Bali is noticeably different from most of the hundreds of other islands making up the Republic of Indonesia. The inhabitants are mainly Hindu rather than Moslem and this is reflected in its buildings, especially in the style of the temples. The paddy fields with their extensive irrigation channels have moulded the hillsides so that every mountain appears exceptionally lush, clad by terrace upon terrace of rice fields. My host was living in a typically Balinese dwelling built of local materials – timber and thatch – perched on a mountain slope with as spectacular a view across a valley as I have seen anywhere in the world. He lived alone apart from his servants, all beautiful young topless maidens, who served a superb lunch of spiced chicken marinated in coconut. I admired my host's oil paintings and watercolours, but must confess my main attention was focused elsewhere for much of the time.

The next leg of my trip by air brought me to Djakarta, the capital city of Java. During my tour of duty in Singapore I made a number of visits there but it never appealed to me. I found it an untidy, busy, dirty and unattractive place, grossly overpopulated and lacking in character. Some new hotels and housing were under construction, but for the most part the city was suffering from a population boom worsened by the poverty in the countryside which had drawn millions to the metropolis in search of jobs. My hosts took me on several trips by car and I could readily understand why the embassy personnel relished the countryside whenever they could get to it. Once away from the city the main island of Java is spectacularly beautiful.

215

Back in Singapore we were nearing the end of the era of British colonialism. Many of the old hands kept the flag flying in the traditional way. They had their clubs and some of these still excluded the native people from membership. At the cricket club on the padang where matches were played almost every weekend, the ambience was akin to that of any cricket club in England. I was not a cricketer, but, fortunately for me, the island was also a haven for tennis players, and I indulged myself in matches and tournaments galore. In June 1954 we had word of a group of Australian players, on their way to compete at Wimbledon, who were prepared to play an exhibition match if we could provide a court. We marked out a square in front of the cricket pavilion that was reasonably level and worked on it for a week. Our visitors turned out to include Rosewall and Hoad on their way to defend the Wimbledon doubles title they had won in 1953.

After about two years I was given leave in the UK and this time elected to travel home on a small merchant ship of the Blue Funnel line. I liked little ships because of the many interesting places they visited on their way, to deliver and collect cargo. On this particular voyage we called at a number of ports not on a tourist map. I particularly remember Djibouti at the mouth of the Red Sea, where I was able to wander ashore with some friends who took me to a leper colony where I saw hundreds of Africans suffering from a disease that was literally eating them away; some without arms, some without legs, but worst of all, I thought, were those whose faces were partially destroyed. The hopelessness of these unfortunate souls was heart-rending and the conditions in which they lived seemed appalling by our standards in the West. They were being cared for, as best they could, by a group of dedicated nuns, and I could only marvel that they retained their faith. We re-embarked feeling humbled and inadequate.

After a few months leave in the UK when I stayed with my aunt and uncle in Brecon, and visited family and friends, I returned to Singapore by air for the second leg of my tour, fully expecting to carry on where I had left off, but life in the FCO was never like that.

CHAPTER NINETEEN

I MEET MY MATCH AT TENNIS

'What strenuous singles we played after tea
We in the tournament – you against me.'

John Betjeman.

On returning to Singapore in December 1955 I was immediately seconded to the Colonial Office and posted to Kuala Lumpur. Many preparations had to be made for the independence of Malaya and we were kept busy. Quite unexpectedly I was greeted on my arrival at the airport by an old friend from my student days, Ghazali bin Shaffie, who had been a member of my Colonial Students Committee in London. He had become a civil servant and was working in the Malay foreign ministry. Later he became its head. We had also met at the MRA centre in Caux on my return from the IUS Congress in Prague in 1950.

Much as I had liked Singapore and enjoyed my stay there, I welcomed the move to KL – a new challenge. The climate was very similar, hot and humid with no seasonal changes to speak of, but I had grown used to it and it suited me well. When I first arrived KL was a small sleepy town with its many mosques and Hindu temples. For me it had the added attraction of being within easy reach of mountains and dense tropical forests. Unlike the bustling skyscraper city it has since become, it was then very much a typical Malay settlement with immense charm and boundless atmosphere.

I stayed for a while at the old Station Hotel with its quaint oriental architecture, but soon afterwards moved into a small modern bungalow and set up my bachelor home. I later met

219

another young unmarried civil servant, John Snelling, attached to the Ministry of Defence, who was looking for accommodation, and he moved in to share the bungalow with me. We engaged an elderly Chinese servant to cook and clean for us. She spoke no English and we no Chinese, but before long we developed an adequate sign language that served us well. She would produce delicious meals and I shall never forget her picnic lunches, plucked as from nowhere, for our friends and us, whenever we needed them.

The colonial work-and-play schedule was well organised to ensure that there was always a good balance between the two. Busy though we were in the office I still found time to keep up my tennis and play in a number of matches and national tournaments. In my capacity as tournament referee – a function that often fell to me – I had one day to advise General Bourne, the land forces commander, that he must complete his next round by the weekend or be scratched. He jokingly remarked that I was the only one in Malaya to give him orders! It was also through tennis that I met and got to know the last Governor of the Federation, Sir Donald McGillivray, who carried on the tradition of tea and tennis in true colonial style until independence, after which he retired to Rhodesia.

It was on the tennis courts at the Golf Club in Kuala Lumpur, where I used to play some evenings in the week, that I was introduced to a young lady, Barbara Webb, who was to become my wife. For an American tournament I was asked if I wanted a partner for the next game, said 'yes please', and kept her for life, or rather, she kept and looked after me! I have since told many a joke about our never having scored off each other: it was certainly a love match.

I was later to learn that Barbara had some interesting ancestors. A first cousin of her paternal grandfather, Sir Aston

Webb, was the architect who, *inter alia,* designed Admiralty Arch and Christ's Hospital at Horsham. Her father married a Pilkington, related distantly to the family that spawned the glass-making empire. Her great-great-grandfather Christopher Pilkington founded the Pilkington & Wilson Shipping Line that became the White Star Line and was later to merge with Cunard. Some photographs and relics from the clipper ships that sailed from Liverpool to Melbourne around 1856 were later passed down to her.

From then on life for the pair of us was idyllic. I had an open-top sports car and, together, Barbara and I would visit the beaches of Malacca – the old Dutch settlement on the west coast – and other resorts. Some had romantic names like 'The beach of passionate love' which I might have chosen to propose marriage, but instead I popped the question on Christmas Day 1956, under palm trees on an isolated sandy beach on the north-west coast of Malaya, which had no special name that I can recall, but which we had that evening all to ourselves. The occasion was somewhat spoilt for both of us because Barbara had been bitten on the nose by a hornet, producing an ominous and none too attractive swelling! In spite of that I went ahead with my proposal and, thankfully, she accepted.

During the sublimely happy months that followed, Barbara and I took local leave and drove from Kuala Lumpur to the east coast of Malaya and then north to the Thai frontier. We started off on a Saturday afternoon driving as far as Kuantan where we spent the night. The route was then little used though construction of a new main road north had already been started. We encountered a few good stretches where it was completed, but it was mostly potholed tracks. We had to cross twenty-one rivers and estuaries by ferry, some of them taking a few passengers, and others where a grizzled old Malay man appeared to pull our car across by means of chains. On one occasion, when Barbara was driving, we had to negotiate a very steep slope down and almost parallel with the river before making a sharp right-hand turn onto the narrow deck of the ferry. We were very relieved not to end up in the water. We stayed the nights in remote government rest houses that afforded fairly austere but adequate accommodation for travellers, conveniently sited by generations of colonial servants at most of the river crossings. We would arrive unannounced to find a Malay or Chinese houseboy ready and anxious to cook for us and provide hot water and clean beds. The journey for most of the way was breathtakingly beautiful and quite unspoiled. We drove for miles along deserted coastal roads and tracks with nothing between us and the sea, except for silver sand and palm trees.

We travelled on to Kuala Dungun and Kuala Trengganu where we saw some of the most colourful markets we had seen anywhere in the world, with the Malay women in their multi-coloured *sarongs* and head-dresses among their stalls of exotic fruits and vegetables. We would stop in native villages of tiny mud and thatch houses and buy fruit, returning to the car to eat mangoes, papayas and rambutans, and to squeeze fresh lemons and limes to provide refreshing drinks. Groups of smiling children would soon gather to see the strange foreigners. Most loved to have their photographs taken but some were too shy and disappeared when I produced my camera. Unfortunately when we sent off the colour slides we took on this trip to be processed; they never reappeared – lost somewhere in some photographic labyrinth.

Our next night stop was at Kota Bahru the chief town of the State of Kelantan, and our final destination Tumpat, close to the Thai border, where we discovered a little used bungalow owned by the Malayan Railway Company. We spent a few days there enjoying a restful time and exploring the local *kampongs*. When our leave ran out we drove to Kuala Krai station where we saw our car loaded onto an open wagon, leaving us apprehensive about its fate perched precariously aloft. We travelled back to KL through some completely unspoilt rain forest. When our train pulled in at stations we used to stand at the window, trying to avoid the smoke from the engine as best we could, listening to the din of the jungle, which intensified as dusk fell.

We were married on 23rd March 1957, by an Indian curate, in the little Anglican church beside the padang in KL. As we emerged from the service we found our friends waiting for us holding an arch of tennis rackets. Our reception, for nearly a hundred guests, including most of the local diplomatic corps, was held at the Selangor Club, known locally as 'the Dog', though we never knew why. None of my family was able to attend the wedding, but Barbara's parents had flown out and we were delighted to have them with us for a few weeks after the ceremony. We had only just left the airport runway, after the reception, when our guests were deluged by a heavy storm that caused flash floods throughout the area. Local superstition had it that this must be an ill omen, but it certainly did not turn out that way. We flew out of the storm into Singapore for the night, before flying on to Hong Kong for our honeymoon spent at the Repulse Bay Hotel in, appropriately, a district named Stanley. This made it easy to find our way home after shopping: we simply boarded the bus or took a taxi to 'Stanley'.

Our wedding presents included many cheques and we used the proceeds in Hong Kong to buy household requirements. In those days it was the shopper's paradise of the East: ivories, jades and Chinese porcelain were available at very low cost and we have since greatly regretted that we had not more to spend at that time. We returned to Singapore by sea on the s.s. Tchwangi, a small Dutch vessel where we shared the captain's table and struggled for four days to keep sober. Loaded with several large packages we made our way to the railway station to board the train for KL. The customs officials delayed its departure to check us through, and even as the train pulled out they were still marking crosses on our purchases while running with them to the moving carriages.

My best man, John Snelling, who had shared my accommodation until the wedding, had obligingly moved out and, on our return to KL we settled in my bungalow. Barbara continued to work for the US army unit at the Medical Research Institute, where she had found herself a job when she first came to Malaya to visit a cousin who was a district officer in the Malay civil service. She had found what she intended as a temporary job for a limited stay; now she had a job for life – and hard work it was to be.

The life of the wife of a diplomat can be very demanding, particularly for those with young families to care for. Few people realise how much time diplomats, and their wives, spend entertaining and being entertained, taking part in diplomatic functions and local activities and generally showing the flag. Parties were given for some specific purpose and were occasions when one had the opportunity to meet other diplomats and indigenous people and their leaders, whom we needed to know and understand if we were to do our job. But it has to be said that circulating amongst the guests offered the opportunity for little more than an exchange of pleasantries. There were also many visitors to posts overseas wanting to meet people, or colleagues leaving and new arrivals to be welcomed. Entertaining is an essential part of the diplomat's life; gastronomy and socialising are vital tools of the trade and the art of exploiting social contacts to find out what is going on and to influence the thinking of others is part and parcel of the armoury of HM representatives abroad. Information is probably the key to much of it, and this is two-way traffic. To provide the minister of some remote country with knowledge or arguments that he might in turn use to further his position within his own government might of itself produce a dividend.

To relieve the monotony of these functions, we tried to introduce an element of fun and make our parties different in some way, and we became adept at devising the unusual. Introductions between guests we hardly knew were always a test of memory, but we once found a way to overcome this. We invited each guest on arrival to pair up with a member of the opposite sex, by matching a word given to each on a card with an associated word given to another. All went well until two failed to match. It transpired that the American envoy's wife had been given a card bearing the words 'Angles on' instead of 'Angels on' and had failed to link with a gentleman frantically searching for someone to match 'horseback'. (Fortunately the Americans thought it was just another peculiar English spelling.)

The well-tended grass tennis courts at the golf club in KL where we spent much of our leisure time proved an oasis for us. They were usually watered each day by a heavy tropical downpour, but dried just as quickly and could be played on within minutes of the rain stopping. I used to fly over the courts on my journeys back from Medan or Penang, while it was still raining, and by the time I had landed and reached the club they were ready for play. Barbara and I competed in a number of tournaments together during our Malaya tour. The most strenuous of these was one played at Klang during one Easter weekend when we had entered some six events. We ended up in four semi-finals that all had to be played on the same day. Starting at 9 a.m. when it was already hot, we played for much of the day. My skin had been burning through my tennis shirt and every movement hurt. Of our matches, we played – and lost – two, but had to abandon the others to take Barbara's parents to Port Swettenham to catch their boat home to England.

It was while playing in one of these events in KL that I broke a small bone in my foot and Barbara drove me to the hospital where we found the customary queue of people waiting for attention. On arrival the receptionist advised us that the doctor had no appointments for at least two weeks. Instead we were given his car registration number and told to wait by his vehicle. This would ensure that we would be noticed and attended to by the Irish doctor when he left for lunch. It was a strange way to make an appointment, but the stratagem worked and my foot was put into plaster. This proved to be a most unpleasant experience in the tropics, not nice for me and unsavoury for others. Barbara went so far as to suggest that I should sleep with one leg out of the window.

We were fortunate to have made friends in KL with the daughters of an affluent family of Malay-Chinese who had a holiday home in Malacca and another in the mountains at Frasers Hill, one of two old colonial hill stations popular with the British. The two, Frasers Hill and the Cameron Highlands, were set in pleasing landscapes which bore strong similarities to the English countryside, with rolling hills, shrubs, many trees common to England, and a variety of less recognisable birds and insects. We used to join our friends there for weekend house parties, to play mah-jong and to walk in the mountains. On other occasions we went on holidays with them staying at their house in Port Dickson, where we once found ourselves the only British amongst a dozen Chinese. We both enjoyed oriental food and their servants knew how to prepare it: there is probably no finer cuisine in the world. After the heat of the lowlands, the air in the hills and time spent on exquisite beaches brought welcome relief. The heat and humidity of the town usually sent us scurrying to the hills or the sea whenever we could.

On the road to Frasers Hill we would pass Batu caves where Hindus celebrate their annual festival of Deepavali. We saw this event on a few occasions and found the rituals somewhat nauseating. Devotees – men both young and old – would pierce their skin with hooks to which they would attach frames and sometimes quite heavy loads and garlands of flowers as they walked long distances, first to the holy caves and then up endless flights of steps to the shrine at the top of the mountain. They painted their bodies with white ash, in part to check the bleeding, and worked themselves into a trance before subjecting themselves to what seemed to us pointless suffering. I was reminded of the dehumanising experience the war must have had on me when my former student colleague, Ralph Blumenau told me many years later, of a letter I wrote to him after seeing the Batu cave ceremonies, when I had expressed an urge to 'use my bren gun on the lot'. In mitigation, I can only plead that I knew little of the significance of these events for the participants.

There was one occasion in the course of my duties when I had to make a call on Tunku Abdul Rahman at his home in Alor Star in Perak in North Malaya. He was then leader of UMNO, the main Malay political party of the time and prime minister designate. I shall remember Alor Star for its piercing winds which blow keenly for much of the year giving residents rather more than a welcome respite from the tropical heat. I took some papers for him to see, stayed for lunch, and then returned to Kuala Lumpur. He was a kindly, wise and tolerant man and was to prove an able leader of an independent Malaysia.

227

It was part of my duties, and a very pleasant one, to pay periodic visits to North Sumatra, where I stayed with our consul in Medan. On one of these my baggage went astray and Malayan Airways compensated me with a free ticket that I used to take Barbara the next time I went. For some inexplicable reason, she was subjected to a rigorous body search at the airport and had to be rescued by our consul. She did not look like a drug smuggler, but something must have aroused suspicion. On this occasion we were taken to see the grandeur of Lake Toba set high in the Sumatra Mountains where we spent a very enjoyable weekend with the consul and his sons. We went lightly armed with revolvers because of raids by dacoits in recent times, but nothing untoward happened to us, which was just as well for it was a remarkably remote, if beautiful place.

On another of my visits to Medan I was inveigled into playing bridge with the consul's wife, an intimidating lady, who began by laying down the bridge system we would play and rules for our partnership. It was not long before I had done something heinous – I think I used her non-trump convention incorrectly. She exploded with wrath and it proved a disastrous evening. I don't think I have since dared to play a hand of bridge; the memory still haunts me. On my last visit to Medan the consul took me to his club where we played skittles. Unknown to me they had a club convention: if anyone knocked down all the pins with a first ball, he stood all present a round of drinks. My first ball did just that and it proved a very expensive evening for me. In retrospect it is strange that I have mostly pleasant memories of my many visits to Sumatra.

The obligation and duty of the diplomat and civil servant to discharge the policies of the government of the day comes under great strain at times like the Suez crisis. The Egyptian government, under President Nasser, had tried to reclaim sovereignty of the canal by negotiation, and when talks broke down the British and French governments, who had financed, built it and claimed ownership, resorted to military force to maintain their control of what they regarded as a vital route to the East. Whatever the rights of the parties concerned, the military invasion that followed seemed to us hard to justify, and was roundly condemned by the American government who acted swiftly to bring the conflict to an end by applying pressure on the invaders. The Anglo-French forces were then withdrawn and Nasser nationalised the canal. While all eyes were focussed on Suez the way was left clear for the Soviet Union to move its army into Hungary and suppress the tide of nationalism that was emerging there.

It surprised me that the detachment of the civil servant from policy-making was so often sufficient in itself to obviate the need for more civil servants and diplomats to resign rather than carry through policies they could not stomach. Suez proved a great embarrassment for me, for other members of the British mission, and especially for Barbara who was working with Americans. From our standpoint British military intervention seemed indefensible and we were under constant attack from our diplomatic colleagues, particularly the Americans, of whom Churchill once said, 'they could be relied upon to do the right thing in the end – having first exhausted the available alternatives'. In this case the British, rather than the American, government must have felt they had exhausted the alternatives open to them. The effect of Suez on the Soviet invasion of Hungary will be for historians to gauge. Perhaps it was because of my days in Eastern Europe, and the time I had spent in Budapest, that I was acutely aware of the implications for that unhappy country.

As the date for independence approached we were conscious of taking part in the last phase of a history of occupation and colonialism in Malaya. India, Burma and Ceylon had already gained their independence amicably, if not without turbulence, but there had been a long campaign of fighting communist insurgency in the Federation to create the right conditions before autonomy could be granted. Now there was to be a new Malay Union – in which, eventually, the nine Malay States would be joined with the two old colonial settlements of Penang and Malacca while Singapore was to become a separate colony. Although our work on the Defence Treaty was at an end, we stayed in KL for the celebrations in August 1957, performed by the Duke and Duchess of Gloucester. So as to avoid the heat of the day we were required to be in our seats by 6 a.m. to witness the lowering of the British flag on yet another of our dependencies. (I wondered what my former communist adversaries would have thought of this as their troops continued to occupy much of Eastern Europe. Who were the colonialists now?)

There were a number of official celebration parties after the ceremony in the stadium to which we had been invited, but we elected to go into the town and mingle with the people on the padang, where the smell of satay and other food stalls filled the air and thousands of jubilant people mixed. Some of my colleagues thought this venture into the crowds might be unwise, but they were wrong. We encountered nothing but smiles, handshakes and warm greetings.

Thus we had seen the launch of the self-governing Malayan Federation which was expanded in 1963 to include Singapore, Sarawak and Sabah in the Federation of Malaysia, but this tenuous alliance was to last only a couple of years before Singapore broke away in 1965, leaving the new territory in temporary disarray.

We sailed from Port Swettenham for the UK in October

230

1957 on a small merchant ship, for me aptly named 's.s. Breconshire', after my home county. During the war my uncle Stanley in Brecon, for fund-raising in our war effort, had a large-scale model made of the first 's.s. Breconshire', a naval frigate, that was later lost at sea. I remember the model stored for years in a shed in the builders' yard at the bottom of our garden.

On the voyage home our ship was delayed in Colombo because of a dock strike. Acting on the captain's suggestion we took a train trip inland on a narrow gauge railway that meandered through tea plantations lining the mountain slopes to Nuwara Eliya, one of the favoured hill stations of the British. While we were there we saw in our hotel a display of magnificent jewels including some yellow sapphires. Later, in Colombo, we were entertained by an American colleague from my student days, who was then director of a youth education programme there, who took us to dinner with a Ceylonese friend of his who was one of the leading jewellers in the country. He turned out to be very anxious, in such difficult times, to make a sale, and we ended up buying a large yellow sapphire, greatly reduced in price. As it happened, I did not have sufficient foreign currency with me to pay him and my American friend offered to settle the account while I agreed to repay him in the UK. We thought no more of it until we arrived at the harbour and declared our stone for export. My reply to the question 'How did you pay for it?' was 'I didn't, my friend did' and this led me straight into a major currency infringement situation. There were strict currency controls in force at that time and only the good offices of my friend saved me from incarceration in some ghastly gaol.

Eventually we were on our way and, at Alexandria, we discovered that our ship was only the second British merchantman to call there since the Suez debacle. In the circumstances we were surprised that the shipping-line agents gave the ship such a warm welcome. They came aboard to take the captain ashore to be entertained, invited us to join the party and took us on an extensive tour of the old city and King Farouk's palace. We were wined and dined in a manner that left no doubt they were glad to see a British vessel back in port. Later we called at Naples and fitted in a trip to view the ruins at Pompeii.

On our arrival in London docks on 31st October, we were at pains to avoid any further trouble over our precious gemstone and took the precaution of displaying it prominently on the cabin table while awaiting the arrival of the customs officer who had boarded the ship. In the event he did not pay us a visit and we disembarked without incident. My first thought was to get the stone valued and insured. But no jeweller we consulted valued it higher than the price of a topaz, which it resembled in appearance, even though we had proof of its authenticity. 'Nobody would believe it to be genuine, it's much too big, so who would pay more? It's all a question of fashion'. We sold it later at Sotherbys – they also insisted on it being a topaz. Having by this time lost the certificate of authenticity we got less than we had paid for it. Another unsuccessful commercial venture!

Barbara was now pregnant with our first child and we stayed with her parents in their delightful 16th century cottage in East Peckham in Kent – a building that sported many old oak beams with square porthole cut-outs still visible, and which reputedly had been used by retainers on their way to join the Armada at Tilbury. For some weeks I commuted daily to London while we looked around for a new home.

CHAPTER TWENTY

SINGAPORE TURNAROUND

'The surest road to health, say what they will,
Is never to suppose we shall be ill,
Most of those evils we poor mortals know,
From doctors and imagination flow.'

Churchill.

We had by this time decided that it would be prudent to buy a house and furnish it before we were posted abroad again, but most of my office colleagues advised against this. They took the view that ownership of a home in the UK would only be a burden, and quoted their experiences with difficult tenants and in managing property at a distance, but how wrong they turned out to be. Because property values soared soon afterwards, our purchase of a house in Redhill proved to be exceptionally rewarding. Many of those who had advised us against buying found, on returning to the UK some years later, that they could not readily afford the homes they wanted. The next two decades proved to be a bonanza for investors – I was already a keen follower of the stock market – and especially for property owners, and we were to make a handsome profit when we sold our house only seven years later.

Our first child, Nicola, was born in Pembury, Kent, on 22nd December 1957, and we moved into our new home in January 1958. The house had been sub-divided into three parts and we bought the largest of these with most of the garden – in all about an acre of land that included an old greenhouse some forty feet long – not enough land for a pony perhaps, but enough for a tennis court and some to spare.

We had hastily to unpack our crates and improvise with just about everything. We spent days at auction sales and picked up the essential furnishings and some treasures at very reasonable prices. My DIY skills were required in applications throughout the house and garden and many repairs and alterations were carried out. We had great pleasure in creating our new home.

It was not only the weather we had to grow accustomed to. As householders we had to rediscover much about living in England. Heating such a large house to temperatures to which we had grown accustomed was a problem. After Malaya we felt the cold intensely, especially Barbara, who suffered from poor circulation. We were encouraged to find that the house had once had gas fires in almost every room and that these fires had been stored in an attic bedroom. I invited the Gas Board to quote for reinstating them. Having accepted their quotation a gas fitter reconnected all the fires before telling my wife as he left the house 'you know there's no gas there I suppose?'. The Gas Board, soon to become the butt of many jokes, knew when they quoted for the work that the gas had been cut off years ago, and that there was no supply to the house. My rather tersely phrased letter to the Regional Gas Board chairman produced a surprising response. When I got home he was waiting for me and, after some negotiating, he offered to share the cost, an offer I refused arguing that they might just as well have connected the fires to the water pipes. In the event they did the necessary work at no cost to us.

On 6th April 1958, when our guests gathered for Nicola's christening – reported to have been the coldest Easter of the century – I decided to light the old dilapidated central heating boiler in the basement for the first time since we had moved in. We only discovered that the chimney was blocked when the neighbours called to ask if we were on fire; the smoke was seeping from behind their skirting boards. But nothing, it seemed, would heat the radiators. It was snowing, but we had to open all the doors and windows to save our guests from asphyxiation.

When we first moved into our new home we found the cellars filled with hundreds of empty wine bottles. Whoever had lived there before us had obviously lived well, and concealed the evidence of their indulgence by storing the empties for posterity that had now arrived prematurely in the manifestation of the Jenkins family. It fell to us to dispose of the evidence. The local authority would not take the bottles and, surprisingly, suggested we should bury them in the garden. Accordingly, before leaving for the office one morning I set my newly found gardener to work digging a pit. When I returned from the office in the evening I was amazed to see old Tom well below ground level and still going down; I had omitted to tell him when to stop. He was that sort of chap. We buried the bottles and I have since wondered whether anyone stumbled across them when planting rhubarb or digging prize leeks on the site of our home that later became their gardens.

I had long cherished the idea of having my own grass tennis court so we engaged a specialist contractor, who brought in heavy equipment to grade, level and sow our front lawn. But it rained all the week and it was not long before the excavator got stuck firmly in a sea of mud. The more the driver revved his engine the deeper the machine sank. Finally the contractors brought in a huge crane to rescue the digger from the swamp they had created. The court construction then had to be postponed until the spring, by which time we had left the country.

We had been home only eleven months when I was advised to prepare to return to Singapore and we began making the necessary arrangements. Just before leaving England, we heard of the sudden death of my auntie Norah. This was sad news. She had been inordinately kind to me during and just after the war. We were able to attend the funeral in Brecon before having to uproot the family.

We now had our first experience of moving being householders and having a small child. It was never easy. There always seemed a hundred and one things to attend to – and those tormenting decisions as to what to take or leave behind, and where to store the rest. And suitable tenants had to be found for our home. Keeping in touch with friends and family as we constantly moved around the world became a major undertaking and we kept printers busy with change of address cards. Such were the trials in the life of every diplomat, and especially for wives.

We sailed from Southampton on 17th December 1958 on the 's.s. Iberia' for my next tour in SE Asia. This time, having our baby daughter with us, our lives would inevitably be different. I was familiar with the Suez route having been through the canal seven times previously, but it still fascinated me to see the desert running close alongside the ship and other ships gliding by as though ploughing through the sand itself.

Much as I liked Singapore I was marginally disappointed to be posted there again. There was always a danger in the office of becoming too specialised and missing out on promotion opportunities for lack of experience. It was policy to move staff around the world every few years to give each a wide knowledge of different regions of the world and to lessen the danger of personnel 'going native'. Later I became more appreciative of the contribution living and working abroad in the same area made to the depth of one's understanding of a region and one's perception of events, but at the time I thought I was perhaps missing some opportunity.

Back in Singapore we engaged as a baby nanny (*amah*), a Singapore Chinese girl, Ah Yair, who had just left school. She was to prove an invaluable help to us as, apart from one break, she lived with us as another daughter for the next eleven years. She was a wonderful cook and our children adored her. (Long after she had left us and her own children had grown up, her younger son became a student at the University of Surrey and she and other members of her family came to visit us in England in 1999, for his graduation, when we attended the ceremony at Guildford.)

A visit by Prince Philip on 24th February 1959 was the occasion for a gala garden party for over a thousand guests at the Residency in Singapore. These were occasions when the protocol books had to be dusted off to ensure that everybody who should be invited was, and that the maximum goodwill was extracted. Everything went well with all the customary handshaking and small talk and presented no problem for those who had the task of preparing a despatch to the FO reporting all the salient points. I often wondered whether anybody at home found the time to read what were almost stereotyped returns, to which each head of mission would add his own literary flourishes.

Our second daughter Caroline was born on 3rd April 1959. Immediately prior to this event we were walking around an exhibition of orchids arranged on tiers of stone steps in a large Singapore stadium when Barbara told me she thought we should proceed immediately to the British military hospital. I left her there in the early evening and drove home – a distance of about 2 miles – to hear the telephone ringing. 'Mr. Jenkins, you have a son.....no wait....Jenkins?....sorry, no...its a daughter'. What a pity I thought, we had wanted a son this time, but there it was. When we took Caroline home a few days later she was painted purple with gentian violet which they

237

used to quell heat rash. She looked positively repulsive: they had even painted the inside of her mouth. We little thought then that she would become a beautiful ballerina.

Lord Selkirk, who was ably assisted by a Ministry of Defence official, Philip Moore, succeeded Malcolm MacDonald as Commissioner-General for SE Asia during my time in Singapore. Philip and his wife were both keen tennis players and we enjoyed many hours of family tennis with them. (Later he became Private Secretary to the Queen and received a knighthood.) Philip would sometimes ring me up towards the end of the working day to ask if I could be available to play tennis with Lord Selkirk that evening. This was by nature of a Royal Command and whatever other arrangements I might have made had to be cancelled. My social life was often in disarray because of this; nonetheless we had many enjoyable games, usually at the Tanglin Club. On the first occasion we played there Philip, the club secretary and I were knocking up when Lord Selkirk appeared from the pavilion wearing, against all the rules of the club, blue shorts, blue canvas shoes and a shirt that matched. He looked more ready for a day at sea than a game of tennis. Not knowing who he was, the club secretary called out 'Who the hell is that moron?' It was as much as Philip could do to prevent his Lordship from being thrown out there and then.

I had experienced something similar – but considerably more embarrassing – a few years earlier when, in Kuala Lumpur, the Sultan of Selangor had been invited to attend a social function at the Selangor Club. When he failed to turn up it transpired that he had arrived earlier and been despatched unceremoniously by a porter on the front door who brusquely told him to 'shove off, you locals are not allowed in here'.

With the sea all around us and numerous tropical islands

within easy reach, a boat was a must. I had sold mine when I left Singapore earlier and for this second tour we shared a small motorboat with an office colleague. With the children we enjoyed many visits to the offshore islands that I found magical places, taking our picnics, swimming and basking in the warm sunshine while the children would take their afternoon nap on a blanket under the palm trees. There were hazards in the sea, but we did not worry overmuch about the danger posed by sea snakes and jellyfish; they were rarely seen. We did see a sea snake further north in Malaya later on, but they were reputed seldom to attack swimmers unless provoked, which was just as well for there was no known antidote. But we never allowed such fears to spoil the sheer delight of swimming and bathing from wonderful tropical beaches.

There were many quaint touches to life in the East. I remember telephoning the wife of one of my colleagues and his *amah* answered the phone to inform me that I could not speak to *memsahib* because she was 'milking the baby'. A friend went on leave and left a pet cockatoo in the care of his houseboy. On his return he was told the bird had died and, to prove it, the frozen bird was produced from the refrigerator!

Diplomats had to oblige their numerous official visitors by escorting them around the customary sights, and family and friends added to the numbers. Barbara's two rather prim, elderly maiden aunts joined us in Singapore for Christmas 1959. They were an adventurous and much-travelled couple who wanted to see everything. A travel-guide's course would not have come amiss. After leaving us exhausted from their two weeks of sightseeing, they went on to visit Japan before returning to Singapore for a further round of exploration. Their visit was uneventful except for an incident when we were all waiting for them to dress for Christmas lunch. They finally emerged from their rooms and were about to take a drink in the lounge when our cat, who decided he was not going to be left out of the festivities, strolled in and deposited his contribution to the feast – a large live rat – on the carpet immediately in front of them. The aunts disappeared into their rooms and did not emerge for some time. It was an inauspicious start to our festivities.

We took the aunts with us on one of our frequent weekend trips north of the Singapore-Malaya causeway to visit some of the resorts in the Federation. We made many such visits to the beaches of Malacca, Pangkor Island, and Mersing. In those days the journey to Pangkor involved a short flight to Ipoh, then two hours by taxi to the West Coast followed by an hour on a small motorboat. There was only one car on the island. We stayed in a small hut on the beach and took our meals in a larger hut that we could only reach by walking through a sea of hermit crabs scuttling for cover. The Australian armed services used this as a leave centre and loved to play with our small children on the beach and in the sea, regardless of the quantity of alcohol they had consumed, where we saw the little ones being tossed several feet in the air. Their shrieks of sheer delight could be heard from afar. An Australian colleague assured us they would come to no harm. A twenty minutes trip by rowing boat took us to Emerald Island. As we approached the shore it was as though the whole beach moved as thousands of crabs headed for the jungle. At the time these islands were virtually uninhabited and undeveloped, offering little but miles of golden sands and palm lined beaches.

My work occasioned my making frequent trips to neighbouring countries, from which I would return with treasures bought in some exotic land. There were so many things to buy and I could not resist some of the temptations placed in my way. The children always greeted my homecoming with huge excitement and expectation. My shopping resulted in accumulating artefacts we have since been reluctant to part with as each holds a special memory.

During this tour of duty in Singapore there was a serious smallpox epidemic. Priority was given to inoculating children, and Barbara had to queue for two hours in the heat of the afternoon sun with a ten day-old Caroline, waiting to take her turn. This epidemic heralded a major and completely successful campaign by the World Health Organisation to eradicate the disease.

One of the many delights of living in Singapore was the range of food stalls and restaurants throughout the island offering all the delights of eastern cuisine and broadening our culinary horizons. We often chose to eat with the children at street stalls that some of the British residents considered impossibly unhygienic. Luckily we came to no harm. The children loved to eat a revolting looking local soya-bean cake liberally sprinkled with tomato ketchup, wrapped in banana leaves, and delivered at our compound gate by a local trader pushing a handcart, the Asian equivalent of the ice-cream van.

As our tour drew to its close we were advised that, following leave in the UK, we would be posted to Vientiane. We again took up French lessons for a while before we sailed home, in October 1960, on the 's.s. Asia', for mid-tour leave. As we were coming into Aden harbour we almost lost Caroline over the side of the ship. She was only eighteen-months old and, as a precaution, we had her in reins, which fortunately, Barbara had securely wound around her wrist. Suddenly Caroline took a header over the side. The sea was some thirty feet below but Barbara clung on while a member of the crew, who had seen the mishap from an upper deck, lowered himself over the side, grabbed the child and brought her back. Fellow passengers were as stunned as we were, and we had many expressions of sympathy for some days. We left the liner at Genoa, took the night sleeper to Paris and stayed with Barbara's cousin, Ursula, for a few nights before taking the ferry back to England. With all this travelling and excitement one would have thought the children had had enough, but they kept asking us if, on their return to England, they could ride on a bus!

We were home for Christmas 1960 and stayed in our house at Redhill. Our leave passed quickly, with visits to friends, and to families in Kent and Wales, proudly showing off our two daughters, before we returned to Singapore by Comet aircraft, on 19th January 1961.

As we were expecting to be posted to Vientiane, our old house in Singapore had been reallocated in our absence, and we stayed temporarily in a small hotel. Inconvenient though this was in many respects, it was at least away from the area of the Chinese cemetery where we had previously lived and where several times a day we used to hear the funeral processions passing. They were elaborate and noisy affairs, accompanied by highly vocal mourners, heralded by small bands and gongs to banish evil spirits.

Both Nicola and Caroline developed mumps soon after we arrived back. Children seem to make a point of choosing the worst possible timing for these things, and we had to keep very quiet about it in case we were evicted from our hotel. As our baggage had been placed in storage when we went on leave and was awaiting shipment, we now had to improvise – another of the hazards of our peripatetic life. While all this was going on I developed a low persistent temperature that initially puzzled the doctors. It was eventually diagnosed as a recurrence of the TB I had had as a child. Apparently an old lung scar had broken down, releasing the previous infection. I began to wonder where this would lead. Was this the end of my career? They would surely not send me anywhere but home now. I was put in isolation for a month in the military hospital and the children were only allowed to wave to me from the garden below. To say I was despondent would be the understatement of all time. But I need not have worried. The drugs available by this time were administered and I was soon on the road to recovery though the medications took their toll. My hearing was depleted by streptomycin and my stomach greatly upset by the drugs: in spite of that I recovered in a relatively short space of time.

We had become attuned to the Vientiane posting when we were told we were to proceed to Rangoon, where we arrived by air in April 1961. Our possessions, that had been in crates in Singapore for some months, were now re-routed, but it was another two months before they were reunited with us and we could recover our clothes and the children their toys.

CHAPTER TWENTY-ONE

LAND OF GOLDEN SPIRES

'Oh, East is East and West is West,
And never the twain shall meet.'

Rudyard Kipling.

B arely a month after I had been discharged from hospital in Singapore we arrived in Rangoon. It was not the ideal place to convalesce and contend with the tedious medicinal regime of tablets and injections I had to endure for the next two years, but we felt privileged to have been given the opportunity to live and work in such a fascinating country. As a member of the embassy staff it promised to be very different from my wartime sojourn, when I had lived in a tent on Mingaladon airport. This was my first posting to a country that was not a British colony and I found myself holding the position of first secretary in chancery, the political department of the embassy. I had previously served in colonial territories in both Singapore and Malaya where the former had a commissioner-general at the time and the latter a high commissioner. There were no marked differences in the way these institutions worked, but it soon became apparent that embassy life in Rangoon was to involve a great deal more by way of representational work than I had experienced elsewhere.

Before we arrived in Burma, we had heard contradictory views about the country, while the post report, prepared by the office, read rather like a catalogue of things to guard against, and was not very inspiring. Rangoon was clearly not regarded as one of the more appealing places to live, and we were told that many of the embassy wives found it particularly uncongenial. We, however, soon warmed to the place. It immediately struck us as an absorbing and magical country. Over the years of British rule, traders had extracted mainly timber and minerals but had done little that changed the character of the place and we had the feeling that nothing much had altered in a thousand years.

Each post had its rules of etiquette and new arrivals generally started off with a round of official calls, usually preceded by the delivery of engraved cards of an approved size. I was duly taken to meet my new ambassador, Sir Richard Allen, one of the old breed of diplomat that was fast disappearing. A colleague had forewarned me that he was something of an expert on, and a fanatical lover of, Shakespeare. He was also a keen yachtsman, always on the lookout for people to crew for him at the local sailing club. Had I expressed interest in either my career could have prospered, but at what price? We had scarcely been introduced when he enquired if I sailed. 'No Sir, I don't'. 'Then your wife does?' he asked hopefully, 'No Sir, I'm afraid not'. 'Oh dear' he said, and then tried again with some question about Shakespeare. I confessed to having little knowledge of the Bard and he turned to Barbara, still clinging to the hope that, even if I did not match up to expectations, my wife would. But she had been alerted to the dangers and I felt my career prospects fading.

We had been allocated a commodious family house on the edge of the Inya Lake, with an extensive garden terraced at two levels and planted with a fine collection of shrubs and trees. There were always flowers in abundance and after the monsoon the jacaranda and flame trees blossomed in all their delicate grandeur.

We engaged six servants – a *mali* to tend the garden; he spent all his time slashing at the coarse grass with a cutlass blade, refusing to use the rotary mower I had bought him – these people were a long way from the mechanical or technological age; a cookboy – an Indian who would produce the most delicious dishes; a bearer – who waited on table and did much of the house cleaning; a baby nanny – a Karen lady of ample proportions who mothered our children as her own; a wash nanny – who did all the laundry, and a driver – who took great pride in polishing the car and presenting himself immaculately dressed in his native costume whenever his services were required. Our staff blended together as a team, without the impediment of trades union restrictions as to what each should do. We found we needed them all.

Shortly after our arrival the British ambassador entertained the Burmese Prime Minister, U. Nu, at the Residency. I had been posted to watch out for his approaching car, so that I could warn of the PM's advance and ensure that His Excellency would be in the right place at the right time to meet his principal guest. After some waiting, I decided to inform the ambassador that the car had still not arrived but, as I approached him, he walked towards me accompanied by a group of Burmese, who all looked very alike to me in their national costume. As I surreptitiously whispered my message in his ear, he turned and introduced me to U Nu, standing on his left, who had arrived by another entrance. Again I felt my career had suffered a setback.

We found the indigenous people we met and came to know friendly and quite charming, but these were mostly Burmese who were resident in Rangoon and spoke English learned in mission schools. Sadly we were to have little contact with the rural population. On every posting we faced a language problem, and Burma was no exception. We could never be sure that the people we could communicate with were representative of the population as a whole; it was virtually certain they were

247

not, a factor that made our understanding of the local scene infinitely more difficult. We went out of our way to meet other than the intelligentsia, who comprised the majority on our invitation lists, but it was not easy for us to move outside this circle. It would have been so much more convenient if we could speak the vernacular, and we were encouraged to do so wherever we were posted. In the case of Burma this was virtually impossible in the space of a tour of duty, and only a select few were allotted the time to live in Burma and study the language. Sufficient linguistic ability, if only to deal with servants and shopping in the market places, was more necessary for wives than for husbands, who invariably had official interpreters to assist them in their duties. In my time in Rangoon we had a new entrant third secretary language student, Nicholas Fenn, living with a Burmese family in Mandalay who was later to return to Rangoon as ambassador.

We soon began to take an interest in the many different multi-racial peoples of Burma. The better known are the Shans, Karens, Kayahs, Kachins, Burmans, and Chins, but there are many others living in remote hill regions, all very distinctive and determined to retain their separate languages and identities. What elegant and colourful people they are. It was fascinating just to stand in the streets or market places and enjoy the spectacular scenes they created. The hill tribes retained an age-old hostility to the Burmans (the Mons and the Pyu) in particular, which they regarded as 'the scum who drifted to the Irrawaddy delta'. Likewise, the Burmans had little time for the mountain tribes. While the Burmese government based in Rangoon engaged in endless campaigns to subdue the hill peoples, whole regions of the country remained under the control of armed ethnic groups. Guerrilla warfare continued all the time we were there, making travel up-country difficult and none too safe. It was hard to imagine these seemingly gentle folk being involved in the most terrible and bloody massacres that have occurred throughout their history: racial rivalries and mistrust having bedevilled progress for centuries, there were few manifestations of modernity to be seen. It was not long before I came to appreciate what a country of contrasts and contradictions Burma was.

Unlike other posts where I had previously served and where we could mix freely, we had little contact with people in Burma other than those we met at the social occasions arranged by members of the diplomatic corps and business community. Entertaining was, for most of us, our main channel for the promotion of better international understanding. Nevertheless, I often felt that the round of cocktail and dinner parties given by diplomats, mostly attended by other diplomats, was of marginal value and sometimes carried to excess. We would sometimes attend as many as three or four diplomatic cocktail parties, followed by a dinner party, when it was possible to find oneself speaking to an identical group of people at three or four different venues on the same evening. The diplomatic convoy would simply move from one location to another. This is where one learned to make a whisky and soda last a very long time. Then there were visiting individuals and delegations, businessmen, musicians, ballet dancers and the like, that had to be looked after and fed, and given the introductions they sought in order to achieve their objectives. And there were always plenty of such visitors, even in Rangoon.

Fortunately we had a hard tennis court in our garden, and it was there that Barbara and I did much of our socialising. Most Burmese rarely entertained foreigners and there were few restaurants where we might have dined them. Indeed we discovered only one small Chinese-run restaurant at Mingaladon airport, but as it was of poor standard we only made occasional use of it. In situations like this the burden of official entertaining at home fell to the spouse, and wives were automatically expected to undertake these duties without any reward, apart from the satisfaction they found in helping their husbands in the exercise of their duties and from meeting people. In this regard I always thought the office took too much for granted and that the role of the diplomatic wife was greatly undervalued.

We were fortunate in that a number of ambassadors and diplomats were keen tennis players and we turned this to our advantage whenever we could. Contact with some missions proved singularly difficult but the Russian ambassador, who lived in a compound adjacent to ours, had a son a little older than our daughters, and they played together crossing from one garden to the other. Members of the Russian embassy staff normally had little or no contact with any of the non-communist missions, but we had – the children broke down all the barriers.

The various injections we had been given before leaving the UK and Singapore offered a large measure of immunity from the many diseases common to the area, but we still had to be careful about what we ate and drank. For drinking we depended on a local water factory from which our driver fetched supplies daily: the consequences of drinking from the tap would have been too horrific to contemplate. We had a deep well in the garden for all other purposes, and when one day it ran dry for about a month, we had to take water from the Inya Lake at the bottom of our garden for everything but drinking, and Nanny took the children down to the lake with a large bar of soap to bath them. We knew there were water snakes there, but had learned to take such hazards in our stride. Scorpions were much more threatening and were often to be found in places such as our dustbins.

At night the frogs and other amphibians gathering on the

edge of the water would join in chorus to drown all conversation as we sat on our balconies. We used to hurl stones into the lake to gain a brief respite from the noise. Leeches were common on the lawns in the monsoon period and occasionally attached themselves to the children who detested wearing shoes. One day we saw blood on our three-year-old Caroline's leg and no leech. She explained that she had 'bashed it with dolly's broken leg'. She was always sublimely practical. The children were never short of such an original remark. Nicola was adept at the quaint phrase and I remember her assailing her mother, in front of guests, with the comment 'Mummy, the baby's nose is raining'.

Unlike other posts where I had served, I sometimes found my thinking deviating from that of my Head of Mission, although we remained good friends. One day he strode into my office and placed a draft dispatch on my desk and invited my comments. I was not overly impressed by what he had written, and with tongue in cheek went in to see him with a list of comments. I presumed to suggest, obliquely, that he was inclined to indeterminacy and to use the word 'ostensibly' to excess. I went so far as to suggest that to tell the FCO that things were ostensibly this or that rather begged the question 'were they or not?'. He listened carefully for a while, but I sensed an unpropitious atmosphere developing – in Burma perhaps I should have consulted an astrologer first. In response to my next observation he politely enquired whether I was questioning his grammar, his syntax or his political judgement. I left it at that, and promptly retired. I was not consulted on his drafts for some time.

The rains in the monsoon months lasting from May to October, encompassing the Burmese Lent, placed severe limitations on what could be done in that period. For us the downpour seemed never ending. They were singularly depressing months, but when the rains ceased and the temperature dropped for a brief while, the trees and flowers bloomed in all their tropical splendour and made everything seem worthwhile. The flowering trees, lining the banks of the Rangoon River and the Inya Lake, were extravagantly colourful, with their huge bracts of blue and red blossoms set against delicate green foliage. Elsewhere in the jungle where the masses of tendrils of climbing plants formed scaffolding for a dense canopy, one could see frangipani, bougainvillea and wild orchids, some in brilliant colours, others in subtle shades, cascading from the trees. Cannas, crotons and marantas of many varieties, which we struggle to grow in England, grew like weeds and were easily propagated.

By the end of the monsoon season the paddy fields were flooded with water and thick brown mud swirled along the riverbeds. The countryside was rich and fertile and yielded abundant crops of rice and vegetables. We used to stop the car to let the children watch the peasants planting and harvesting the paddy after the fields had been ploughed by half-submerged water buffalo, which our little ones insisted on calling 'moo cows'. It was not uncommon for the fields to yield two crops in a season, and as each ripened, the green fields turned gold. Crops were harvested by peasant women wearing brightly coloured *longyis* and wide-brimmed hats. It was an artist's paradise.

I thought I had learned in the army never to volunteer for anything, but I was caught out in Rangoon when we attended a cathedral meeting to organise a fete. I foolishly made the suggestion that a plant and flower sale might help to raise money and the vicar welcomed my 'most generous offer' and invited me to proceed! We promptly recruited everyone connected with the cathedral, and set them and their *malis* to work preparing plants and pots for the sale. One of our friends had perfected the art of grafting several varieties of bougainvillea onto a single stock, resulting in standard trees bearing swathes of flowers in several different colours. In that climate one had only to break bits off, stick them in the ground and heypresto! they took root and grew. On the day of the fete we sent a lorry to collect contributions from the various gardens and were astonished by the response. Within hours our garden was filled with magnificent orchids, shrubs, and young fruit trees. I cannot remember the figures for the takings at the end of the day, but we did very well and, as I feared, were invited to repeat the sale the following year.

One of the consequences of this excursion into gardening was that word got about that I was an expert in horticulture. This led to telephone calls from friends and complete strangers asking my advice on the cultivation of this or that. I hadn't a clue on most of the points raised but am told I was most reassuring with my advice to all and sundry, to 'spread a good layer of water buffalo manure around each plant and leave the rest to nature'. Some reports of the results of this well-intended advice were none too encouraging!

Schooling for diplomats' children was often a matter for concern at posts overseas, but we were lucky in Burma. Our two girls attended an international nursery school presided over by a Burmese lady, Mrs. Iris Gauld, married to a British businessman. She had infants from twelve different countries in her school of twenty pupils and, with all the other activities, she taught them to sing songs from their respective homelands. Ours soon learned ballads and nursery rhymes from many other lands that they would sing to our visitors and us wherever we went by car. (Mrs Gauld and her husband had to leave Burma after the coup d'etat in 1962, when her husband's business was nationalised. She settled in London and we kept in touch until she died in 1999.)

Diplomatic wives usually had their hands full, not least in coping with the children of the diplomatic corps and their social calendars. Our children seemed to have parties to go to every other day, and the demand for presents for them to give was ceaseless. Since offence might be caused by not inviting all those children in the same age group, the number of children attending each party meant that the host child ended up with anything up to twenty presents on each occasion. Our children had so many from so many parties that they were able to take some of them to a local orphanage at Christmas to share their good fortune with others who, we were told, would be getting no more than a few sweets.

One of the attractions at these parties was a donkey brought by a little man to give the children rides. He would arrive in a tiny three-wheeled taxi with, to our astonishment, his donkey in the back. There is no doubt in my mind that the warm climate contributed to the ebullience and wellbeing of our children and it was sheer joy to see them healthy and happy even if they were somewhat spoiled by the generosity of the diplomatic corps and the business community.

On 27th November 1961, we enjoyed a three-day visit from Princess Alexandra, and we were delighted by her charm and informality. Barbara and two other 'expectant mums' were talking to her when she insisted they all sat down, not wanting them to stand because of her. In the afternoon there was a garden party at the Head of State's house, and in the evening a regal ball, held in her honour at the Residency. On these occasions we became quick-change artists, dashing home from each event to change into the next outfit. What a spectacle that ball was with the Burmese and diplomats from many lands mostly dressed in their national costumes – the Burmese costume consists of a *longyi*, jacket and slippers while the men wear *longyis* and shirts and headgear in brightly coloured silks.

For us it was pleasing to be able to dance again, in the old-fashioned way. By now the modern world outside had adopted new forms of dancing which seemed entirely alien, even to my generation, but none of this had penetrated into this secluded country.

Many years later our Burmese friend, Mrs. Gauld, told me of an incident at the sailing club where the Princess spent her second afternoon. When the royal guest arrived, the British ambassador looked around for suitable people to present to her and, seeing no one he immediately recognised, he went up to Mr. and Mrs. Gauld and said 'well I suppose I might as well present you two'. The Gaulds were not amused.

During my tour in Burma I enjoyed a visit by my old friend from my student days, Ralph Blumenau. Being an historian he particularly wanted to see the old Burmese city of Pagan, the former ceremonial capital of King Anawratha, built in the 11th century south of Mandalay on the dry central plains of Burma. It was not easy to get permission to visit this remote site and, as so often happened, we used to cover ourselves by applying for permission and then going. The flight took just over an hour and as we came in to land on the plain to the west of Mandalay we could see the panorama of Buddhist temples stretching for miles in all directions. It was the Pagan dynasty that had vigorously promoted Buddhism in the country. I had not visited Pagan before this and I sensed something akin to a cosmic change in the stillness and antiquity of the impressive scene laid out before us. Some of the huge white temples, covering many square miles along the Irrawaddy River – there were once over four million of them – stood hundreds of feet tall. Sadly most had been badly damaged over the years by time and vandals, but many still contained Buddha figures faced with gold leaf and imitation jewels to remind us of their past glory. Previous earthquakes had badly damaged many structures and a major shock in the 1980s exacerbated matters, but the site was still very impressive. Mountbatten was said to have personally decreed, during the Japanese occupation of Burma, that the Allies should not bomb Pagan, though for the life of me I could see no military point in anyone doing so. The old city appeared at first sight to be totally isolated and abandoned, only occasionally a solitary Buddhist monk in the familiar saffron robes, or a worker in a *longyi* would be seen tending a shrine or resting in the shade. I remember particularly how remarkably clear the air was and how stunning the silence. It was an outstanding day for both of us.

In December 1961, Barbara's parents, both in their late 70s, visited us and we began the sightseeing rounds yet again at the beautiful Shwedagon pagoda in the centre of Rangoon with its imposing gold spire towering above the city. It was said that anyone who gazed on this pagoda would at some time return to Burma. It stands 360 feet high and can be seen for miles around, with the sun glinting on its golden pinnacle. It is truly impressive and we found ourselves taking our visitors to see it time and time again. The spire of the pagoda transcends the shrines at its base, representing the eight cardinal points or planetary posts. Eight, because in Burmese astrology the week has eight days – the Wednesday being split into morning and evening, with each day represented by both a planet and an animal. Nats or spirit gods play an important part in the everyday life of a Burman – some are said to be of violent disposition but most have a more gentle side – and all this mythology is represented in the architecture of their temples. The traders' stalls around the pagoda were selling incense, sweet smelling flowers and trinkets, and there was always the sound of gongs being struck and of bells, that were moved by the breeze or the worshippers as they passed the shrines of their ancestors. Our children did not seem to mind walking on the marble mosaic paving: the slabs were often too hot from the sun to bear and the adults had to manage with bare feet as best they could. It was amusing to see the reaction of the Burmese to our children with their blond hair. They are brown or yellow skinned and have dark or black hair. They thought blond hair unusual and loved to touch it out of curiosity and this made our children furious.

Another port of call for visitors was the slightly smaller Sule Pagoda, near the centre of Rangoon, which formed a traffic island that I was driven past each day on my journeys between home and office. My driver would weave his way around numerous potholes in the road – for they were never repaired – and dodge the children playing 'chinlon' in the streets – a game played with a small rattan ball, which they tossed and bounced about their limbs with great dexterity.

Barbara's parents celebrated their ruby wedding with us and we presented each of them with small items of jewellery made up from Burmese rubies I had purchased on one of my many visits to Bangkok.

Although we were a long way from Whitehall we did not altogether escape its influence. We experienced one highly amusing example of Whitehall bureaucracy in the form of a post inspection by a team sent out by the Ministry of Works. We were told that the Rangoon mission and housing had been selected for refurbishing with modern British manufactured office furniture to promote exports and we were to become a display centre. The idea that Burma would offer any sort of market for modern western furnishings seemed ludicrous at the time. The ambassador was on leave when the team arrived and his large Burmese teak desk and furniture were replaced, in his absence, by tubular steel desks and tables and mauve curtains adorned his windows. On his return he walked into his office and immediately demanded that his room should be restored to its original state. After some searching, his desk was recovered from a downtown market, and only when he was satisfied did the mission resume its functions. The rest of us had to adapt to modernity.

We were informed that our lounge was a few square feet smaller than that prescribed for a first secretary, and that we were allowed only ten rather than twelve dining chairs. Our loyal Indian cookboy refused to let the inspectors remove the 'surplus' chairs in our absence and we were able to keep them. We did most of our entertaining during the dry season on the lawns by the lake but we needed the extra chairs when we entertained inside during the monsoon months. Nevertheless, our fine house was given up when we left, and was promptly taken by the Soviet ambassador as his official residence.

Our next child was due in January 1962 and Barbara had not been at all well early in the pregnancy. The Burmese doctor tending her was very concerned at her continued sickness, loss of weight and dehydration and, on his advice, she was sent to the British Military Hospital in Singapore where they had the means to treat her. She was soon able to return to Rangoon where Nina, our third daughter, was born on 21st January at the Prome Road Nursing Home. There was apprehension about the birth at the time because the wife of the British consul, who lived next door to us, had died there in childbirth only a week earlier. Blood of the right group had not been made available and the omission proved fatal. This did nothing for Barbara's blood pressure, or mine for that matter. But all went well for us. The name 'Nina' we chose was derived from the name used by our Chinese nanny to describe small pieces of cloth she gave to our children to take to bed as comforters – a sort of Chinese version of the teddy bear.

There was little of western cultural interest in Burma, but in

February 1962, we enjoyed a visit by the Chinese National Ballet Company. In an open-air theatre in the cool of the evening they presented the whole of Swan Lake. We were impressed by the high standard of the production and the dancing. This was a rare treat in a country where there was so little of theatrical interest for us though we did attend many cultural shows or Pwe, based on Burmese folklore where the movements of the traditional dances depicting love, concentrated on sentimentality rather than sex. Ladies bedecked with flowers in their hair, displayed coyness and passion in their dances through sighs, glances and movement of feet rather than by touch. The costumes worn by both men and women were kaleidoscopic. However, lacking knowledge of the traditions, we found the limited and repetitive steps, common to Burmese classical dance, monotonous in the extreme: they went on and on for hours, and we invariably had to sit to the end.

We visited many monasteries and pagodas – the countryside was dotted with them; with some 800,000 monks to accommodate they were never hard to find. I had not previously appreciated the extent to which Buddhism permeates every aspect of Burmese life. Possessions are of no importance to the devout, who strive through life to achieve merit for the next incarnation. The horrors of a Buddhist hell, depicted as being boiled in oil, of flesh being torn off the bones by monstrous dogs and vultures, and bodies being dismembered with red-hot knives, were sufficiently frightening to ensure that children did conform. For most poor households merit is earned through service within the family and to this end members will go out of their way to pay to see relatives through school and university.

It was not usual for the Burmese to invite outsiders to their more intimate ceremonies and we considered ourselves

259

privileged to have been asked to attend a Buddhist initiation. This ceremony, usually held during the summer school holidays, is where the novice receives a name in the Sanskrit language to mark his 'accession to the full dignity of humanity', a name which he abandons when he returns to the world outside. The new entrants to the monastery are usually boys of twelve or a little older, but at the ceremony we attended there were some who seemed no more than five. The initiation is regarded as the bounden duty of the parents to their son who believe that until a Buddhist has entered the fraternity he cannot claim to be more than an animal. Thus the entry into the monastic order is probably the most important religious event in the life of a Burman.

We saw the boys wearing their finest clothes, adorned with all the family gold chains and jewellery, carried in procession on the shoulders of the parents, relatives or well-wishers, to join the carriages and horses waiting to take them to the temple. The horses were suitably garlanded and the families moved under a sea of brightly coloured umbrellas. We all gathered around the novices; the young men dancing and singing, the girls laughing and smiling with heavily powdered faces and brilliantly coloured dresses, as the column wended its way through the crowds. In a part of the ceremony that we were not allowed to see, we were told that the novice had to have his head shaved and washed. Then, prostrating himself before the head monk, he had to ask in Sanskrit for admittance to the monastery. Once accepted he was given his robes, and begging bowl and, the next morning, would walk decorously through the streets wearing his long saffron robe, keeping his eyes fixed on the ground six feet before him. The more devout would stay within the monastery for some months, but most of the novices would return to their homes after seven days. As the procession moved off, we found ourselves whisked away to our host's home to join in a feast, which lasted until dawn. We were never much attracted to Burmese cuisine that relies to a large extent on the flavour of *ngapi,* a paste made from prawns and seafoods tasting like a concentrate of anchovy, usually served with rice in bowls or wrapped in banana leaves. Durian, pomalo, marian and other indigenous fruits were offered in plenty.

We learned that a monk's material possessions were limited to eight sacred items: three pieces of yellow cloth which make up the robe, a leather belt for securing the robe, a needle to keep it in good repair, a begging bowl, an axe for splitting firewood and a water filter to ensure no animal life was taken in drinking water. Additionally it was deemed essential to have a palm frond to protect the monk from looking at females and giving rise to carnal thoughts – women being considered disturbers of tranquil meditation! We made our excuses and left long before the festivities ended.

Another ceremony we were invited to witness was the ear piercing of young girls. This is something of a parallel with the putting on of the yellow robe for the boys and marks puberty; but nowadays it seems to be carried out on infants, and is more akin to Christian baptism. The astrologers would consult the horoscopes of the parents and the children and choose a day and time that seemed auspicious. My wife was allowed to witness the actual piercing but I was not. The professional ear-borer waited for a signal from a soothsayer, indicating that the propitious moment had arrived, and then moved swiftly to pass a needle through two fingers to pierce the lobe of the ear. The girl, who had been worked up into a high state of excitement by all the preparations, was expected to resist while the women around her enjoined her to proceed. Outside the band played music supposedly to drown her lamentations. We were told that it was inauspicious to treat an even number of girls on the one occasion: to the Burmese only odd numbers bring luck. After the ear piercing, the girl is regarded as mature and from that time forth her mother, an aunt, or a married sister, acting as a chaperone, would invariably accompany her. When she had passed from girl to woman she could develop what I have seen described in books on Burma as, 'the impish glances and coquettish walk, so popular with young maidens'.

The New Year Festival, or Water Feast, held on April 12th, 13th or 14th, depending on the moon, is an occasion few can avoid. It is celebrated all over Burma and it became a great favourite with our children who joined the young people who lined the streets with large syringes, hoses or buckets of water ready to douse all who chanced to pass, as we did on one occasion when formally dressed and on our way to some diplomatic function. My wife learned then that care had to be taken by the ladies not to wear garments that might become transparent when soaked! To leave the car windows open was to invite a dousing. While we saw only the visible manifestations of these ceremonies, for the Buddhists they had deeper significance. I used to think it was a bit like a Buddhist seeing our celebration of Christmas – the crib and the fairy on the Christmas tree – and trying to comprehend the significance of Christianity to us.

In September 1961 we had a visit from the Lord Mayor of London and his wife, Sir Bernard and Lady Waley-Cohen, and were entertained at a banquet by the Municipal Commissioner of Rangoon attended by Prime Minister U Nu with whom I had a brief talk about his student days when he had been an activist in Rangoon university; this gave us some common ground. On this occasion the guests assembled on the lawn of the Residency and when the meal was ready a signal was given and the guests rushed to take their seats at tables laid out in the open air. It was a bit like musical chairs. The prime minister and his host moved to their seats with admirable decorum, only to find that, while the ambassador's place had been left vacant, the seat allocated to the PM had been amply filled by the thighs of another guest's wife. However, the servants were used to coping with such situations and, as though from nowhere, another chair appeared, but only just in time.

I again met U Nu at one of the ambassador's social functions held at the residency in March 1962. We knew nothing of it at the time, but preparations to overthrow his regime were already advanced. Two days after that party I made one of my periodic visits to New Delhi, only to be informed on arrival that General Ne Win and a military junta had staged a coup and that U Nu and members of his government had been incarcerated.

As we lived in Ady Road in Rangoon, and the general lived in the compound adjacent to ours, we had to pass his well guarded front entrance to reach our house, I was naturally concerned for my family living so close to the powerhouse of the coup, but they were entirely safe and the day passed without violence or loss of life. The only immediate change we noticed was that the sentries outside the general's house had fixed bayonets from then on. But I was stranded in New Delhi, the airfield at Rangoon having been closed, and it was not possible for me to return for two more days.

This was the second occasion on which the military had seized power in Rangoon and we were apprehensive about the future. We optimistically hoped that they would soon return the country to democratic government, as they had done on the previous occasion. Our worst fears were soon realised when there was no declaration of any intention to give up their authority. The new regime – calling itself the 'Burmese Socialist Peoples' Party (BSPP)' – was essentially a single party military junta – professing to a policy they named 'The

Burmese Way to Socialism'. They imposed a military dictatorship and in the chaos that followed began to nationalise everything they could, even cigarette stands and tiny shops were taken over. The whole Indian population and most other foreigners, apart from a few professional people, especially doctors who were required to attend the army's needs, were expelled from the country. Some, including our physician, managed to escape from Burma before this fate befell them. British owned firms were taken over and their expatriate staffs were required to leave. We saw some of the wives of these old Burma hands having their wedding and engagement rings cut from their fingers when they left the country because they could not produce evidence of having imported them. It was both cruel and irrational but there was nothing we could do but protest.

The military regime has continued in power ever since, first denying the people a vote and then ignoring the will of the overwhelming majority who voted against them when the first democratic elections were held in 1988. It turned out to be a repressive and unpopular regime though I had, at the time, some sympathy with those who had seized power who, we were told, were genuinely seeking to exclude external influences and preserve all that was good in traditional Burmese life. I could understand their fear that western culture could so readily dilute, and even destroy, much of their tradition. In the context of their religion, the material things we almost expected them to have were of no relevance whatsoever. Unfortunately few in the New Order held such altruistic views.

Shortly after the 1962 coup the British army C. in C. based in Singapore visited Rangoon where he hoped to talk to General Ne Win, and the ambassador arranged a dinner party for him to meet the whole Revolutionary Council. We waited and waited for our guests but the Burmese did not turn up, and they sent no apology or explanation. The Burmese were never good at replying to invitations, not only did they come, or not, – as perhaps the astrologers advised – but they might bring along their entire family, if not their visitors and friends. However, this rebuff was inexcusable. After the coup the local people had even less contact with foreigners and fraternisation was positively discouraged.

From this time the Burmese army resorted to repression and ruthless military campaigns against the minority peoples and there have been countless recorded instances of violations of civil liberties. When Ne Win seized power, the economy of Burma was at a low ebb and we could not believe it could get much worse, but it did, and has remained at an appallingly low level. The country was of little economic consequence to the West, we sought nothing from Burma and, regrettably, a blind eye was turned to much that happened there.

During my tour I witnessed the total failure of the new regime's ambitious 'Burmese Road to Socialism' schemes, such as the import of cattle from Australia, which did not survive the Burmese environment; the purchase of vast quantities of cooking oil from India, for which no storage arrangements had been made, and the arrival of dozens of tractors made in Eastern Europe, quite unsuited to the paddy fields they were intended to work and for which there were no drivers or mechanics. We saw and smelt the oil rotting in open drums on the quayside. The competence of the former regime was never high, but the incompetence of the new army administration was indescribable. The Burmese army never had any mandate to rule, but they clung to power for the rewards it brought to their own.

For months following the army seizure of power we were

virtually cut off from any contact with Burmese officials, and few civilians would agree to come to our houses: most were too frightened. As we could do little that was useful in Rangoon I decided to take a trip north to Taungyi in the Shan States to see what the situation was up there. This being an area considered off-limits by the government, we asked for permission to travel and, as usual receiving no reply, we went. In the event we found nobody in an official position willing to take the risk of being seen talking to us, so we enjoyed the vacation. The children loved visiting the nearby Hopong Springs to picnic and swim, but to reach them we had to enter 'prohibited territory'. The word 'swimming' seemed to act as a password to the armed Shan guard who appeared on the mountain track as if from nowhere. On seeing the children and their costumes we were greeted with a big smile and waved on. The water in the deep rock pools was ice-cold and a welcome relief from the heat and humidity, even in the mountains where we were staying.

Another of many unforgettable trips we made took us high on the Shan Plateau to the Inle Lake renowned for its leg rowers. The largest village in the lake, Yamaw, was unlike anything we had seen before. It is actually a web of canals with islands connected by arched wooden bridges and causeways. There we saw the Intha people, mostly fishermen whose homes were built on stilts on the lake, standing in their long shallow craft, hewn from logs of wood, propelling themselves using a long wooden oar, around which they wrapped a leg to row while standing on the other, a skill developed to keep the hands free for casting their fishing nets. The only access to parts of this remote area was by means of wooden craft, some powered by outboard motors. Few white visitors ever reached these parts and wherever we went with our small blond children, the local people would stand and gaze at us in wonderment. We watched the craftsmen in remote rural areas making their traditional lacquer-ware bowls and trays for sale from their floating craft and we brought home a collection of these momentoes. Years later we learned that, following the army coup in 1962, many of the indigenous crafts had been stamped out and in some areas the making of lacquer-work had been prohibited.

When we had an opportunity later on, we travelled south of Rangoon to Moulmein in Karen country, a centre of the hardwood industry. The tree trunks were mostly transported to the sawmills by floating them down great rivers and waterways. We saw the elephants working in the timber yards. With small boys riding on their backs, these enormous animals showed remarkable dexterity with their trunks and tusks, selecting logs and planks and neatly stacking them in another part of the yard. One old bull elephant had been taught to pick logs up and load them end-on onto the saw bench and to push them towards the rotating saw, stopping only when his trunk was within inches of the rotating blade.

Earlier we had seen teak logs being raised from the bed of the Rangoon River where they had lain for a century or more, and in a nearby sawmill we saw them being cut into slices and made into coffee tables. We brought two of them home with us. In a nearby shed men worked with the rich red wood of the padauk tree, extensively used in the construction of bullock carts. While this seemed a waste of magnificent timber, the way they fashioned the carts did credit to the material. Every piece of wood was beautifully sculptured by hand to curves that harmonised with the wheels and the shapes of the animals that pulled them. There was poetry in their craftsmanship.

U Nu, the deposed prime minister, was to remain a prisoner in Burma until 1966, when he was allowed to leave the country. In captivity he turned to meditation and prayer. In his memoirs, 'U Nu Saturday's Son', he recorded that:

> 'While still prime minister he visited Russia where he
> was taken to visit the mausoleum housing the bodies of
> Lenin and Stalin. Although disgruntled by Stalin's earlier
> interference in Burma when he gazed at Stalin's remains he
> felt a change come into his heart. He reasoned that Stalin,
> who in life had oppressed, tortured, and murdered so many,
> could not possibly find happiness after death He must have
> gone straight to hell and must at that very moment be
> suffering great torment'.

Not only did we have a hostile and largely irrational regime
to contend with, but the country still held its own hazards for
the unwary. One Sunday morning Barbara was preparing to
take the children to Sunday school when we heard a scream
from the garden and found our four-year-old, Caroline, on the
ground with a small dog mauling her throat. Rabies was always
a danger and we were terrified. Not knowing whether it was
akin to a snakebite we did not know how much time we had,
and we were some six miles outside Rangoon. We rushed by
car to the Pasteur Institute, only to find that, being a Sunday,
there were no doctors on duty. But we knew the American
embassy had a full-time nurse and rabies vaccine and we
turned to them. In the event they had only two day's supply
and they immediately called for fresh vaccine from
Washington. It was delivered to us in Rangoon within forty-
eight hours. Meanwhile our own doctor had started a course of
injections.

Staff at the Pasteur Institute said we must catch the dog so
that tests could to be made, but the animal had already run into
the next compound where General Ne Win lived. I took two
servants and asked at the gate for permission to catch the dog
and was refused entry. But we were not to be deterred and,
with bayonets pointing at us, we walked in and caught the dog
that was found to be rabid. The price the servants paid for

touching it was for each to have two weeks of painful inoculations. We took Caroline for hers every day until the doctor could hardly find another place on her stomach to inject his needle. Thankfully, no harm came from the bite – except that both Barbara and I felt that we had aged considerably.

I was glad that I was not responsible for security in the embassy, for in my time there were a number of problems. First we learned that one of our military attaches had been having a homosexual relationship in Bangkok with a young man who turned out to be a member of the Soviet embassy there. Later a young lady in our embassy was found to be going out with a young man from an Eastern European embassy. Both were sent home. I had not encountered these subtle methods of subversion during my earlier days behind the Iron Curtain. These incidents served to remind us that the Cold War continued and that we were under attack from the communist bloc, even in such remote places as Rangoon.

At one of the Queen's birthday parties I was deputed to look after Brigadier Bernard Ferguson, a visitor from the UK who was passing through on his way to New Zealand. I had heard of his exploits with the Chindits during the war and was looking forward to talking to him. I met him at the airport and took him to his hotel, and later to the garden party at the ambassador's residence. I saw to it that he was introduced to all those he wanted to meet, or those whose names I could remember – I was never very good at that, especially with Burmese names and their individual titles – was he a Thakin or a U or she a Daw? At the end of the party I took him back to his hotel where he invited me to share a bottle of whisky. He had spent much of the war in northern Burma and was able to tell me a great deal about the Shan, Kachin and other leaders with whom he had operated behind Japanese lines under the leadership of General Wingate. 'Ah yes' he would say, 'so-and-so – a splendid man, an alpha plus in my book', or, 'so-and-so, a beta minus in my book'. In no time he had them all suitably categorised in the manner of the military. He was an accomplished raconteur and kept me enthralled with his dissertation on the hill tribes: it was riveting stuff. The evening wore on and at each point when I suggested I might retire, he insisted on our having just one more drink. It was close on midnight when he asked if he might let me into a secret. He was obviously dying to tell someone, and he told me that he had been appointed as Governor General of New Zealand and was on his way to take up his new position. I thought it was the whisky talking and suggested he should turn in. The following day the *London Times* reported his appointment and I was able to offer my congratulations as I accompanied him to the airport.

We left Rangoon on mid-tour leave by air in June 1962, accompanied by our Karen nanny, who had never left her homeland before. We had already let our Redhill home and spent our leave in Ferring, a small village near Worthing in West Sussex, where a friend had made the holiday arrangement for us. During our stay there we bought a small timber and thatch cottage built about 1920, intending this to be a holiday base when we visited the UK. We had not planned to live there ourselves having been told that Ferring was a place where people came to die and then forgot why they had come! But it did become our retirement home later on. We moved in temporarily in July 1962, towards the end of our leave. A survey had shown some woodworm in the roof timbers so I tore the house apart, taking up floorboards and removing the roof lining. I then flooded the woodwork with an appropriate treatment and left the fumes to do their deadly work.

Years later the lady, Mrs. Morcom, who had occupied our cottage earlier, told us something of its history. In particular, she said that the Prince of Wales, and a circle of friends he had made associated with the West End stage, would visit Ferring for occasional weekends in the 1930s, and that the Prince used to meet Mrs. Simpson (later the Duchess of Windsor) there when she was staying with a member of the Dodge family from the USA. She recalled that the Prince had stayed in a number of Ferring houses, including ours, during his visits. I always wanted to put a plaque over my bed 'The King Slept Here'! We also learned that the house next door to ours, named 'Erin', which we later bought and demolished to make a tennis court, had been a private school that some of the young Royals had attended when visiting Ferring in earlier times. Miss Turnbull, the headmistress of the school, told me that the old tithe barn in the village, which later became the Tudor Close Hotel, had also been a private school during the 2nd World War, and that some of the children of Haile Selassie of Ethiopia had been boarders there. She remembered the Emperor and his entourage visiting his children.

Confirmation of the date when our cottage was built came from a surprising quarter. On one of many holidays in Spain we entered into conversation with a Mr. Street who told us his father had been a builder in Worthing and that, on leaving school, he had helped with the construction of two timber and thatch cottages in Beehive Lane, Ferring. These turned out to be our cottage and the school building 'Erin' we had demolished. Further confirmation of the date came on our demolition of 'Erin', which I accomplished over several weekends with the help of a friend and neighbour, John Pallister, when we discovered the score of the 1920 cricket test match chalked on the raw timber under the staircase.

On 13th August, I made my way back to Rangoon by air, stopping off to see my old student friend, John McNab, who had also joined the Foreign Office and was then stationed in

Peshawar. He had visited us in Rangoon a year earlier. One day he took me by car through the Khyber Pass to the Afghan frontier. Every village we passed through on the mountain route seemed to be little more than an arms factory comprising dozens of little family owned shops, each making a variety of small arms out of scraps of metal cobbled together. I found it immensely interesting and colourful.

Barbara returned to Rangoon with our children and nanny a few weeks later. Our isolation following the coup seemed more complete than ever as we were now mostly cut off from the Burmese people and remote from the rest of the world. The postal service was slow and we depended for contact with the outside world on telegraphic communications via the embassy, and on the weekly diplomatic bag service to and from London that was routed to Australia via Thailand. Our bags were dropped off and collected at Bangkok and members of the embassy took it in turns to make the courier run. Most of our personal mail came by this means. Because supplies of most things we needed in Rangoon were limited, each courier had to do the week's shopping for everybody else. The lists of requirements were often long and certainly varied. I remember having to search for presents for our ambassador to give to departing colleagues, to find gold slippers for little girls for their parties, and even for nappy pins. Without knowledge of Thai this called for a discreet demonstration! There was a superb and well-stocked cheese shop in Bangkok that was always visited, to stock the Rangoon larders. When I was waiting for my return flight I would often sit in one of the many jewellers' shops in the city and browse through trays of fine rubies and other precious stones. I ended up buying a number of rubies that were then plentiful and cheap, which we subsequently had made into pendants or rings.

One of our favourite excursions from Rangoon was to

Sandoway on the Arakan (west) coast of Burma, a place with one of the world's most beautiful beaches. There the embassy had a chalet, as did a number of other diplomatic missions and business houses. The children loved it. We always took our Indian cookboy with us and he would appear mid-morning, when we were swimming in sapphire blue water, carrying iced drinks and cubes of various cheeses bought in Bangkok. He worked miracles with the most primitive wood-burning stoves that he constructed out of rocks found on the beach, and would arrange heated stones over his dishes to brown them or to toast the cheese.

On one occasion when I was sent from Rangoon to attend a conference in Melbourne, I decided to visit an old friend from my Singapore days, Ernest Eaton, who was living in Perth, and routed myself accordingly. He was then a housemaster at a large public school and I have one lasting memory of that establishment. I was standing on the front lawn conversing with members of the faculty while waiting to attend morning service at the school chapel when the bell tolled, the signal for staff and students to enter the building. As I strolled to the entrance with the staff, the students surged forward and pushed their way past us. Members of staff, barring their way, were summarily jostled aside. At that time it would have been hard to imagine such a scene at a British public school. I had another experience of Australian attitudes when I tried, early one morning, to buy a shoelace in a large store in Melbourne. Seeing a group of sales staff conversing in a corner I enquired where I would find a shoelace. 'You've got b....y eyes haven't you?' was the response. It was even more surprising and most welcome to me, to find on a return trip to Australia some thirty-five years later that attitudes had completely changed. Nowhere did we find greater courtesy than on that second occasion. This prompted me to comment that it was as though the whole Australian nation had been sent on a good-manners course. I wondered where we could send some of our own nationals for similar training!

I had not appreciated the vast distance between Perth and Melbourne, and it came as a shock to find that the flight would take almost all day. Consequently, I arrived rather late, in fact very late, and missed half the conference. On the way back to Rangoon I broke my journey in Djakarta, where I stayed with a colleague and his wife whom I found greatly distressed at just having been burgled. Their house had been broken into when they were out for only a few hours and they had lost everything. Even the furniture had gone.

The post coup period in Burma was decidedly frustrating for all of us and when, in late 1963, the teacher at the nursery school our children attended offered us her bungalow at Kalaw in the Shan hills, for a holiday break, we were happy to accept. We sent the car and cookboy ahead and travelled by train. Leaving at 4 p.m. from Rangoon we arrived at 11 a.m. the following day. We had three small children with us and when we stopped at stations there were vendors on the platforms selling food and drinks. We bought boiling water in coal black kettles passed through the station windows to make the baby's bottles. As dawn broke we gazed from our train windows at fascinating and colourful station scenes as we wound our way north into the mountains. This was the real Burma, totally unspoiled and immensely appealing. The bungalow where we stayed in Kalaw was set in pine trees and we enjoyed long walks in the hills in cool mountain air, and trips to the fascinating market where the hill tribes meet and trade, dressed in their contrasting national dress, creating a most colourful scene. Occasionally people from remote and rarely seen tribes came into these markets – they were just as curious to see us, as we were to see them.

We had started to collect the small brass weights shaped like Burmese chinthes, or sometimes monkeys or chickens, used in the market places, and we found some in Kalaw market we wanted. The local people could not comprehend why we wished to buy the things on the wrong end of the scales. Often we had to wait until the market closed before we could strike a deal. We brought home to England a collection of these weights in thirty different sizes and many years later, to our surprise, our collection caught the eye of an oriental expert who was visiting us, who considered it unique.

During my tour in Rangoon my ambassador was the most senior diplomat and thus Dean of the diplomatic corps. It fell to him to provide a chairman for the diplomatic secretariat, to handle certain protocol matters, and he nominated me for that task. The Chinese, Indian and Russian missions each appointed a first secretary to complete the secretariat, and we used to meet periodically in our embassy. The odd thing about this set-up was that I was the only one able to speak to any of the others. The Indians were having a frontier war with the Chinese, and the Russians and the Chinese had also fallen out. We used to sit around a table and they all talked through me, never to each other however hard I tried to achieve this.

When my ambassador left Rangoon, apart from the official diplomatic corps dinner, we arranged a farewell party for him mainly for his Burmese friends. I remember that he made a long and erudite speech laced with many of his favourite Shakespearean quotations – most of which were over the heads of his audience, but he seemed not to notice. His departure marked the end of an epoch. He was succeeded as doyen of the corps by the Chinese ambassador. As the Chinese were not then speaking to any of the non-communist missions, the new Dean asked me to continue as chairman. From then on we met at the Chinese embassy, in a walled compound that few of the

Chinese staff were ever allowed to leave, and into which very few Burmese or other diplomats ever entered. The Chinese ambassador had little contact with anyone outside his embassy compound and seemed to enjoy my visits. We had many lunch parties together and, through his interpreter, we had long and interesting discussions. He told me that he had accompanied Mao Tse Tung on his 'Long March' through China. How I wished I had had the capability to speak some Chinese dialect familiar to him and could bridge the language gap.

The day came when it was the turn of the American ambassador to depart, and a farewell party had to be arranged. The Chinese ambassador informed me that he would definitely not attend. After consulting my Secretariat, I had to return to him and deliver an ultimatum on behalf of the Diplomatic Corps. Either he accepted his duty as Dean of the Corps or he should resign that position. He then agreed to attend and made the farewell presentation, but his speech was a classic in brevity – the translation amounted to a few syllables and he sat down almost before he got up.

When I was due to end my duties as chairman, the Chinese ambassador, by way of saying 'thank you', arranged a dinner for me at his embassy. He was not intending to ask anyone else from our mission and I had to persuade him to invite at least a few of my colleagues, including my ambassador. Thus we – the ambassador, our head of chancery, myself and wives – tore down the wall for a brief moment, and dined in splendour within the Chinese fortress – some twelve courses in all.

Gordon Whitteridge (later Sir Gordon) succeeded Sir Richard Allen in November 1962. We got on well – he was a tennis player after all – and we kept in touch long after he retired. (After he died in 1996, we often visited his widow who lived in Surrey, with whom we had played tennis in Rangoon, when she worked as his personal assistant, and she gave us a few Burmese carved wooden artefacts covered with gold leaf, from his collection. Later, when her sight failed we helped to move her into a nursing home where she died in 1999.)

We had a never-ending stream of visitors and numerous functions to attend. We enjoyed a Chinese banquet in Rangoon on the occasion of the visit by the Chairman of the People's Republic of China, Liu Shao-Chi, on 25th April 1963. This was a formal occasion held at the State guesthouse in honour of General Ne Win, and it proved to be an unforgettable occasion. The Burmese wore their splendid formal traditional attire and the Chinese their familiar boiler suits! The menu was incredible and we lost count of the number of dishes served. We had learned that the secret of surviving a Chinese banquet lay in taking very small quantities of each course, so that one could last until the end, when something very special would be offered. The next day General Ne Win returned the compliment to his guest, and we again indulged ourselves, but this time it was western food and the menu was printed in French.

In January 1964, I was sent to New Delhi to meet and brief Admiral Lord Louis Mountbatten for a visit that had been arranged for him to talk to General Ne Win. Mountbatten had stopped off to attend the India National Day celebrations and I linked up with his team there. The next morning at dawn I found myself seated in the grandstand with him and the Indian Prime Minister, Pandit Nehru, watching the spectacular march-past of troops from all the states of India, including the magnificent camel corps and elephant bands. The parade lasted for hours and included some ingenious and beautifully decorated floats representing all the diverse cultures and provinces of India. In the evening we attended a costumed display of native dances performed on a floodlit stage in the open air. I had my cine camera with me and my first ever colour film.

The day after the celebrations I joined Mountbatten on his flight to Rangoon and was invited to take breakfast with him and his daughter Lady Brabourne. He had already sent an aide to check whether we had met before, and I was able to remind him of our three previous encounters. He was very good at this sort of thing and, having been briefed, greeted me like an old friend. As I tried to tell him of our main concerns in Burma he was (a) eating his breakfast (b) conversing with his daughter (c) signing thank you letters to his Indian hosts (d) checking with his valet as to what clothes would be needed for his visit and (e) trying to listen to me. In spite of all the distractions he had obviously taken in what I had been saying about our hope that he would be able to persuade the General to look favourably at compensation for the British interests that had been nationalised. He asked me if I thought he should pursue this point, and I said it was very much the view in London that he should. 'Yes' he said 'but what do you think?' I made clear that my view was of little consequence, but he persisted. I said that I felt undue pressure at this time could prove counter-productive. 'So do I' said Mountbatten and that was that. However, when he reported on his discussions with Ne Win to my ambassador, he went out of his way to comment on the advice I had proffered and commended me for it! As a result I was reprimanded. With hindsight, I served our commercial interests well, however unwittingly, in that British firms received some compensation later. Whether they would have received a penny had Mountbatten forced the issue at that juncture is open to question.

There was an amusing incident during breakfast on the aeroplane, when Lord Louis asked for a mango and it was served iced with a small spoon. He looked at it and asked for a mango spoon. The waiter looked puzzled – he had clearly never heard of a mango spoon, nor had I, – and went off to find one. He returned with a long face to announce that they did not have such a spoon on board. Mountbatten pushed his mango aside saying, like a petulant child, if he could not have a mango spoon he would not eat his mango. His daughter chided him, but he would not eat it.

As we approached the foothills of the Himalayas, Mountbatten ordered the pilot to change course so that he would get a better view of some part of the West Coast of Burma, the scene of one of his campaigns, while his staff were frantically searching for some maps he wanted. Consequently, we landed in Rangoon rather late. The great man had just changed and was now resplendent in his white Admiral of the Fleet uniform, bedecked with ribbons and medals. He was viewing himself in a long mirror in the aisle, as his valet adjusted his dress, when the pilot asked if he should open the door for his exit and was told 'No, not yet'. The Revolutionary Council, headed by Brigadier San Yu was left waiting a little longer in the blazing sun. This was all done for effect. When the admiral descended from the aircraft he spotted Barbara and my daughters Nicola and Caroline and walked straight over to them, ignoring the Revolutionary Council lined up to receive him. They had to wait while their visitor had a word with Barbara and shook hands with our little girls and only then did he turn to meet his host and members of the new Government. Initially Barbara had been refused access to the tarmac, but the children had insisted on seeing their daddy and the guards had relented. Barbara recalls that as she stepped over a small retaining wall onto the tarmac the Brigadier was passing close by and he ducked for a moment, perhaps suspecting an attempt on his life.

One of my many pleasant memories of our stay in Burma was a sedate trip Barbara and I made down the Irrawaddy

River – the main artery of Burma – from Bhamo in the far north to Mandalay. This time we left the children behind and flew from Rangoon to Bhamo. We then sailed south on a small trading paddle steamer that called at many isolated villages along the one hundred and fifty-mile journey, some comprising little more than a dozen or so wooden huts topped with reeds or palm leaves. We were aware that our route was entirely off-limits to us as diplomats, and that we were not supposed to travel in an area that was largely under insurgent control. We had asked for permission to travel and had no reply, and were greatly amused by the endeavours of the security forces to keep tabs on us during our voyage. At every stop along the river a policeman would come aboard to ensure that we were 'comfortable'. We had the tiny first class deck to ourselves but to get ashore at each stop we had to balance on slender planks and jostle with people and animals loaded with provisions. The landscape was dotted with white pagodas, with golden spires, each marking the devotion and piety of a Burmese family or dynasty. The pilot of the vessel navigated the river with the aid of long pole markers carrying white canvas lanterns placed at every bend and shallow. The river was prone to silt-up and many boats could be seen stuck on mud-banks, victims to the shifting mud and debris. Our boat grounded once and had to be freed by a gang of men pushing with long poles over the side.

We spent hours at the rail watching the ever-changing scenes – the life of the river people fascinated us and we marvelled at the skill and dexterity of the boatmen we saw steering massive rafts of logs through repeated hazards as they plied their loads between jungle and sawmills. This was Burma as it must have been for centuries past and we loved it.

When we arrived in Mandalay – the city of seven hundred pagodas – a friend of mine from the American Embassy greeted us. He had volunteered to show us around, but instead

280

he brought the sad news of the assassination of President Kennedy only a few hours earlier. Our schedule for the day had to be rapidly reorganised and we spent the time quietly shopping and sightseeing on our own. Little in Mandalay seemed to have changed since my triumphal march through the streets some twenty years previously with my African company. I wondered how many unusually dark-skinned young people walking the streets were the consequences of my soldiers fraternising with the local girls two decades earlier.

During our tour of Mandalay we chanced on a somewhat dilapidated temple where we found a smelting shop in which a group of men were melting down old temple bells and other beautiful bronze and brass artefacts, and converting them into small Buddhas for other temples or the tourist trade that was just opening up, albeit slowly. On the floor we spotted a brass temple bell handle ornately carved with figures of dancers and musicians with their native instruments, about to be melted down. It was plastered with red paint and mud but we could just discern through the patina what it was and bought it for a nominal sum. We took it back with us to Rangoon on the plane; it weighed heavily but luckily our baggage was not checked in. When we arrived home we cleaned it up and it is now part of our treasured memorabilia. On the same trip we ordered and had made a fifteen-inch diameter silver punch bowl embossed and decorated with Burmese scenes. Another treasure.

While we loved much about Burma and its people there were a few 'cultural' differences that made us squirm. Being Buddhists the Burmese would not kill animals and their way of dealing with a surfeit of wild dogs was to round them up and chain them individually to stakes in a field where they were left to expire 'naturally'. At night we would hear the plaintive wailing of these poor animals as they were left to die from hunger and thirst in the tropical heat.

After two years it was time for us to return home and the night before we left Rangoon we held a farewell reception. Although the new regime had made clear its attitude to foreigners, we had issued the usual invitations and hoped that some Burmese would come. There were a few who remained loyal to us, in spite of their fears, and having to pass the General's house to reach ours. We were especially concerned as to whether any Burmese would come because our ambassador had asked if he might bring Lord Carrington, then Defence Secretary, who was visiting. That evening we had our children dressed in their pretty little Chinese pyjamas, meeting the guests at the top of a long flight of stone steps that led down to the lower lawn skirting the Inya Lake, where Barbara and I were waiting. We were both suffering from bad throats and I remember that our voices failed completely and Carrington jokingly rebuked our ambassador for working us to the point where we could not even speak.

It was with great sadness that we said goodbye to our servants and made our way to Singapore via Bangkok. We all knew that we would probably never meet again. The servants and we had formed a happy and united family. Nanny especially had grown to love the children as her own and it was quite a wrench on both sides. In Bangkok we made straight for a doctor and were injected with penicillin. We stayed for a few nights in Raffles Hotel, Singapore before embarking on the 's.s. Oriana' for our journey home via the Suez Canal. I got off the ship at Suez for a spot of sightseeing, leaving Barbara with the children, and travelled overland to Port Said via Cairo. I had always wanted to see the pyramids and the Sphinx which I did, following a short camel ride. Barbara had her turn to leave the ship when we sailed into Naples, then I stayed with the children while she visited Rome.

One night when we were at dinner on the ship we had a call from the cabin and rushed down to find that Nina had taken a bite out of a glass tumbler and had her mouth full of what she called 'ice'. It was certainly chilling for us. We had longed for the rest the journey home would give us, but protracted sea voyages with small children are never restful. We next called at Lisbon and spent a day sightseeing with a couple who lived there, whom we had met on the boat.

A Burmese friend of mine told me some years after we left Burma that General Ne Win was told by his soothsayer, on whom he depended for advice, that he needed to move the country 'more to the right'. Rumour has it that his response was to change the 'drive on the left side of the road' rule to 'drive on the right'! If true this would not surprise me – Burma was like that, never easy for the westerner to comprehend.

The name Burma has since been changed to Myanma and Rangoon is now known as Yangon, changes that will do nothing to detract from all the pleasant memories we will always associate with the names by which we knew a fascinating country.

Back in the UK we were again living in suspense. Would we be posted abroad immediately or would we have time to settle in England, and if we were to stay at home, what desk would I get? The life of a diplomat always held that element of uncertainty.

CHAPTER TWENTY-TWO

SETTING UP HOME

'Where we love is home,
Home that our feet may leave,
But not our heads.'

C.W. Holmes.

We were to stay in England for the next three years. In that period the most notable event was the birth of our fourth daughter Alison, but there was also a rewarding transaction for me in the property market and the move of our home from Surrey to West Sussex.

Before leaving Rangoon in April 1964, for the last time, we had received correspondence from our neighbours in Redhill urging us to agree to sell the house we had bought seven years earlier. The site had attracted developers who wanted the area for housing and we occupied a major plot of land at the very centre. None of the other landowners could sell and benefit from the generous figures being offered, unless we agreed to fall in with them. Having made so little use of the place, and particularly after spending our leave working on it and investing in our tennis court, we were most reluctant to sell, especially as the house and garden were everything we wanted for a family home. We both felt that families need a home base, it being particularly important for us living such a peripatetic life, in order to provide the children with some roots. We had already procrastinated for several months over the proposed sale, waiting until we were home and could look into the matter ourselves.

We had barely landed at Southampton when we were confronted by neighbours irate because we would not fall in with their plans and demanding that we should. The way this transaction developed is worth relating. We had bought the house in 1957 and were now offered more than twice what we paid for it. Even so we did not want to part with it. But it was clear that the other owners of the divided property we had bought were going to prove troublesome if we did not agree.

I got in touch with my old army friend, Reggie Underwood, who was by now established as a surveyor with his own practice, and he arranged for us to meet the prospective purchasers at Redhill to check the price and see if it could be bettered. After a good lunch at Lakers' Hotel – once owned by one of Barbara's ancestors – they made some rapid calculations under the table on the back of a matchbox and, without hesitation, offered a figure more than double the earlier offer. I then accepted, but there were still problems to be overcome.

The many solicitors engaged on the transfers of the houses discovered some awesome covenants on the land, which had to be disposed of before the sales could proceed. This took over a year and, as we approached the next budget, there was talk of an impending capital gains tax. Rumour had it that this could take up to half our profit, and when by budget day contracts had still not been exchanged, I instructed my solicitor to advise the purchasers that the deal would be cancelled unless contracts were exchanged before 3 p.m. when the chancellor was due to begin his speech. I was greatly relieved when he confirmed that the exchanges had all been effected at 2.55 p.m., precisely, just five minutes before the chancellor rose. In the event there was no mention of a capital gains tax, and CGT was not introduced until two years later. We now felt that our decision to purchase had been fully vindicated, and my office colleagues, who had so strongly advised against any house purchase, had to agree that they had been decidedly unwise to defer buying their homes.

We already had our cottage in Ferring and hastily moved some of our furniture and half the garden stock from Redhill to the coast, and sold the rest. For the next series of weekends I travelled back and forth with the car loaded with conifers and shrubs and all the furniture I could carry. I also salvaged the wrought-iron front gates, which survive at our cottage today. Our new grass tennis court was never to be used and the site was bulldozed for the erection of rows of town houses. It broke our hearts to see the heavy oak panelling from our dining room, the oak parquet flooring and the magnificent staircase, tossed onto a bonfire. For those of us who had learned to scrape and save throughout the war years such waste seemed sacrilege.

Utilising some of the money we had from the sale of our Redhill property we then bought a small house in Camden Town, London where it was intended I should stay during the week, while commuting to the coast at weekends. It never worked out that way, but after I had rewired the house, put in central heating, etc. the house served later as a base for our children and their friends. When we sold it, some fifteen years later, we made another substantial gain on our investment.

I had been abroad for much of the 1950s and 60s and in those years television had assumed a significant place in most households. Our first memory of the 'little screen' was the funeral of Sir Winston Churchill in January 1965. After a long sojourn abroad we were able to see how profoundly television was affecting our national life. The whole nation from Lands End to John o'Groats, was now seeing the same events, and hearing the same interpretation of them, at the same time. We could already sense the impact this was to have on shaping national views, and particularly politics. Television was just starting to give the media the extra arm it needed to play a significant role in the coming decades. As we watched the funeral procession and the service in Westminster Abbey, we were conscious of the deep sense of loss and mourning the nation felt. To every ex-serviceman it seemed a very personal loss. The simultaneous lowering of the great cranes on the banks of the river Thames was an emotional experience for those of us who saw it or viewed it on television. As I watched I remembered how, at so many points in the war, when our morale needed uplifting, Churchill was there, resolute, never doubting victory and the epitome of everything we were fighting for. He had his political rivals but I doubt if any Englishman in my time was ever better loved and respected. This was an epic occasion that did not need national television to unite the nation in sorrow, but it certainly helped.

I spent some time moving the contents out of our home in Redhill while Barbara was in hospital in Rustington in West Sussex, awaiting the birth to our fourth daughter, Alison. When the hospital rang, on 23rd August 1965, to give me the news of her arrival I was in Ferring papering the lounge ceiling and when I sprang to the telephone a length of well-pasted ceiling paper drooped around me and stuck to everything. As this was a daughter and I had again rather wanted a son I did not think it such good news at the time, but Alison, like all our daughters, was to prove a great joy to us all.

Even when we were ensconced in our new home we could never settle down: there was always the expectation of another overseas posting, with the possibility of another move at short notice. Few people outside the Diplomatic Service appreciate how disruptive a diplomat's life can be. Such frequent changes of scene and the constant prospect of being sent to some far corner of the earth, present a host of problems that do not normally confront those who choose less volatile careers. Each posting, and these were normally of two to three years' duration, meant packing up the complete household, changing the car or shipping it with you, taking the children out of schools and settling them in others, saying goodbye to friends and making many new acquaintances in some foreign land. In many ways it was easier for the more senior diplomats, who were invariably provided with drivers who helped them to find their way about a new city, and for whom houses, fully equipped and staffed, were ready for occupation. For junior staff who lacked these advantages, it was more difficult. The burden on the wives was every bit as great as on the husbands, probably more so, as I am sure the wives would agree. On our return to the UK, in order to store all we had accumulated abroad, we bought two large cedar-wood sheds and erected them in the garden. Between tours we unpacked everything we needed and left the rest in our sheds on standby. Both Barbara and I are magpies by nature: we tend to keep rather than dispose. And knowing that we might have to help furnish homes for our girls at a later stage, we tended to cling to everything we had. While we were still unpacking and setting up house we started our infants at the local C of E school in Ferring: they were too young for boarding school; that was to come a little later.

For a while it seemed that I was destined to commute from Ferring to Whitehall for the rest of my working days; a prospect I did not relish, but there were too many contemporaries around from the post-war intakes, and with seniority counting against me, the competition for postings was intense. Few wanted to serve in England if they could land an alternative. Thus I was fortunate, in 1967, to be offered a posting as first secretary at the high commission in Nicosia, Cyprus. In spite of all the disruption this would entail, Barbara and I decided that it was too good an offer to refuse.

By October 1968, following the protracted amalgamation of the Foreign, Colonial and Commonwealth Offices into the FCO, the problem of too many chasing too few vacancies was exacerbated. It remained that way for some time after I had retired, but when that logjam had been cleared, the younger men and women made rapid strides up the promotion ladder.

CHAPTER TWENTY-THREE

APHRODITE'S ISLAND

'What thin partitions sense
from thought divide.'

Pope.

A fter our time in the sunshine of the East we had found the English weather dull and depressing. I recall the dismay we felt on our return from Rangoon as we came down through the blanket of cloud over London, leaving the sunshine above and landing on a sodden airstrip at Heathrow. We wondered then how anyone could choose to live in the English climate. A posting to Cyprus seemed ideal for us with a family of four small girls. I had found daily commuting from Ferring to London very tedious and tiring, and Barbara and I had both longed for another overseas assignment, especially to a place in the sun. Barbara had never liked the cold: it made her curl up and want to do nothing: she seemed quite a different person in warmer climes.

On this occasion I went ahead of the family and arrived at Nicosia airport in July 1967. An old friend from my student days, George Peleghias, greeted me. This was almost a repeat of what had happened on my arrival in Kuala Lumpur some years earlier. It was strange how these old student contacts kept turning up in different corners of the world. George had been on my student colonial committee in London and was now a confidant of Archbishop Makarios, president of Cyprus. He was then head of protocol at the Cyprus Foreign Ministry and, having heard of my posting, had come to the airport to greet me and invite me to have tea with the president. Naturally I said I would be delighted, but this proved a mistake. I was soon to discover that relations, at that time, between our high commissioner, Sir Norman Costar, and the Head of State were at a low ebb and, when I announced that I was going to have tea with him, protocol asserted itself, and I was required to find some excuse to cancel the arrangement. I saw this as a lost opportunity to mend fences, but I was only a first secretary.

Each posting offered us a new world to discover and explore. Most tourists visiting Cyprus have time only for the highlights, and few concern themselves with the intrigues of the island's politics. But the diplomat has to settle in, learn about the country and get to know its people, especially its leaders. While most countries are too expansive to explore in any detail Cyprus could be covered from end to end in the space of a brief tour of duty. The whole island covers only 3,572 square miles. My lack of Greek and Turkish did not present much of a problem, but we started Greek lessons as soon as we arrived and had a lot of amusement trying out our limited knowledge on the locals who clearly appreciated that we were at least trying. Cyprus is another land of contrasts, ranging from the beautiful beaches, especially those in the south of the island, to the Troodos mountain range in the west. Each offered a variety of different landscapes with its own individual appeal.

The office had found me a spacious family house at Strovolos on the outskirts of the old walled city of Nicosia, and when I was taken to see it I thought how much it resembled a battleship. It was built of concrete all painted white, with wide verandas on every floor resembling the decks of a ship. The house had remained unoccupied for some time and in one large room with a slightly sunken floor I found layer upon layer of dead cockroaches; they had crawled in and could not get out. I had the whole place and the drains fumigated before the family arrived a week after me. Had they seen the corpses I am sure they would never have agreed to live there.

Barbara's arrival with the children and our Chinese nanny at Nicosia airport was traumatic. On their arrival at Heathrow with our cat, Domino, and armed with all the necessary papers, an airhostess had said, in front of the children, 'You won't be allowed to import that, you know. They'll put it down on arrival'. The tragedy deepened in Nicosia when the cat box could not be found. After hanging about for hours waiting and searching for it, I took the family to our new home with the children crying their eyes out. I had spent a week getting the house ready for them; now all attention was focused on the missing cat, nobody noticing the rest. After we had put the sobbing children to bed, Barbara and I returned to the airport where a porter confirmed that there was a cat in a box in one of the warehouses: and there he was. We had to summon a vet, get clearance and take our treasure home. The next morning the children's faces were radiant. The cat flap was over. The excitement of a new home in a new land was dwarfed by the recovery of their much-loved Domino.

Barbara's immediate priority was to ensure that the house was equipped with all we needed for the family and our entertaining commitments. This entailed repeated visits to the shopping centre around Metaxas Square in Nicosia. Servants usually had to be found and interviewed, but we were fortunate in being able to take over an excellent Greek maid from our predecessor. We lost no time in joining the local tennis club where I arranged to play for half an hour each morning before attending the office.

The BBC retained a relay station at a place called Ziggi in the centre of the island where I was taken on a visit by our high commissioner the day after I arrived in Nicosia. We travelled by helicopter and this gave me a spectacular overview of part of my new territory. I was to use this mode of transport for many subsequent visits to the military bases in the south of the island, to attend routine meetings.

The history of Cyprus and the conflict between Greeks and Turks is a matter of record and it is not my intention to delve into it. Suffice it to say that we found ourselves living near Nicosia, a capital city divided by an artificial 'green line', patrolled by United Nations troops, wearing their blue berets, striving to keep the peace between the ever hostile forces of Turkish and Greek Cypriots. To reach the high commission I had to cross, many times a day, from the Greek side of 'the line' into a stretch of no-man's land secured by UN troops, and then into the Turkish sector, crossing no less than four checkpoints. There were minor incidents throughout the island from time to time requiring UN mediation, but a tenuous peace was being maintained.

We found everything on the Greek side reasonably normal. The Greek Cypriots were industrious and had managed to maintain a high level of tourism in spite of the division of the island. On the Turkish side of 'the line', however, there was every sign of decay and virtually no industry or commerce. The contrast was striking. The Greek Cypriots, who imposed whatever restrictions they could to make the life of the Turkish Cypriots impossible, exacerbated the hardship they already faced. I was to witness such absurd episodes as Greek guards insisting on a lorry load of water-melons being off-loaded and reloaded one by one for inspection, before being allowed to cross to the Greek controlled area.

I often felt that the situation in the island could have been resolved amicably had there been any semblance of a desire on the part of the leaders on both sides to find solutions. But no progress was made, and many opportunities for a peaceful settlement were allowed to slip away. In the high commission we tried to keep tabs on what was happening. We worked closely with the UN peacekeeping force that had the unenviable task of keeping the hostile factions from inflicting too much damage on each other, but there was little we could do without laying ourselves open to accusations of interfering in the internal affairs of what was an independent republic.

The political situation came to a climax when, in 1967, General Grivas, who had led the insurrection against the British, decided, with support from the military junta in Athens, to attack a small Turkish village roughly half-way between Nicosia and Famagusta. We had driven through that area only a few hours before he moved his troops, on one of our return runs home from Famagusta where we had rented a flat by the sea. An hour earlier and we may not have lived to tell the tale – another of those strange quirks of fate.

The high commission building was in a vulnerable position close to the 'green line' that separated the Greek and Turkish zones, and when the danger of a Turkish invasion seemed imminent, as a precaution against military action, we set about destroying some sensitive office papers. This precipitated something of a minor crisis in that the local press, having seen the incinerators in our compound, anticipated that we knew something they did not, and read into it imminent conflict. Some British residents panicked and started the drive south to the safety of the British bases, only to be turned back when they arrived. Had the Turks launched an attack at that time, with many exposed on the only highway between Nicosia and the south, the loss of life could have been serious.

The circumstances and the political and military background to these events are beyond the scope of this narrative, but the consequences were to impinge on our lives in a variety of ways. As the crisis deepened we were faced with a situation where we could not be sure of our safety, or that of our families, and plans were hurriedly dusted down for the possible evacuation of all British personnel to one of the two British military bases – Episkopi and Dhekelia. As I was living in the suburb of Strovolos I came under pressure to move closer to the high commission, but in the event I stayed to save packing up the house, and instead took the children out of school and the family to our flat in Famagusta which was but a few miles from one of our bases. I had arranged with Barbara to telephone her each evening to convey, in a coded way, any warning we might have of impending Turkish military action, so that she could make her way to safety. If I told her to kiss the children for me she would know that, as far as we knew, all was well, and if I did not, she should get moving. We knew from reports coming in that the Turks were loading assault craft on the mainland; the question was whether they would set sail. This tense situation lasted for a few weeks during which the Americans and others struck a deal in Athens and Ankara which, temporarily, took the heat out of the crisis, and enabled us to resume our normal lives. In former times we would have resolved such disputes by sending in a gunboat or military force. Now the best we were able to do was to contain such situations by diplomacy so as to limit the damage to British interests as best we could, and get on with our lives.

Only a few weeks before Grivas moved against the Turkish village of Ayios Theodoros, I had been sent to represent the high commissioner at an important wedding, the groom being a man of some standing in a local trades union. I was mingling with the guests when there was a rustle of anticipation in the crowd and I found myself standing next to General Grivas, a man of diminutive stature. Remembering the crimes against British soldiers in Cyprus of which he stood accused, I wished I could have settled the account with him then and there. When

I told this tale to officers in the British bases they wondered why I had not, wedding or no wedding, and I could understand their feelings.

On another occasion I had cause to call on the editor of a local Greek-Cypriot newspaper, Nicos Sampson, another notorious figure from the emergency days when the British forces had been under siege from elements in Greece seeking to drive us out. He chided me about never inviting him to any social functions and I asked him if he really thought we could after all that had happened in the past. 'Why not' he said, 'you British invite and deal with Makarios, you invite many who did worse to you than I ever did, why exclude me?'. I asked 'What if I did invite you – would you come and who else would agree to come if they knew you were coming?'. He laughed. I never invited him or visited him again. (Following the coup against Makarios in 1974, Nicos Sampson assumed the office of president temporarily.)

With all the different time zones around the world, staff in London were not immune to forgetting the time differences and occasionally would send telegraphic traffic at the most inconvenient hours. Nothing was more infuriating for the duty officer of the day than to be called into the office at some ungodly hour to receive a telegram that had been given too high a precedence and been transmitted in the depth of the night.

One late night call roused me from my bed to deal with a message from London informing us that the chancellor of the exchequer, Roy Jenkins, was somewhere on the island on an unofficial visit, and that the prime minister wanted him to make contact with Downing Street without delay. This was the first I had heard that the chancellor was on our patch and it fell to me to trace him. The Cypriot police tried a number of resort hotels in Famagusta and Kyrenia and eventually found where he had booked in. I immediately drove north and located the chancellor in a swimming pool in Kyrenia, he having just had his breakfast. I remember walking around the pool trying discreetly to attract his attention, not wanting to give a scoop to any inquisitive journalist who might have been watching. Eventually I succeeded and passed my message. As there were no confidential communication facilities from Kyrenia I was left to relay a series of messages between Nicosia and London. We learned afterwards that a sterling crisis had blown up and that the PM had wanted to consult his chancellor. That financial crisis, negotiated from the edge of a swimming pool, was the nearest I ever got to a floating pound!

On some of our journeys north, to the coast near Kyrenia – formerly a haven for retired English people - we used to visit two colourful characters, Major Betty Hunter-Cowan (Women's Royal Army Corps) – a proud Scot – and Major Phillis Heymann (Queen Alexandra's Royal Army Nursing Corps) – a feisty Yorkshirewoman – who lived in the Kyrenia Mountains, in a cave they had converted into a comfortable home. They were known locally as 'the cave ladies' and described themselves as 'Wracks and Cranks' from the initials of their respective Army corps. I first met these redoubtable ladies at an embassy cocktail party in Nicosia when they introduced themselves and enquired what I drank. I cannot remember my reply, but they insisted that I should stick to brandy while in Cyprus and buy it by the cask. I had visions of alcoholic orgies in their cave!

At one of the many cocktail parties we attended in Nicosia I found myself in conversation with the Lebanese ambassador – an anglophile if ever there was one – who expressed some surprise when I said I was returning to the office that evening to draft and despatch a report to London. 'My dear boy' he said, 'you should do as I do. It's all been reported before you know. I simply tell my secretary to send them despatch 67, or whatever we have on file that suits the occasion'. Here, I felt, was a man who had perfected the art of diplomatic reporting.

Our weekend outings included visits to many sites of considerable historical and archaeological interest. The leading monastery of Cyprus at Kykko, with its ornate chandeliers, iconostasis, and gardens, set in the cedar-clad Troodos Mountains, proved singularly attractive. At Curium we saw Shakespeare performed in an open-air theatre dating from the 5th century BC, recently restored with seating for 2,000. The beach at Ayia Napa, a great favourite with the children, took us past the old deserted monastery where the children climbed over the remains, and where we sometimes picnicked. In those days we reached the beach by way of cart tracks and had it to ourselves except for a minute fisherman's hut and a small beach restaurant. When we returned there many years later we found Ayia Napa a highly developed resort with trunk roads, high-rise buildings and swarming with foreign tourists and soldiers on leave. Fig Tree bay was another favourite, long before the tourist boom. We took our many visitors on trips to the far corners of the island, from the eastern tip of the 'Pan Handle' to the 'Stone of Romios' at Kouklia near Old Paphos.

After long days in the sun and on the beaches the children slept well. It was at this post that I developed the habit of telling, rather than reading, them bedtime stories. I found this an effective way to put across lessons of various kinds. If there were any points we felt needed to be taught I would contrive to incorporate the moral into one of my stories, with surprising effect. I have often wished that I had recorded the best of these; they would have made interesting reading now.

We were fortunate in that a friend of ours, Major M. Gibbs,

owned a number of orange groves near Famagusta and we used to visit him frequently. Exporters rejected any fruit that was even very slightly damaged or marked and all this so-called substandard produce was piled in the orchards and, if not collected, left to rot. We were allowed to gather as much as we liked and from it we used to squeeze gallons of orange, grapefruit and lemon juice to freeze for use throughout the year.

I was listening to the local radio one morning in Nicosia when I heard a familiar voice describing a visit to Taiwan. The speaker described how, during his visit there, he had been told about a persistent propaganda campaign mounted against the Taiwanese by Mainland Chinese. Thousands of balloons were being despatched daily, carrying propaganda leaflets to the island. But, the raconteur reported, the Chinese had not realised that the prevailing wind was always in the wrong direction and that all the leaflets were being carried out to sea. Then I recognised the voice; it was unquestionably my old debating colleague, Colin Jackson. Only he could tell a joke like that. By then he was a Labour member of parliament. I spoke to him briefly on the telephone, but we were unable to meet before he left Cyprus and I later read in the press that he died not long afterwards.

With the threat of invasion behind us we felt reasonably sure that the solution negotiated by the major powers would endure. At that time the high commissioner was interested in buying a house in Kyrenia and I to purchase a flat in Varosha, the modern area of Famagusta. In addition, the UN chief of staff was anxious to buy a plot of land in the north with the idea of building later. To buy land or property we had to get permits from the Cyprus government and there had already been a long delay. The occasion to further our plans came at a dinner at the high commission when our guest was the Cypriot Minister of the Interior. (There could hardly be any connection, but the Minister was assassinated a few years later.) After dinner we edged the conversation in the direction of our interests and voiced our concern about the delay in granting our permits. The Minister promised to look into the matter and within days we received authorisation and proceeded with our respective purchases, only to regret it later.

We used our new flat on only a few occasions while we were still in Cyprus and did once return for a holiday, but when the Turkish Army invaded in 1974 the new town of Varosha fell to the Turks and has remained abandoned since. We have never been able to go back there and the modern town has been left to revert to jungle. Trees have grown through the road surfaces, the sewers are choked with vegetation and the buildings, some suffering war damage, have been left to decay.

When we lived in Nicosia Cyprus seemed to be on the route of every traveller going east and we were inundated with visitors. It was not unusual for us to be alerted late at night to pick up some VIPs from the airport or the British base at Akrotiri, and take them home for the night and return them to the airport the next day. Friends and family also visited us, including Barbara's parents who came out for a brief spell. As ever we took them all to see as much of the island as we could.

The most interesting and certainly the most indefatigable visitor I had to host for a day was the head of the Foreign and Commonwealth Office at the time, Sir (later Lord) Gore-Booth, a man with an unlimited fund of intellectual and physical qualities. By the time he reached us at the high commission he had already visited a few monasteries on his way from Famagusta where he was staying, and was overflowing with questions he wanted answered. I was charged to look after him during his visit and I rushed him around the museum and other sights in Nicosia before taking him home to have tea with Barbara. It was hot and he was not a young man, nevertheless, he wanted briefing on just about everything, including a list of monasteries he had not yet explored, prior to visiting them on his way back to Famagusta. To my surprise I had a long letter from him a few days later, written in the early hours of the day following his visit to us. Apparently he needed very little sleep and dealt with his correspondence long after most of us had gone to bed.

We took leave from Cyprus to visit Israel and the Holy Land where I had a good friend in the embassy – this was a plus side to the life of every diplomat. He and his wife took us to many interesting places such as Nazareth, Jerusalem and Bethlehem and many other biblical and historical sites. I remember how shocked we were by the commercialism we found in even the most holy places. A group of American tourists were trying, in the midst of some praying catholic sisters and other devotees, to arrange themselves around 'the manger' for a photograph. 'Would it be alright if I sat on the corner?' asked one.

A day trip to Masada, the scene of the last stand of the zealots in their revolt against Roman rule in AD 66-73, was quite an adventure in those days and we made the journey in an open truck along dusty roads to the site some 30 miles south east of Jerusalem. Almost 1,000 men, women and children withdrew to this remote mountaintop and, after a two-year siege, killed themselves rather than surrender to the Roman Legions. We climbed to the top of the ancient fortress and marvelled at the courage of those who had held off the invaders until their final sacrifice.

We were impressed by what we saw of Israel, a vibrant young multiracial state, where miracles of irrigation, agriculture and horticulture were being performed. We so enjoyed our visit that we were sorry we had not taken our children with us and, to make amends, we sent the two elder ones to visit Israel later with their Chinese amah and an Indian nanny she had befriended.

During one Christmas vacation we flew from Cyprus to Istanbul. It was snowing heavily as we touched down at Ankara to disembark some passengers, and as their baggage was being offloaded the pilot announced that he must leave within ten minutes or the snow on the wings would become frozen and too heavy to allow take-off. Suitcases were being hurled in all directions and it was not until we landed in Istanbul that it was discovered that ours had inadvertently been left in Ankara. We were booked at an hotel, overlooking the Bosporus with a view of the bridge linking Europe with Asia, where it was still necessary for ladies and gentlemen to dress for dinner, but we had nothing to change into, and it was desperately cold. We did not recover our baggage for another three days. Nothing, however, was allowed to curtail our avid appetites for seeing all there was to see – the Topkapi Museum, the Blue Mosque, the Basilica of Saint Sophia, the covered market and many other sights were included. It was strangely romantic to stand on the Galata bridge linking the old imperial town of Stamboul with the port quarter of Galata, and listen to the cacophony of sounds and sights of large and small craft plying up and down the river. The children were soon bored with all this sightseeing and culture and, loudly protesting, were kept going with freshly squeezed orange juice that we found on sale at every street corner.

One day, when returning to our hotel, we boarded a local bus, which took an entirely different route from what we intended. It was difficult for us to ask the way but the driver seemed able to read our address, and his gestures suggested that we would reach the right destination eventually. Our faith in him proved ill-founded and we ended up in a face-to-face confrontation with another bus in a narrow lane in some suburb of the city. The drivers indulged in a ferocious altercation before our vehicle had to back down to let the other one through. An hour later the journey ended in a remote village where the passengers and driver got out and went their respective ways, leaving us sitting there. After he had been refreshed in a café, and had brought himself up to date with all the local gossip, the driver returned to his vehicle and took us back into Istanbul – stopping at the front door of our hotel.

In spite of this worrying experience of local transport we decided to travel by coach from Istanbul to Ankara and to fly back to Nicosia from there. This turned out to be a hair-raising trip, over spectacular snow-capped mountain roads, in a vehicle that would undoubtedly have failed its MOT in the UK. We were the centre of attention, sitting with our children in the front of the bus amongst all the local people. The scenery compensated well for the risk of the vehicle disappearing over one of the many cliffs we circumnavigated.

While in Ankara we were taken by another friend in the embassy for a picnic at the site of King Midas's tomb. There was no longer any gold lying around, but the children were encouraged to search the site. Fortunately the snow had cleared by the time we returned to Ankara and we left for Nicosia on schedule.

I had been in Cyprus for about a year before I met President Makarios. This was at the presentation of the credentials of a newly arrived British high commissioner, Peter Ramsbotham (later Sir Peter). This ceremony was another first for me. I had left the UK unprepared for the occasion and found myself having to borrow full morning dress from the Australian high commissioner, who had become a regular tennis opponent and who, fortunately, was much the same build as myself, except for being some inches longer in the leg. It took a few safety pins and a restricted gait to get me through the formalities when our new high commissioner, supported by his senior staff, stood some feet in front of His Beatitude and his entourage, while he delivered a formal address, declaring his appointment and conveying felicitations, to which the president replied. We all shook hands, partook of light refreshments and departed.

A visit from the Mayor of Camden Town shortly afterwards landed me with a tricky escort assignment. He had initially to present himself to President Makarios and then to Rauf Denktash, the leader of the Turkish Cypriots. The first part presented no problems and I duly presented His Worship to His Beatitude, but our visitor was not willing to tarnish his image in Camden by having any truck with the Turks. He was a rough diamond and made it clear that he was not visiting the Turkish side. 'Not b....y likely' he kept telling me. He claimed that he had more Greek Cypriots living in Camden than lived in Nicosia. I suspected that he was a bit worried about all those votes. However, these things had to be done, and I eventually persuaded him to accompany me across the 'green line' for what turned out to be a cordial reception, with numerous cups of black Turkish coffee, with Rauf Denktash and other Turkish Cypriot leaders.

In spite of the political upheavals during our time in Cyprus we relished the experience and loved exploring new territory. I had colleagues who hated Burma while we loved it: some even disliked Cyprus. But in all our postings we would seek out the things that interested us and make the most of them. Delightful though Cyprus was it could be very hot and oppressive in the summer and cool and damp in winter. It was not altogether a healthy climate and we seemed to have more than a fair share of colds and sore throats, which detracted somewhat from our enjoyment of a beautiful island.

When we eventually left Cyprus, George Pelaghias gave a farewell dinner for us and presented me with an illustrated history of Cyprus. Following the overthrow of Makarios by Nicos Sampson in 1974, he accompanied the deposed president to London, but I did not see either of them again after I left the island in 1969.

I had expected to complete a second leg of our Cyprus tour but instead found myself recalled to take another post in Whitehall. I had by now been elevated to the rank of Counsellor and had joined the elite band listed in 'Who's Who'.

Taking our car with us on our return home we travelled from Famagusta to Venice on a Greek liner, calling at Rhodes, and then drove home via Italy and Switzerland, where we spent a few days at Lake Como. It was at a roadside café in Italy that we saw, on a small television screen, the first moon landing by the Americans.

CHAPTER TWENTY-FOUR

ADAPTING TO ENGLAND

'When clouds are seen,
wise men put on their cloaks;'

Shakespeare.

Barbara had been fascinated by the rich variety of minerals that litter the landscape of Cyprus and had started collecting pebbles and crystal of all kinds from the mountains and beaches from the moment we arrived there. She had bought a tumbling machine and started what I mistakenly thought might develop into a profitable enterprise, polishing stones for brooches, earrings, etc. When we left Cyprus she still had a large collection ranging from asbestos to jasper, in many sizes, and insisted on taking them all home. On arrival in the UK in July 1969 the customs officials were hesitant to accept that a diplomat would carry a huge box of pebbles around the world and demanded to examine the contents of each of our many boxes. As ever on these occasions, we arrived home with huge wooden crates that had to be unpacked and homes found for the contents.

Each time we came back to Ferring we discovered that there had been yet more building on almost every vacant plot of land and began to question whether we had chosen the best place to settle, but we could not face another move. Barbara's parents were still living in Kent and with their advancing years we contrived to persuade them to move nearer to us. We had originally bought the cottage in Ferring with the idea that they might move into it to be near shops, at least until such time as we returned to the UK. As we seemed unlikely to be moving abroad again, we bought a small house for them near to us, and

I embarked on major renovation works before they moved in. Sadly, Barbara's mother died in 1972, soon after they moved in, but her father continued to live there alone until 1980 when he moved in with us and we sold his house. He was active to the end and for his 95th birthday, with a little help from the family, he organised a garden party in a marquee in his garden. Having the old folk on our doorstep made it increasingly difficult for us to take another overseas posting and we stayed in the UK until I retired in 1978. I spent my last nine years with the office commuting each day to and from Ferring.

Our children had been fortunate in Nicosia to attend an excellent school where they had made good progress and, on their return to the UK, we found them academically well ahead of their respective age groups. It was now time to start the two older ones in boarding schools and the level they had reached was to serve them in good stead.

In 1970 we revisited Cyprus with the children for a holiday, the only occasion on which we were able to use our Famagusta flat before it fell to the Turks in 1974. At the time of the invasion my nephew and his new bride were staying in our flat on their honeymoon. He had undertaken to collect for me from the Land Registry Office, the title deeds that were not ready before we left. But the Cyprus war started and my documents remained unclaimed. His bride, being a doctor, was recruited at the Dhekelia military base to screen refugees as they poured in. Some fifteen years later I engaged a Turkish lawyer to seek legal recognition of my ownership of the property in the Turkish courts and, after a protracted wait of three years, secured a judgement in my favour. I thought this a wise precaution in the event of Varosha ever returning to the Greeks, which seemed, by the year 2000, little more than a remote possibility.

Our growing family was already putting pressure on the space available in our small cottage so we decided to extend it by adding a dining room and extra kitchen on the ground floor and another bedroom upstairs. This required planning consent and we engaged an architect to prepare and submit plans. In the event the plans were rejected. When our architect sought an explanation he was surprised to be informed that the application had failed because (a) no rainwater gutters were shown and (b) the proposed extension was within a prescribed distance of the neighbour's fence. This led to an on-site meeting with the planners when the architect was able to enquire as to where, on the thickness of thatch shown on the roof, the rainwater gutters should be fixed, and also to point out that the land on both sides of the fence actually belonged to us and was not therefore a boundary. I am sure he thoroughly enjoyed that meeting. Planning permission followed swiftly and a builder carried out the work in the winter months leaving us protected by little more than a plastic sheet while the end of the cottage was removed.

My next nine years in the office were especially busy. I had in turn responsibility for a number of different desks and dabbled in personnel management, training, recruitment and communications. It was all very interesting and instructive and essentially different from the political desks I had held earlier. Those were the days when the Treasury started to turn the financial screws to rein back on public expenditure and we had to find ways to live within strict financial constraints. I had a hand in finding scope for economies and found there was quite a lot of slack to be taken in, but doing so proved altogether more difficult as there were some extremely well entrenched positions to undermine. Suffice it to say that those changes I did succeed in implementing won me few friends. The dawn of information technology was also at hand and there was scope for economies with the introduction of new means of communicating, use of word processors, etc. I learned a lot from serving on a number of committees in Whitehall and working with people of outstanding ability.

I particularly enjoyed the time I sat as a departmental representative on the Civil Service Selection Boards (CSSBs). It was a challenge to play a part in selecting people for roles in our national life. Each month these boards interviewed a number of those aspiring to enter the civil and diplomatic services, who had passed the civil service entrance examination. Candidates participated in three days of interviews, cognitive and intelligence tests set by psychiatrists and others, to determine their suitability. To be seen by one of these boards was itself a mark of quality: to get a good grade was indicative of the highest potential. One of many things I learned from this experience was how unreliable the face-to-face interview is as a means of selecting personnel. Time and again the highly presentable candidate, who scored a top mark in interview, would show up badly in the other tests. At the outset I was sceptical about the value of the process in assessing candidates, but when I had personally experienced its efficacy I learned to respect it highly. The Whitehall selection system had already won the seal of approval of many major city institutions, including the top merchant banks and the leaders of industry, and we found that such employers, often at the expense of the diplomatic and civil services, would accept without question a candidate who had got a good CSSB grade. Industry and commerce poached some of the best talent, but we got our share.

The standards set by the selection boards were very high and there were no class barriers in the search for talent. The door was open to those of either sex who had the personality and intelligence for the job and showed genuine interest in making a career in the service of the crown. The search for suitable candidates took me to a number of universities and colleges I had visited some forty years earlier in my student-leader days. I thoroughly enjoyed being closely associated again, this time with another and different generation of graduates and undergraduates.

In July 1977, Barbara and I, together with our eldest daughter Nicola, were invited to an afternoon tea party at Buckingham Palace, one of the many garden parties Her Majesty holds each year to meet her subjects. On arrival at the palace the first couple we met amongst the guests were Fred and Anne Jarvis, old friends from my student days. Accompanying the Queen and other members of the Royal Family as they strolled to the lawns at the rear of the palace, was our old friend Philip Moore (now Sir Philip) from Singapore. No time for tennis on that occasion or even to speak to him.

We had many an enjoyable holiday during this period. On one occasion the couple who had introduced us to each other in Kuala Lumpur in 1956, invited us to visit them. They had settled in Malta and gave us the use of one of their cars, which we used to tour the island extensively. Our visit coincided with a major religious festival in Valetta where we saw the most spectacular firework display we had seen anywhere in the world. As we pressed to find a vantage point in the street to view the proceedings, a Maltese family came to our rescue and invited us to their second-floor flat to watch from their balcony. Apart from the fireworks there was a colourful parade of religious statues that processed through the streets from the churches where they were normally closeted.

Neither Barbara nor I had had any previous close association with the world of dance but our children were to change all that. Two of them, Caroline and Alison, were

311

trained by a redoubtable lady, Mrs. Jean Butterworth, who ran a dance school in Worthing. Both showed early promise and we sent them, in turn, to the Bush Davies School of Education and Theatre Arts in East Grinstead as boarders. Caroline then went on to train at the Royal Ballet School and both became professional dancers, Caroline preferring classical ballet and Alison modern dance. Nicola became a boarder at Ancaster House in Bexhill, and Nina followed her there. Once the children were away at school our weekends were usually tied to fetching and carrying: and there was usually a sports day, a parents' day or school show that required our presence.

While I was beginning to think of all the things that I would do if I could retire, my thoughts turned to acquiring another overseas property. When the Turkish army invaded Cyprus in 1974 we had lost access to our flat in Famagusta, and as prospects of any settlement of the Cyprus question seemed remote, and with Barbara craving for a holiday place in the sun, we finally decided to buy a chalet on the Costa Blanca in Spain.

At the time the purchase of property overseas was additionally complicated by the dollar premium – a levy introduced by the British government to conserve sterling, but this was nothing compared with the problems we encountered over the transfer of funds to Spain. On one occasion I had deposited an instalment in cash into my bank at Torrevieja against a receipt, but the money disappeared into the Spanish banking system. I later visited Spain to sort this matter out, only to be told at Torrevieja to 'try Bilbao or Madrid'. It seemed the bank had no means of locating the money I had paid in. I ended up at a bank in Alicante sitting on the manager's desk with Barbara and the children, refusing to move until our money was traced. We returned to England still unsatisfied, but a few months later the money was paid into the account of the property vendor without ever passing through my bank account. We have never discovered how this happened and the bank offered no explanation. The problem of securing the deeds (Escritura) for the property seemed insurmountable, but eventually, after no less than eight years, a clerk arrived one night at our chalet, where we were on holiday, to deliver the document to us. The Spanish have their own ways of doing things.

Our first trip to Spain to see our chalet was made by coach from Victoria station. The return fare from London to Alicante was just £29. We loaded our trunk of household effects at the coach station, and did not see it again until we arrived at our destination. We then hired a taxi and set out in search of our acquisition somewhere in the heart of a new urbanisation some forty kilometres along what was then an undeveloped coastline. With some difficulty we found it and, in the two days we had allowed for the task, we organised electrical wiring, curtains and furnishings and made it habitable. We were lucky to find that we had a most helpful German neighbour who, it turned out, had been a Luftwaffe pilot who had been shot down in England at the beginning of the war. Although officers were not required to work he had elected to labour on a farm. He had been so well treated by his captors that he had acquired a genuine affection for all things British and, in some respects, had become more English than the English and still returned regularly to his wartime farm to spend his holidays.

I was devoting much of my weekends to making alterations to our house in London, maintaining our home in Ferring, fitting up the home for Barbara's father, and negotiating the sale of some cottages outside Dover that Barbara had inherited from an aunt. We also found ourselves making frequent visits to Barbara's two maiden aunts living in Dorset and, trying to meet the needs of our own four children. In the middle of all this I was offered a posting to South Africa but felt obliged to turn it down, principally because we had Barbara's elderly father living close by, and we could hardly leave him behind. I seemed to have so much to do at home that attending the office became of secondary interest, and with so many of my generation bunched above me in seniority, my ambition had dissipated.

Commuting from Ferring to London each day, especially in the winter months, was becoming increasingly intolerable as the years wore on. Trains were cold, dirty, and uncomfortable and invariably ran late. I spent hours in anguish at East Croydon station on my journey north not knowing how late I was going to be for some important meeting in London, or, on my journey home, thinking of Barbara sitting in a cold car at Goring-by-Sea waiting for me. There was no telephone at our station and there were no mobile phones in those days. This was no life and I had had enough.

Consequently Barbara and I started to talk about early retirement and whether we would have enough income to live comfortably into a ripe old age. Fortunately, my various forays into the stock and property markets had been mostly successful and we came to the conclusion that we had enough in the piggy bank to ensure that I would not need to work again. At the time we still had our home in Ferring, a flat in Cyprus – which the Turks had taken – our London house and our chalet in Spain which left me with what I considered to be a reasonable schedule of maintenance tasks.

Thus, when the opportunity presented itself in 1978, I decided to call it a day. The office was supportive of those retiring early and offered me introductions to a range of alternative careers, but I had already decided that what I wanted most was some of that all elusive commodity – time.

314

Now at last I should have more of it to spend with the family, to enjoy the garden and engage in the many activities for which I had never had the time to enjoy.

After a good service the doubles team leave the church.
Kuala Lumpur - March 1957

Singapore bound on the Tchwangi on return from our
honeymoon in Hong Kong – April 1957

The newly-weds relax on the Beach of
Passionate Love, Malaya – 1957

Nicola our first-born with her grandfather
Douglas Marshall Webb – 1958

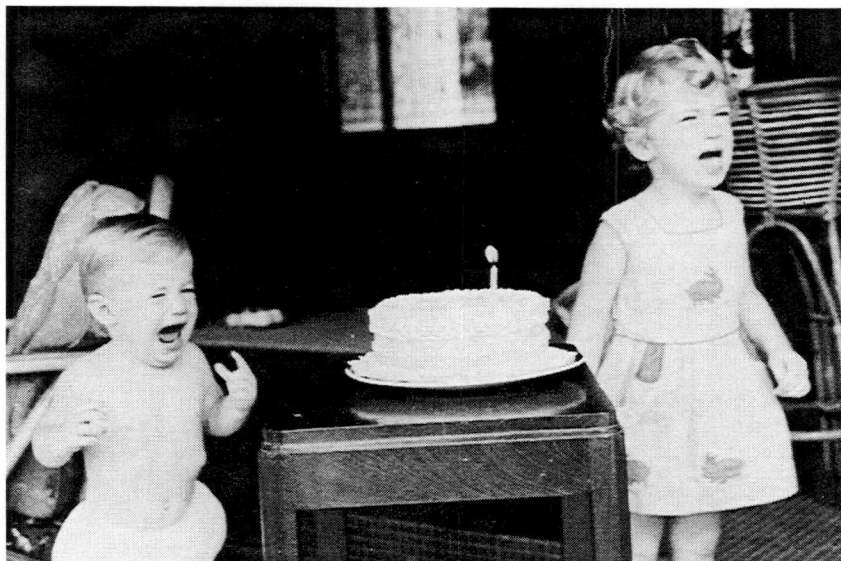

Nicola and Caroline 'enjoying' a first
birthday party! – Singapore 1960

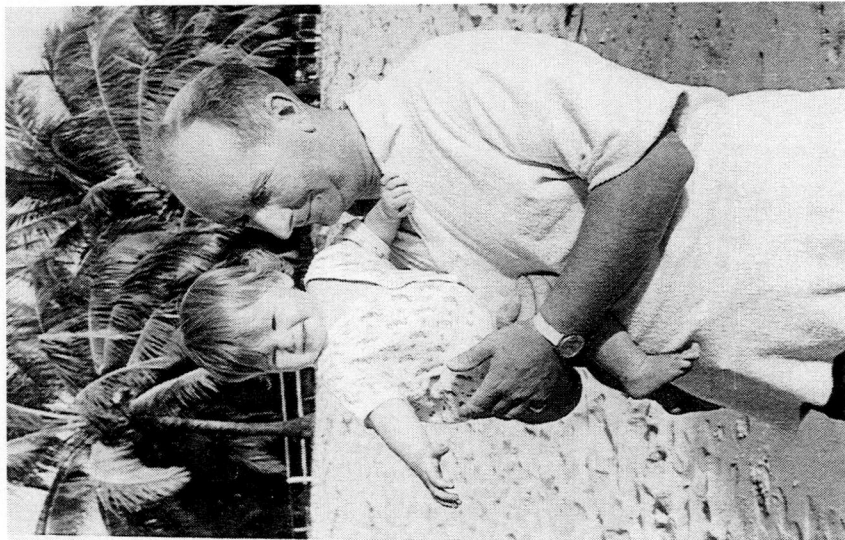

Nina with her godfather John
McNab – Rangoon 1963

On leave in the UK with
Nicola and Caroline – 1962

Christmas in Rangoon – 1963.

Barbara, Nicola, Caroline and
Nina – Sandoway, Burma, 1964

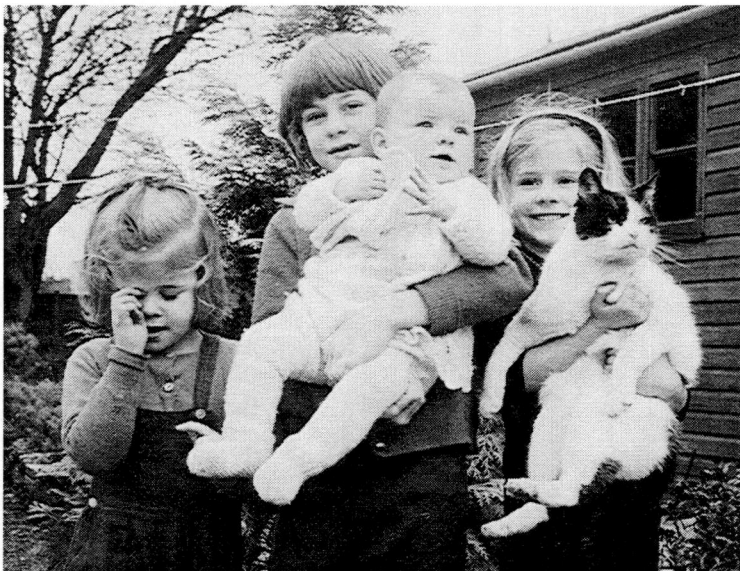

Our children with their pet Domino – Ferring 1965

Our children, Nicola, Caroline, Nina and Alison
in school uniform – Cyprus 1968

Discussing the Cyprus Question – 1969
L to R. T.Empson, self, Col.Wilson and Rauf Denktash

Children skiing in the Troodos Mountains – Cyprus 1969

Caroline, Nina and Alison
with their grandparents – Cyprus 1969

Family picnic on the roadside – Cyprus 1969

So Much To Do
So Little Time

. . . .

Part V

Winding Down

CHAPTER TWENTY-FIVE

FALAJ AND FRANKINCENSE

'Anywhere, anywhere,
Out of the world.'

Hood.

After living for some years in our cottage Barbara and I thought it would be an ideal place for our retirement. We had many ideas for improvements we wanted to make to achieve the sort of home we aspired to and as soon as I could I began a programme of alterations and redecoration with enthusiasm, starting outside by building a rock garden, incorporating a pond and a waterfall. We then upgraded the swimming pool I had built earlier and gave the grass tennis court an overhaul. The cottage thatch had to be renewed and Barbara wanted me to build a conservatory, so that she could continue her gardening in all seasons and this, she decreed, was to be my first task. Before long I was digging out the foundations.

Much as we liked Ferring when we first knew it, we were sad to see that the village was changing, and not for the better. It had always been typically 'sea-side' rather than 'country' and never a pretty place, though its residents kept their gardens immaculately. The area had its attractive features, like the Downs to the north, the narrow bands of open land on either side of the conurbation, and the sea to the south, but the building boom that had led to most of the development, especially that in the southern part of the village, post 1920, was architecturally unappealing.

Much of the change was due to the escalating value of building land in the Worthing area which rocketed throughout the 1960s and 1970s. Many residents had sold up to exploit the situation and taken their profits. We were constantly urged to lodge objections to developments taking place around us, but it seemed irrational to us to object to others wanting to settle in the very area we had chosen for ourselves, as though we had some divine right to live in the place of our choice and then deny that right to others. The coastal strip had long been christened 'geriatrica', and with the trend towards demolishing the larger houses to make room for small bungalows, the age balance of the population had swung even more towards the elderly and retired though the number of children increased in holiday periods when families visited grandparents.

The village had already lost its bowling green and its tennis club by this time, and almost every available plot of land had been built on. We also observed a change in the kind of people who were moving into the village. When we first bought our cottage there seemed to be more who had travelled and lived abroad and were perhaps better used to entertaining. This had changed in the relatively short time we had been away and Ferring appeared to us to have developed a decidedly more inward-looking atmosphere. But, having our cottage there, we still thought it a good choice.

Barbara's father had moved in with us when he could no longer continue to live alone and we were happy to have been able to look after him in the closing years of his life. He was a wonderful person in every way and much loved by his grandchildren. He had served during the First World War in the Honourable Artillery Company and had been invalided out after a mustard gas attack in France. It was my pleasure to take him in the last few years of his life to the annual HAC reunion dinners at Armoury House in London. On the last occasion, when he was ninety-five, he was far and away the oldest veteran of the First World War present, and was accorded the rare honour of a "salute of fire", a ceremonial toast of the HAC. The ancient dining hall was packed with veterans of two world wars greeting each other and enjoying renewed acquaintances while the regimental band, occupying a small balcony overlooking the dining chamber, played throughout the proceedings. Such occasions are becoming increasingly rare. The old soldier had been accorded a richly deserved honour.

I shall always remember the old gentleman, especially for his wonderfully humorous stories. He once told me how he had been stopped by a policeman for speeding and asked if he was in any particular hurry. He replied, 'Oh no officer, no hurry at all if there is anything I can do for you'. And again from his days during the Second World War when, working for the Ministry of Food, he had visited their offices in London looking for the Homegrown Cereals Division. He enquired of two elderly ladies, in the first office he looked into, if he had found what he was looking for. 'Oh dear no' came the reply 'we are the dried fruits'.

Having travelled so much, I was content never to make another foray overseas, but Barbara still had the urge to see the world, and she was mainly responsible for getting me on the move in the years ahead. It was not that I had tired of the poetry of travel, but rather that I wondered about the value of indulging myself further at my time of life. When I first retired I felt strongly that I did not want any commitment for at least a year; I just wanted time to tackle the many things I had for so long set aside.

Then, almost exactly twelve months after leaving the office, I was invited by an old friend and colleague to join him in Oman, where he had taken an adviser's post on leaving the FCO. He wanted me to undertake a few studies to assist him and made his offer sound most attractive. With no experience of the Middle East, and having caught up on many of the tasks at home that had been neglected for some time, I decided to go. Barbara's father was living with us and, because of his great age, I made clear that I could only be away for a few months at a time. Over the next two years I made three short visits to the Sultanate, and on two occasions, when we found someone to care for her father, Barbara was able to accompany me. Barbara's father died in 1981 aged 97.

It was only a short flight from England yet, on arrival, it was as though I had stepped into another world. Coming in by air to land at Muscat for the first time, the feature that caught my eye was what seemed to be dozens of small green circles dotted over the city. From the air they looked like tiny green oases, but I later discovered that they were grass-covered traffic islands watered constantly from a secondary irrigation system using reclaimed water, piped throughout the city. Alongside green standpipes, providing drinking water, were red ones, supplying partially treated water for uses other than drinking: water conservation is a matter of life or death in these parts and none can be wasted.

I was allocated a government guesthouse with a swimming pool and an Indian cookboy. When I told him of my time in the East and my love of Indian food, his face lit up and from then on he used to go out of his way to see that I got the best of everything. He also taught me a number of the secrets of Indian cooking, a favourite cuisine.

Knowing that I did not have long to see the sights of this relatively closed society I took every opportunity to travel wherever and whenever I could. Almost everything was different from other countries I had known and I was captivated by it, and especially by the gentle and unostentatious Omanis, who exuded tranquillity as they went about their daily business with a smile, deporting themselves with majestic dignity. Their dress, especially the civil servants, all wearing traditional long white dish-dashes and turban headdress, differentiated them from the peoples of other lands I knew.

I found the landscape as varied and as attractive as the people. While much of the countryside is arid desert, there are some spectacular mountain ranges where one can see richly coloured and deeply fissured rock formations. It must surely be a geologist's paradise. Ranges of hills enclose areas of grazing that support tribes who can be seen tending their sheep and goats as their ancestors have done for generations. Visiting Oman was to step back a century or two. At the same time it was fascinating to see how this previously undeveloped country was being transformed by an enlightened ruler. The proceeds the government derived from a limited oil discovery, which they began to exploit in 1967, were being sensibly used to provide a basic infrastructure that included schools, roads and hospitals. Up until then there were only three schools (boys only), one doctor to look after the Sultan and only lanterns to light the streets.

Sultan Qaboos bin Said – who had summarily deposed his reputedly despotic father with the aid of a British army officer in 1967 and flown him to London – was, I thought rightly, concerned that too rapid a rate of development could do more harm than good. The many changes, particularly in regard to health and education provisions, that were being made to many aspects of the Sultanate had to accord with the strict Moslem traditions of the country and the new Sultan sought to modernise only where he safely felt he could. He remained sensitive, perhaps sometimes paranoid, about the external threats to his borders, especially after earlier incursions from the Yemen in the south, and about the danger he perceived in having too much contact with the West. Consequently, the borders of his country were mostly sealed to the outside world. Some fine modern hotels that had been built were little used, and miles of new highway appeared to be going nowhere. I felt lucky to have been given unrestricted access to such a secret world. (The deposed Sultan lived in enforced exile in the Dorchester Hotel in London until he died in 1972.)

The renaissance began in earnest in about 1970 when attention was given to the needs of the people in every walk of life, especially for improving the ancient *falaj* – a network of stone cisterns and channels carrying water from nearby springs and wadis to the villages and fields – that remains the main system of irrigation. The *falaj* spawns over the cultivated areas branching at intervals into subsidiary channels to distribute water to another field or another landowner, the flow controlled by nothing more than temporary stone interruptions, adjusted according to age-old rights to share the precious water. At some of the sites of old forts and battlements I visited I saw how ingeniously the *falaj* had been constructed underground so that its waters could not easily be poisoned or diverted by hostile tribes in days long past.

The extraordinary wealth of these oil rich states was brought home to me vividly when I made a study for the government on border controls. After visiting all the points of entry and egress I recommended the installation of a computer-controlled system to link all the frontier stations to a central computer in Muscat. It so happened that there was a major international computer exhibition in Kuwait at the time to which I wanted to take a few senior Omani officials to show them what might be done with the aid of the new technology. Within hours of my suggesting this, a government aeroplane was standing by to take us. Sadly, when we arrived in Kuwait we learned that the exhibition had already moved to Dubai. This entailed an overnight stop at the Sheraton Hotel before flying on. After brief discussions with a few exhibitors, the Omanis became impatient to place a firm order for an extensive computer system regardless of cost. I advised them of the preliminary work that would be necessary – the analyses, the planning and the costs, but they would have none of this. 'What is the problem, order it now and we can sort out the rest later?' That the cost was likely to be of the order of £2m. did not seem to worry them at all. In the event they did order shortly afterwards, and I heard later that the equipment did not turn out to be exactly what was required and it was all replaced a few years later. After the tight-purse-strings of Whitehall this was a salutary experience.

On two of my visits to Oman Barbara accompanied me and we were taken on a number of journeys of discovery. We especially enjoyed a trip with some friends, who took us on a two-day camel safari through the desert where we slept under the stars. We both have unforgettable memories of waking as the sun rose, and of seeing our camels tethered on a distant skyline. The still night air had condensed on the outside of our bedding and we could ring the water from the outer layers. Never had breakfast tasted so good as when cooked in the open by our Arab hosts. At the end of each long camel ride we were all suffering: those of us inexperienced in the art found great difficulty in dismounting and our hosts were amused by our anguish as we tried to straighten up our tortured limbs.

On another occasion we were taken to visit Nizwa in the north, a trading, religious and silver craft centre with a seventeenth-century round fort, one hundred and twenty feet in circumference. Our visit coincided with the holding of a camel market and we had the rare experience of walking amongst the animals and their vendors and listening to the animated bargaining as they tried to reach agreement on a price. Another trip took us to some remote Arab villages where we visited many houses and sat cross-legged on the floor and joined with the menfolk drinking Arab coffee and eating slices of orange. At lunchtime the women appeared only to bring us dishes of sumptuous fried spiced chicken, goat or lamb served with rice and slices of mango. Crossing the desert we travelled mostly in an open four-wheel-drive truck driven at incredible speeds. We were told that to drive slowly could lead to getting stuck in the loose sand but we took the view that the drivers were slightly mad! After sitting on hard wooden benches and travelling at such speeds, without cushions, we were to nurse bruises for days.

An American government official who, like myself, was in Oman as an adviser, and whom I met in Muscat, took me on my first ever deep sea fishing trip in a powerful motor boat that he kept moored in Mina Qaboos, the picturesque port off the Muttrah Corniche. As we roared out to sea at high speed I wondered if there could be anything more exhilarating than to drive in a powerful motor boat in such a superlative setting. Nobody was more surprised than I when I cast a line and had a bite. It was judged to be a big one and my host helped me to land an enormous grouper. Later, he cooked it simply by soaking it for twenty-four hours in lime juice and herbs and it was delicious. I learned afterwards that this was a typical South American speciality called 'seveche'. Another friend with a motor boat took us for picnics to largely deserted islands off the coast but, as I always suffered badly from sunburn on these outings unless I was very careful, some proved a doubtful pleasure. We found little or no shade on the beaches and I used to sit in a huddle covered with towels and anything else I could borrow to protect my skin from a searing sun. Any part of me that was exposed for more than a few minutes would invariably scorch.

I never tired of visiting the many market places, especially

324

in the more remote villages in the desert areas and I found the bazaars (the souks) of Mutrah close to Ruwi, the main business centre of Oman, particularly entertaining and intriguing. The long narrow passageways were flanked with traders of many nationalities; the Indians with their fine silks and saris, the Lebanese with their gold jewellery and Baluch and other Middle Eastern merchants with their cottons and artefacts. The peoples of the Middle East all seemed to be represented in those secretive passages, which held all the fascination and mystery that one associates with an eastern bazaar.

The souks were also recognised as the places to change money at advantageous rates, and there were many illicit moneychangers hovering around or sitting aloft above the merchandise ready to strike a bargain. The sights, the sounds, and the smell of exotic spices, incense, scented teas and tobaccos were unforgettable. The little shops in the souk, including those retailing gold and silver of considerable value, were secured at night with little more than a light-gauge metal grille and a small padlock. As a friend pointed out, theft was virtually unknown; convicted thieves were subject to the harsh penalties of the Islamic Shariah Court that, not so long ago, would have demanded amputation of the right hand. That I could leave my car unlocked and my small change on the bedside table left me wondering if, after all, such harsh measures had some justification.

A more endearing feature of the Omani people was their love of football. Perhaps this was more true of the men than the women, but whether they liked it or not the ladies had football thrust upon them in large measure on their television screens. The news for the day slavishly followed a set pattern. Starting with a detailed account of the day's programme for the Sultan and his ministers it would end with an excerpt from a recorded British home league soccer match, often one that had taken place some weeks earlier!

I was present in Muscat for one of the National Day celebrations held each November, on the Sultan's birthday, in the Royal Oman Police stadium. This was very much a military affair. He and his entourage arrived by helicopter to deliver his National Day address to the nation. This was followed by displays and marching routines mainly by police and armed forces contingents. The Sultan, who had been trained at Sandhurst, obviously loved British military traditions and music, and the bands did their best to render some of our regimental marches. I say, did their best, because it was not always easy to recognise what they were striving for. Their repertoire was decidedly limited and every other march they played resembled 'Sussex by the Sea'. At least this made me feel at home. I was weary by the end of the day that had begun for me with a dawn call to accompany some friends to the local camel races, which turned out to be a sort of national Derby Day, except that they had to be finished before the full heat of the mid-day sun. The Omanis liked to have a flutter amongst themselves on their favourite mount and it was hilarious to see these ungainly creatures guided by tiny children sitting astride them, hurtling along in the sand between columns of people cheering wildly. Some of the animals followed the appointed course for the race while others had minds of their own.

I paid one visit to Salalah in Dhofar, a unique corner of Arabia situated at the extreme south of the Sultanate. On the aeroplane, I found myself sitting with a BBC correspondent who had spent some years in Cyprus in the army during the time when the British were under constant attack. He was flying there to make a documentary. That evening we took a swim together and spent the rest of the time at the hotel bar that we had almost entirely to ourselves, talking about Oman and reminiscing about Cyprus. The next day we strolled through the streets of the town lined with plantations of bananas, date palms and coconut groves and were struck by the enormous potential for tourism that Oman had to offer. We speculated on how long the beautiful stretch of deserted coastline would remain as completely unspoiled as we found it: the sand was almost pure white. Together we visited the Sultan's Al Husn fort and the food souk with its many stalls offering seafood including shark, vegetables and fruit and many spices: myrrh, sandalwood, cinnamon, and frankincense stacked in great pyramids of many colours. Other stalls offered a range of silver and gold artefacts, silks, cotton goods and aluminium kitchenware. Whenever I travelled alone, chance meetings with complete strangers were always a bonus. This is one of the delights of travelling solo: when accompanied, one rarely meets or establishes a relationship with anyone.

During my visit to Salalah I was taken by a group of young Omani servicemen and a young British army NCO attached to the Omani forces, for a picnic in the mountains, where I first saw frankincense bushes growing wild all over the hillsides. Reaching our destination involved a hair-raising journey in a four-wheel-drive truck, partly along mountain tracks and partly along the bed of a dry wadi where we seemed to bounce from boulder to boulder. We arrived at our picnic site in the mountains in convoy and, to my astonishment and dismay my host dragged a small goat from the rear of his truck and asked if I would like to slit its throat. Not knowing if this was the custom and wondering if it was offensive to refuse, I hesitated. On balance I decided that I would prefer to offend and politely declined to take the knife. My host proceeded to cut its throat in front of me, and dismantle the carcass. The meat and the whole head were then put on top of the embers of a fire with the eyes of the poor animal still gazing at me. We had to eat it, but I cannot say it was one of the meals I have enjoyed. Eventually only the bones were left – I noticed the eyes had also been eaten, but not by me.

Although our hosts were Moslems they were fond of alcohol and saw their picnic as an occasion, away from their elders, to indulge themselves. As the evening wore on they became rather aggressive and let slip that they did not approve of the way in which the British still ran so many facets of their country. Prior to this I had seen nothing but happy smiling people and no dissent from the policy of their ruler to make full use of foreign advisers. They left me in little doubt that, although the British were only there at the behest of their Sultan, there clearly was an undercurrent of resentment that they still occupied so many of the higher posts, particularly in the Sultan's armed forces and the civil service. The hostility of our hosts began to worry my colleague and me and we thought it prudent to beat a hasty retreat. While the others were continuing their eating and drinking we surreptitiously made our way to our truck and drove off into the night. We began to fantasise about what might have befallen us had we stayed. I had visions of being treated like the goat with my head roasting on the embers, and never being seen again.

Before leaving Oman I was offered a two-year government contract but declined it. I had little desire to become another of those unwanted advisers and thought that any protracted stay would soon lose its appeal. There was no cultural life, and after all the sightseeing had been done there was little else that attracted me. Anyway, I wanted to settle down and do other things at home.

CHAPTER TWENTY-SIX

A VILLAGE OF CONTRADICTIONS

'Where is the man who has the power and skill
To stem the torrent of a woman's will?
For if she will, she will, you may depend on't,
And if she won't, she won't, and there's an end on't.'

Anon.

Just before I retired friends had suggested that I should stand for election to either the county or district councils. I had already decided to join the Conservative Party, where my political instincts lay but, remembering my student days, I had set my mind against any deeper involvement in politics. I was also anxious not to take on anything that might prove too time-consuming. A fellow commuter on the train to Victoria, who was chairman of the Ferring Ratepayers' and Owners' Association, (FROA), wanted me to join his executive committee and as this did not sound too onerous and being a firm believer in playing my part, I agreed, and was duly co-opted until the next AGM. Two years later I became chairman. The consequence of this was to involve me, albeit only marginally, in local politics – which was about the last thing I had intended.

The FROA had been set up to enable property owners to contribute collectively for the maintenance of the network of roads throughout the village that had not been adopted by the local authority: they were still classified as privately owned public highways. This seemed to me a worthwhile job and I was happy to help where I could. Each year for the next seven years I was returned unopposed as chairman, mainly because nobody wanted my job, but we had no complaints either. I was fortunate to have good committee members and together we made a useful contribution. Each year I tried to find a successor so that I could take a break, but none was forthcoming. It was not an office that involved very much – except when people would ring me at lunch time on a Sunday to ask for advice about a blocked drain, or to complain about someone having parked across their driveway, which was nothing whatever to do with the association. In the circumstances I was happy to carry on until a suitable successor could be found but there were no volunteers and I was to spend much of the next ten years working for the village.

Apart from maintaining roads, we found a number of things requiring attention that might normally have fallen to the parish council, but at the time they refused to set a precept and had little or no money to pay for anything. In consequence residents tended to write to us and we would refer the matter to the council, wait a while, and when as usual nothing was done, we would set about doing it ourselves. Sadly, unbeknown to me until much later, everything we did for the village was building up resentment within the parish council. They appeared to take exception to others doing anything they ought to have done themselves and some councillors apparently thought their authority was being threatened. When one appreciates how little jurisdiction they actually had, the absurdity of this attitude makes this hard to understand.

As I came to the end of my eighth year as chairman of the ratepayers' association, my committee agreed that we ought to update our constitution, which had remained untouched since it was first drafted some two decades earlier: there was much that needed clarification and revision. Accordingly, we set up a subcommittee that produced an excellent document which we submitted to our legal adviser. When he commented that he considered it 'a masterpiece' we decided to put it to members for approval.

This happened to coincide with another development in the village, namely, a move by a group of individuals who approached me, seeking help to establish some local sports provisions. I agreed to this, little realising what a poisoned chalice it would turn out to be. I had always been keen on sport and considered the residents of Ferring to be ill served in that regard. I had my own grass tennis court and a swimming pool, where we used to let the village children swim, but there were no such facilities for other residents.

When I looked into the matter, I discovered that we had some nine acres of recreation ground within the parish borders, all owned by our district council. Approximately one third was being used by a football club and one third by a cricket club, but only in the winter and summer months respectively. I was surprised to find that only three Ferring residents played at these clubs, the rest being from elsewhere. It was obvious that neither cricket nor football was likely to involve many from a largely retired population. When my wife and I first came to Ferring we were particularly attracted to a small tennis club near where we bought our cottage, but when we returned later from Rangoon, it had been taken over for housing. Whilst chairman of the FROA I was informed that Fred Perry once played tennis at this club so I wrote to him and he replied saying:

> 'I do believe there was a tennis tournament in Ferring many years ago and I do know many of the better players of that time used to compete. The tournament was held after the championships at Wimbledon. As I was always out of the country once we had finished the Davis Cup I never had the opportunity of playing in either the Ferring tournament or coming down there to play exhibition matches. Too many of the pleasant tournaments have fallen by the wayside in England. It is a great pity.'

In earlier years, when the population of Ferring was half

what it was in the 1990s there was also a bowling green, but that too had fallen victim to developers. Apart from a small area set aside for children to play, the rest of our three large recreation areas were used only occasionally, mostly by casual walkers and their dogs. To the north we had the South Downs, to the south the sea and on both east and west sides of the village we had land designated as 'strategic gaps' to prevent coalescence with neighbouring developments. Few coastal settlements enjoyed more open spaces.

At the outset it seemed to me that there would be no disagreement about providing facilities for bowls, croquet and tennis. There must have been few villages the size of ours, with a population of about 4,000, without at least a bowling green. I thought that what was needed was a group of capable, dedicated and competent individuals who could cause things to happen. But I had not reckoned with the fact that many elderly British people value the past more highly than the future. We are, after all, a nation with more industrial museums, preserved steam railways and listed buildings than any other on earth and we all wallow in nostalgia, conservation and preservation.

Oblivious to the fact that change was almost certain to be resisted, my colleagues and I set to work with enthusiasm. We were advised by the Regional Sports Council to prepare a constitution for a local sports association and to incorporate it as a private limited company, to be best placed to receive grant aid and to give the committee financial protection. The parish council appeared to support us at this point and nominated a representative to our first meeting. The ratepayers' association nominated me and we recruited representatives of those who supported tennis, bowls and croquet, together with officers from the existing cricket and football clubs. At our first meeting I was elected chairman. (I was subsequently re-elected each year for the next eight years.) We thought we were away to a good start, and one would have expected our efforts to have won wholesale support and approval. As it turned out, this was to become the most frustrating period of my life. I cannot recall any other series of events, in which I have been personally involved, that have done more to undermine my faith in human nature.

We next called a public meeting to explain our ideas and invited parish councillors to attend. We were surprised to find instant opposition to our proposals from a few members of the latter. It seemed that the village Luddites were having nothing changed in *their* village: anyway this was not *their* idea. Objectors claimed that the three recreation grounds were in constant use, were invaluable for village children to play and should be kept entirely for informal recreation. (At a later stage we took photographs throughout normal and holiday times to prove that use of these areas was minimal.)

In spite of these objections, we pressed ahead with enquiries to establish what facilities were most needed, and there was a consensus that priority should be given to bowls, preferably indoor rinks, croquet and lastly, tennis. There were already two disused grass tennis courts on one of the recreation grounds 'maintained' by the parish council, but these were sadly neglected, more suited to grazing goats than tennis, and badly needed refurbishing.

At the time we had our eyes on a possible site that would have left the recreation fields undisturbed, but the planning authority turned this down, because it fell within the 'strategic gap'. They asked why we wanted to go into the 'gap' when we had so much under-used recreation ground within the village itself. In turn we invited them to indicate where we might put an indoor bowls centre and they suggested some partially wooded land adjacent to our cricket circle, where trees had been extensively damaged in the great storm of 1987. We began to prepare plans for the village to consider.

But within weeks of our discussing an indoor bowls centre a local opposition group had been formed 'to protect the village open spaces'. We should have anticipated this 'normal' British reaction, but failed to do so. (My mind harked back to the communist technique of hijacking good causes such as 'peace'.) Residents were now told that 'developers' were threatening to take over the village, that a 'private limited company', and I personally, were going to make a lot of money out of exploiting the open spaces, and that the value of their properties would be affected adversely. Moreover, the bowls facility was likely to become a drinking club and would result in a lot of drunkenness. Not surprisingly, residents flocked to join a new conservation group that was soon to speak vociferously 'in the name of 1,500 members'. It consistently opposed every proposal advanced by the sports association. After all is said and done we are all conservationists at heart; the aim of the sports group was to conserve what we considered to be some of the best elements of village life.

Our adversaries had all the skills of wartime propagandists and proved very effective in whipping up opposition to something that could have proved to be of enormous benefit to the village. Overnight I became some sort of terrorist with people expressing to my wife their horror at what her husband was proposing. We could hardly believe what was happening.

Showing immense flair and imagination, those who opposed our plans were not long in organising an exhibition in the village hall, displaying *their* version of a new bowls complex, before we had finalised a scheme for discussion. According to them, villagers were faced with the prospect of a massive structure, smack in the middle of the cricket field, and most of those who saw the exhibition believed this.

Then all hell broke loose. Had the scene been set in a French context, barricades would have been erected on the streets. I had convened a meeting to adopt the new FROA constitution that had already been approved by almost a two-thirds majority in a postal ballot. Word had been put about by our opponents that this was part of some sinister plot to throw the resources of the Ratepayers' Association behind the 'development of the village open spaces by a private limited company'. Crowds turned up. We had never seen such a turnout, not all could be accommodated and, having regard to fire regulations, I felt obliged to adjourn the meeting to a larger hall at a later date.

When we did meet, parishioners came baying for blood. There was uproar. One of my colleagues remarked 'they looked like a crowd waiting at the guillotine, they only lacked their knitting'. Their behaviour suggested that their very lives were in jeopardy. Our new constitution, which we had worked so hard to prepare, was summarily rejected. In consequence, I did not offer myself for re-election, nor did any of my colleagues. We were left wondering what the fuss was all about and how such virulent opposition could have been engendered.

There was little acceptance on the part of our opponents that the village recreation areas were for the benefit of the whole community, and that the district council who owned the land supported our views about improving sports provisions. There was no willingness to share the abundant space we had. In effect we were told that we could have any sports facilities we liked, but 'not on our patch'. One lady expressed astonishment when I told her I did not play bowls, nor did my wife. 'Then why are you doing this?' she asked. There was little sense of altruism.

PART V - WINDING DOWN

As I saw it, the arguments about preserving open spaces were fraught with contradictions. I felt that those supporting conservation should have been campaigning for local facilities if only to get cars off the roads, but they were telling us to use our cars and go to play on someone else's patch. I argued that what we were offering would encourage wider participation in healthy outdoor exercise as well as providing an attraction for local spectators. But logic played no part in any of this and the hypocrisy implicit in many of the arguments was conveniently ignored.

The accusations being made against the sports association were sometimes outrageous, sometimes melodramatic but never justified. I was reminded of the words of Mark Twain 'A lie can be half way round the world before truth gets its boots on'. I thought it especially sad that a number of honourable people living in the village, listening to the outrageous accusations being made against my colleagues and me, knowing them to be false, and forgetting that veracity is at the heart of morality, said nothing. There is a saying that 'Evil flourishes where good men stay silent' or as Emerson once wrote, 'Society is a masked ball, where one hides his real character, and reveals it by hiding'. Many people said to me that Ferring had more than its share of 'fence-sitters'. It is understandable that retired folk should want to live quietly and keep out of controversy, but where, I asked, should one draw the line on matters of principle? An insidious aspect of these developments, or so it seemed to me, was the fear expressed to me by one councillor who supported the idea of improved facilities that, 'to offend the conservationists could cost him a lot of votes'.

Whereas we wanted a relatively small area for indoor bowls, the intensity of the campaign launched against sports provisions suggested that – as one committee member pointed

336

out – we were advocating at least a string of brothels and a few discos. There was something quite unreal, and often highly amusing, about the whole thing.

The sports association decided at this point that residents ought to know the facts, and I was asked to write a pamphlet that was published under the title 'The Ferring Saga'. This told something of the bigotry and selfishness of those who were opposing our plans for the village, and showed how people had been misinformed. But the seeds of doubt had been sown and had taken root and the pamphlet had little effect.

But worse was to come. We kept two cats, and one day I found a basket with two drowned kittens at the bottom of our swimming pool. But they were not ours. Whoever did this had caught our neighbour's pets, often seen in our garden, and drowned them in our pool. Later the glass on our sports association notice board was defaced with some form of etching paste. And all this was about the provision of a bowling green. Our village policeman, who thought both these incidents were calculated to intimidate me, told my wife to tell her husband to 'watch his back'. It was so reminiscent of my earlier days in Eastern Europe, but this was a quiet English village where we had then lived and worked constructively for the community for some twenty years.

Backing the local vendetta against the sports promoters was a concerted campaign of letters to the press and to the planning authority, some of them libellous. I ignored these for some time, but when a local free newsmagazine, the *TV Review*, published an article that was damaging, I passed it to a solicitor friend because every accusation made against me was entirely false. Within hours of my solicitor's intervention, the editor of the magazine called on me to apologise and offered to settle the matter out of court. I agreed to accept a published retraction and cash payment of £2,000, which I arranged to be paid directly to the sports association, though it was my reputation that had suffered. We were left wondering who the source of the article had been. I suppose every village has its 'crackpots' but this was something manifestly evil. I remember at one of the overseas missions where I had previously worked that we had a file marked 'Nut Cases' where we filed all letters that fell under that heading. They were usually from those we categorised as frustrated ancient Brits. – mostly ladies I regret to say – writing to complain that they had not been invited to the Queen's Birthday Party having already bought a new hat, or objecting to something they had heard on the BBC.

At one of the parish council meetings held at this time, a senior parish councillor made an impassioned speech against having croquet lawns in the village. He declared that he had once lived near a croquet club and knew from experience that 'the noise of wood on wood would drive the people of Ferring insane'. I wondered how he felt when his observation appeared in a press report!

In the fraught atmosphere of the time we did not pursue the indoor bowls project, and I feel sure that future generations will deplore the loss of such an amenity. The building we had in mind would have been largely below ground level, with car parking on the roof space and facilities for indoor bowls, an assembly hall, snooker and table tennis rooms. It would also have incorporated a café and a fine cricket pavilion facing the cricket circle, and all on land that was providing little amenity. But projects of this kind required people of vision and few of them were in evidence in Ferring at that time.

We then prepared plans for an outdoor green with parking provision on the main recreation ground, known as 'the Glebelands'. The next developments to counter this plan were

338

decidedly Machiavellian. At the height of the controversy, in order to prevent the sports association or anyone else putting any sports facilities on that site, the parish council asked the district council to lease it to them. This was agreed, but only on condition that the parish council provided two hard tennis courts within three years and a bowling green within seven. The two councils then entered into a legal agreement to that effect, and a year later the parish fulfilled its undertaking to provide the tennis courts, paying for them entirely out of its own funds. No attempt was made to get grant aid, which was available on application.

To meet its obligation to provide a bowling green the parish council then levied a precept, and raised £20,000 towards the cost. Having done that it decided to conduct a poll 'to determine whether to proceed'. The order of events might seem confused! The vote went against bowls by about two to one, but less than half of the population bothered to participate, and there was some evidence of chicanery over the voting, where some hundreds of voting papers that were not deposited in the official ballot boxes, and oddly, all negative votes, were accepted as valid. The parish council then petitioned the district council asking to be released from its undertaking to provide a bowling green, claiming that the people were opposed to it, and this was accepted. The £20,000 raised for bowls was retained but, shrewdly, the district left the parish with responsibility for the maintenance of the Glebelands, which entailed a sizeable grass cutting cost they had not previously had to carry. Without the bowling green there was no income to offset this, and the village was left with a continuing financial burden it need not have incurred. The village precept was increased accordingly.

As we live in a democracy our supporters felt that the way ahead lay in fighting the next parish council elections. We had earlier tried to persuade individuals to stand, but few would allow their names to go forward. As the next election approached, the sports association started to canvass possible candidates. A few thought it unfair that we should ask others to serve, if we were not prepared to stand ourselves. Thus, I agreed to become a candidate, along with five others.

A vigorous campaign was mounted against us and we were all directly, or by implication, branded as from the same group of 'property developers' seeking to take away from residents their last remaining open spaces. Lists of 'them' and 'us' were issued to the voters, many of whom arrived at the polling stations carrying their chosen list. In a low turnout candidates nominated by our opponents each got votes of the order of 700 against our 500. The result was a council heavily weighted against any sports provisions. But this was how the system worked and we were obliged to accept the result. I felt it was a sad day for democracy.

Later, the parish council decided to set up a subcommittee, on which I sat representing the sports association, to look into the use of the recreation grounds. After meetings held over two years, at which the case was examined and debated, it was agreed by a small majority to recommend that bowls and croquet should be provided for on the Glebelands. However this was clearly not the outcome expected and, before it could consider the recommendation, the parish council arbitrarily disbanded its subcommittee. To members of the sports association this was seen as disgraceful chicanery and a waste of two years' work.

Having exhausted every possible avenue to persuade the council to make provision for either bowls or croquet on the existing recreation grounds, we were advised by Arun district officials to look for an alternative site. This led to negotiations, that lasted a year, to use a derelict piece of land, a former building site, now overgrown, on the edge of the village, but within the 'strategic gap'. The owner was sympathetic to our case and offered us a long lease at a nominal rent.

Overnight this site was 'discovered' by the conservation lobby and presented as a site of major ecological and conservation significance, threatened by developers. My colleagues and I made a planning application and hundreds of protest letters resulted. Our application was first supported by, and then opposed by, the parish council, opposed by the conservationists and finally, rejected by Arun on the grounds that the land lay within the 'strategic gap'. Part of our case was that the site would inevitably fall prey to development if it was not secured for some village use. (Three years later the planning authority was faced with a plan to build 139 houses within 'strategic gap' land on another site. As I write this is under consideration.)

When our application came before the district council planning committee, the Chair made clear at the outset her view that the application should be rejected. There had been extensive lobbying of councillors and a tape recording of bird song, 'recorded that morning at the site', was produced by the chair – so much for impartiality. (The recording could have been made anywhere of course, and I am sure I have more bird song in my garden.) Our application found little support and we were advised to go to appeal, which we did.

The campaign against our appeal was pursued within the village with vigour, yet I doubt whether anyone who attended the hearing that followed would have been left in any doubt that the case put by the parish council and conservation lobby was other than seriously flawed. Many felt embarrassed to see their representatives struggling to make a case. We produced expert witnesses to show that the site was not of ecological or environmental interest and the opposition case against us was demolished in cross-examination by our legal representative. This was the first time the issue had been aired in any impartial forum and we had won the arguments hands down. Then an extraordinary thing happened. The parish council representative, who perhaps surmised that they had lost their battle, led the inspector conducting the appeal to suppose that, following the next imminent parish elections there would be no impediment to having a green on the Glebelands. The inspector asked to see the site, obviously thought it suitable, and rejected our petition. But we knew that there was virtually no likelihood that the local council would agree with their representative's assertion and, at the first meeting of the new council, which consisted mainly of members of the old one, an overwhelming majority vote confirmed this. The wrath of our sports committee knew no bounds. We had spent almost all of our meagre funds on the appeal and lost, because of what we understood to be a thoroughly misleading statement made to the inspector. Our members thought the decision a travesty of justice and good sense, and, in consequence, the village became more divided than ever.

The chairman of the Arun leisure committee then suggested that we should conduct a survey or petition to establish the support that existed for bowls, and we did this by calling door to door asking individual householders for their views. We found overwhelming support. Out of the village population of 4,000 we had 1,077 signatures, having surveyed only one third of the village. Convinced that this would finally persuade our parish council the Arun chairman addressed them and made clear his view that they should reconsider the matter. He emphasised that, if only a few hundred in an electorate wanted some provision it would be normal for that request to be given very serious consideration. He also debunked the parish council's contention that, if a majority did not want a facility it should not be provided, and pointed out that, judged by that criteria no facilities would be provided for anything. The meeting reluctantly thanked him for coming, but continued to ignore the findings of the petition, except that they 'agreed in principle to having a bowling green in the village' while arguing that an alternative site should be found. Yet they knew that we had already spent eight years looking for another site without success. They then set up a subcommittee, which wasted a further six months, looking again at all the sites we had already investigated and, surprise, surprise, came to the conclusion that none was available. If this had been some sort of farce on the West End stage it would have run and run.

We were able partially to meet the demand for additional village sports facilities, by establishing a successful carpet bowls club and a thriving tennis club with around one hundred playing members, making use of the new hard tennis courts. The parish council initially rebuffed all efforts by the sports association to form a tennis club, then, after two years we prompted two 'neutral' players to approach the council with a plan to form a club. This was agreed and I found it amusing that they applauded the constitution presented by the 'neutrals', little knowing that it was the same document that I had previously drafted, which their subcommittee had rejected.

We were left wondering how it was possible for a small group to influence opinion in the way they did, and mainly on the basis of false information and innuendo. And how did they manage to sway the parish council, as they apparently did? The apathy of the electorate provides some of the answers, but there must, we felt, be more to it than that.

Although I was operating only on the fringes, the more I saw of local government the less enamoured of it I became. It seemed to me inexplicable that we should entrust so much

343

public finance and the running of our affairs to groups of people, many of who had little or no background or training for any of this. If one wanted anything done and done efficiently, the last thing any sensible person would do would be to hand it to a group seemingly lacking the necessary experience, ability or aptitude for the task. But that is precisely what we do when we operate our democratic machine, particularly at parish council level, where the situation is aggravated by reason of there being few or no paid officials to guide the elected members.

The scarcity of those able and willing to participate in local government is always a problem. Some excellent people come forward and serve, but far too few. The way in which I had been persuaded to join the ratepayers' association committee, illustrated to me how very difficult it is to find people willing to take on voluntary work. Apart from those who have the best of qualifications and motives, there are always those who want to push themselves into the limelight; those who seek office for the prestige they think this affords them, or those who think they have some God-given right to a seat on every committee in the community. Others may seek such positions because they have achieved little in life, and are looking for some satisfaction in later years; but whether these are the right people to be in charge of public affairs is another matter.

In my experience the best-qualified people rarely come forward to volunteer their services, and it usually falls to those who already carry the burden of unpaid work in any community to seek out others to fill gaps as they occur. Ferring was no exception, and each year when it came to election times all the local associations had to work hard to find individuals to fill places on their committees. Where you had a team of good volunteers content to do the work, it seemed to me highly irresponsible to get rid of them, but we often heard the view that no-one should be allowed to serve for more than a year or two. If an office was filled satisfactorily, to me it made sense to retain the incumbent, if not, the ballot box could provide a remedy. The practice of limiting terms of office had the effect of throwing away scarce and willing talent.

I soon found myself puzzling over other aspects of local government. In particular, I found strange the unquestioning belief held and professed by many that because a group of individuals was duly elected under a local government act, they were *ipso facto* representative of the whole electorate, a contention that often led such individuals to suppose that their views should prevail. It was James Madison, the American constitutional expert who, at the time of the drafting of the American Constitution, made the point that the great weakness of democracy was that it legitimised the right of the majority to ride roughshod over the minority. Had he lived long enough he would have seen this amply demonstrated in Ferring in the 1990s, when minority views on sports provisions were largely ignored.

Sadly, in our local elections, only apathy is the winner. Sometimes as many as 70% of the electorate do not bother to vote, and those who do, tend to vote for individuals they happen to know, or know of: mostly, they have little information about the candidates or their policies. Vacancies on councils and committees, when they occur, are usually filled by co-opting a volunteer, and the tendency is to co-opt 'one of our own' rather than to seek out representative viewpoints. Especially at the parish level there are frequently no election manifestos, political party affiliations are mostly unknown, and voters have little or no idea of the qualifications a candidate might have. It seems to me that such elections border on the absurd. Madison held that:

'To profess against these truths that elected people are in any sense representative of the people simply because they were elected is surely the height of nonsense'.

I could not agree more.

Denis Healey in his autobiography *The Time of My Life* puts the point clearly:

'I sometimes think that the critical difference between a democracy and a dictatorship is that in a dictatorship there are only two people out of every hundred who take a personal interest in politics; in a democracy there are three. The political parties must depend for their organisation largely on voluntary workers. But a man or woman who will give up night after night after working all day to argue politics in a draughty schoolroom or to canvas from door to door in the wind and rain, is exceptionally rare, and is by that very fact untypical of the ordinary voter'.

I was fascinated to see how our parish council worked. In the main I found their attitude entirely negative, and the way in which business was conducted often beggared belief. It used to be said that committees were gatherings of individuals who, as individuals can do nothing, and as a committee agree that nothing can be done. How true that seemed at the time. The very fact that parish councils have virtually no responsibilities of any consequence ensures that, with some exceptions, individuals of ability do not feel attracted to serve at this level. Fortunately, few of the decisions taken at the parish level are of much significance, but these bodies do have legal powers and responsibilities. In the case of our local sports facilities it was this unrepresentative group, elected by a minority of voters, who were determining the issue.

Whereas, within central government members share at least a political party outlook, at the parish level there is little cohesion of any kind between those elected. Members of a parish council generally lack common goals or policies and when they meet they do so as individuals. At the parliamentary level there exists a process for selection, and candidates present themselves at the polls with policies from which electors can make a choice. This is not the case at the parish level where voters tend to support candidates who have been recommended.

I also observed a tendency for groupings of local councillors to emerge whenever a vote was taken, and for these groups to perpetuate themselves over a range of matters, almost as though loyalty demanded it. There is some horse-trading – 'You support me on this and I'll support you on the issue of interest to you'.

Committee standing orders have their place, but for reaching rational solution of local problems, they often prove to be a straitjacket. As a chairman, both in my Whitehall days, and later in the village, I always sought to ensure; (a) that the problem was clearly defined; (b) that all relevant information was before the committee; (c) that there was a full and frank discussion. Only then would I call for either a motion or, in most instances, I would take my responsibility as chairman and summarise the consensus of the meeting. This procedure ensured that we rarely had to vote against each other in committee, a procedure that is, by its very nature, divisive. There is also a strong case to be made for training councillors and chairmen. The Ferring parish council suffered more than most with six different and mostly untrained clerks in as many years. But was this symptomatic of some of the problems I have been describing? I suspect that it was. The strict application of parliamentary conventions is mostly inappropriate to the conduct of parish-pump business.

When it came to decision-making, I became aware of a clear

difference between work at the parish level and that at the district or county level. Both the latter employ professional staff and their committees have the benefit of essential information and background studies carried out for them. Technical advice is at their disposal and they are thus far less likely to reach bad decisions. At the parish level, everything I had seen convinced me that it was a case of 'the blind leading the blind'. Matters were introduced by councillors without warning or any proper research, and decisions were reached entirely on the basis of individual views, knowledge, ignorance or prejudice as the case might be. This was a procedure that any business college would cite as the wrong way to conduct public affairs.

During the upheaval over sports provisions, I was particularly grateful for the support my colleagues and I had from many quarters, especially from those individuals who had perhaps done more for the village than anyone else. I may have made enemies as a result of my efforts to provide for the sports lovers, but I also made a large number of friends. Together we enjoyed many a laugh over this ridiculous village situation, which, in some respects, reminded me of the epic French farce 'Clochemerle', which told the hilarious story of an attempt to build a urinal in a French village.

A friend of mine working in the television industry suggested from my account of parish councils and their work that the subject matter should be turned into a successor to 'Dad's Army'. However, another TV series called 'The Vicar of Dibley,' beat me to it, by portraying a parish council, much as I had experienced it.

Since I first came to Ferring nearly forty years ago there have been many changes. The population has nearly doubled and almost every plot of land has been developed. (Imagine my consternation when a builder called on me one evening to ask if the rough plot next to my cottage was for sale: he was referring to my prized tennis court!). We have seen the narrow roads widened and improved, and traffic has increased immeasurably. Most of the shops have changed hands, not once but several times. Shop rentals have soared and the impact of closures has eroded the fabric of the community. We consider ourselves lucky to have retained those few shops and services so essential to village life. But the threat of the out-of-town shopping malls, bulk suppliers and e-commerce now place a question mark over the future of villages such as ours. The lack of sports facilities matched to the needs of the residents can only hasten the decline.

While I was still chairman of the ratepayers' association, Arun district council made a point of acknowledging service to the community and I was pleased, in 1989, to have been one of three recipients of an award for service over some ten years to the village. It was gratifying that someone had understood what my committee and I had been trying to do. Ferring had turned its back on what we saw as progress and improvement, but there was nothing more we could do about it and I put the matter on a 'back burner', for the time being. Eventually, I think it inevitable that the village will have its bowling green and a happier community will ask, 'Why did we have to wait so long?'

CHAPTER TWENTY-SEVEN

SENIOR LEGAL ADVISER

'The lawyer is a gentleman who rescues your estate
from your enemies, and keeps it to himself'.

Lord Brougham.

I spent some months during 1992-3 visiting and helping an old friend living in Jersey who had worked with me in the office of the commissioner general in Singapore in the1950s. She was godmother to our second daughter Caroline, a factor that had helped to ensure that we kept in touch over the years. After the tragic loss of her husband, who did not return from a bombing run over Germany early in the war, she campaigned for and won a long battle to secure pensions for war widows, but not, she once told me, before she won the support of her member of parliament, Margaret Thatcher, who helped to push through the necessary legislation when she came to office.

My friend remarried after she retired but soon afterwards her husband suffered a stroke and became severely disabled. She nursed him at their home in Jersey for some years before he died, during which time his own children, from an earlier marriage, had little to do with their father.

His will bequeathed everything to his widow and nothing to the children, who reappeared after his death and laid claim to the estate. They argued in court that the old man was not capable of making a will when he did and, as there had been no medically qualified witness present at the signing, the court upheld the children's appeal against the widow's right to the estate. Under Jersey law, which was still based on Norman-French law at that time, the widow was entitled to little other than dower rights on the family home and, while she could

351

continue to live in part of it, she, ludicrously, had to share the only kitchen. She called on me for help in the interminable battles she was having with solicitors and accountants and I was delighted to do what I could. She was also having problems with her eyesight that was failing fast. I made a number of visits to Jersey and was appalled by the failure of the professional people she had employed over two years to resolve her problems. It seemed to me that they had already taken a large part of the sizeable estate in fees, charges and expenses and were not close to resolving anything.

In the event a solution was not hard to find in that the widow had one trump card to play and I played it for her, namely, that the family could not sell the palatial matrimonial home while she still had dower rights to live in part of it. I was soon able to strike a deal that seemed remarkably straightforward: she would relinquish her rights and move out and they would give her a sufficient share of the estate to buy a house and carry on living in Jersey.

But that was not the end of it. Distribution of the contents of the house presented another intractable problem. After some negotiations all the parties agreed that the artefacts should be divided between the widow and the three stepchildren, but to best meet the wishes of all four beneficiaries, each should have the right to select an item, taking turns and starting with the eldest. To give effect to this plan we assembled in Jersey – the widow and I plus the three stepchildren and their individual solicitors when, to my astonishment, my friend introduced me as a senior legal adviser to the Foreign & Commonwealth Office. I was too flabbergasted to say anything and thought it prudent on this occasion to stay silent. As a result I was accorded a degree of deference that my non-existent legal training should not have attracted. We then proceeded to divide the contents of the house, with each member of the family taking turns to nominate an item. The allocation went on for many hours as we sat in the magnificent dining room of the family home overlooking St. Lawrence bay, breaking only for meals, as we worked our way through lists of works of art, china, glass, jewellery, etc. The widow and the stepdaughter both wanted certain objects of sentimental value to them and, naturally, I wanted my friend to select those which were of the greatest financial worth, at least until her finances were assured and she had secured a fair share of the whole. When, for example, it came to a choice between her old bed and the valuable crystal chandeliers, she preferred the comfortable bed! There were several disputes along the way, the swift resolution of which resulted largely from my accorded high profile in the legal profession; whatever I suggested the other solicitors accepted with some deference. At the end of a harrowing day we all parted on good terms.

After the emasculation of her home my friend still had enough to carry on living in much the style of yesteryear and soon afterwards the big house was sold and she was able to buy a smaller one. With an adequate income to go with it she has lived in comfort for many years.

Some time later, largely as a result of the publicity arising from the legal battles, changes were made to Jersey law bringing it closer into line with UK legislation, and ending the age-old dower rights system that had blighted the lives of many Jersey widows. Perhaps I missed my vocation and should have been an advocate.

354

CHAPTER TWENTY-EIGHT

NOSTALGIC JOURNEYS

'What though youth gave love and roses,
Age still leaves us friends and wine.'

Moore.

In the years that followed my retirement, Barbara and I were largely preoccupied with our own family – four very different young ladies – and many but, I hasten to add, not all of their activities. Thankfully we had this pleasurable task to help us to keep our feet on the ground and our values intact, at a time when so much in the world seemed to be going awry. The Cold War was far from being over, the spread of AIDS was causing universal concern, lawlessness was replacing the rule of law in many parts of the world, and in spite of global warming, the British climate seemed to be deteriorating rather than improving. On the bright side there was a growing awareness of the interaction and interdependence of everything in our universe and of the need to conserve resources.

With four daughters we could hardly complain about the ever expanding world population, but numbers were increasing at an alarming rate, and no politician seemed willing to face up to the consequences of this for the universe at large. At the end of the millennium I was beginning to think that nothing short of a global policy to reduce the population by about half would guarantee any sort of decent future for our descendants.

Retirement gave me more time for the family and as they came of age and needed homes of their own we were able to help them with accommodation and later in making each more habitable. We shared with the children in all the hassle of

355

property buying, making frequent dashes here and there to view flats and houses as they came on the market, and were snatched up almost overnight in the crazy property market of the time, when house prices were soaring and gazumping was common. The time I had spent in the building industry, some forty years earlier, proved invaluable as I was presented with an ever-increasing list of jobs to be done. And, luckily, our accumulation of furniture from the family houses we had liquidated proved immensely useful in giving them a start. At the time my little trailer was in use almost daily moving furniture from Ferring to their new homes in London.

Until my late seventies I undertook all of the maintenance on our house and the children's flats and took some pride in never having to call on the help of a tradesman. In later years I had to relax that rule to some extent, but in earlier times I had tackled anything from central heating to re-wiring and redecoration. My DIY efforts were not confined to the UK either. Our second daughter, Caroline, danced professionally with the Ballet Royale de Wallonie in Belgium for a number of years, and Barbara and I used to visit the continent frequently to watch her performances. On one occasion I went over to decorate her flat by day and in the late afternoons I would join the ballet company convoy and accompany them to watch their performances in France, Germany and the Low Countries. It was fascinating to witness the stage sets being unloaded and assembled at speed and the backstage preparations made before the curtain went up. Sadly for me the repertoire for that whole week was *'Les Dames aux Camillias'* – not one of my favourite ballets, certainly not after five performances on consecutive evenings. We made a number of other trips to the continent to see Caroline dancing, once to Paris where she danced in a performance with the legendary Nureyev.

Predictably, having four daughters made weddings inevitable. Three of these took place at our little parish church of St. Andrew. Nina, our third child, who had been born in Rangoon, was the first to leave home. For her reception we erected a marquee on the tennis lawn in our garden. Caroline was next, but she held her reception at Goodwood House, near Chichester. Nicola also elected to have a marquee on our tennis lawn. After these events I was mortified to see my court covered with confetti and cigarette ends and, to the amusement of the neighbours, I cleaned up with an old fashioned Bissell carpet sweeper. Alison, the youngest, has remained single.

Barbara had an eccentric elderly aunt, Lillian, living in Dover whom we visited from time to time. She was best remembered for the occasion when she attended a memorial service in Canterbury Cathedral having just collected an alarm clock from her watchmaker. At a most solemn moment during the service the alarm went off causing enough commotion to arouse the departed spirits as she scurried beneath her pew in search of the offending timekeeper.

Barbara was always keeping an eye open for our next break from the routines of home life, which she found arduous after a life abroad with servants to help her. We had kept our chalet in Spain and usually managed to spend a few weeks there at the end of each English winter, often in company with my eldest brother, Leslie, and a friend, Betty Tanner, from our Rangoon days. This too became the scene for building and decorating as we improved the facilities. Over the years we had grown to enjoy self-catering holidays and found them especially suitable when the children were small. We stuck to the habit and acquired a few time-share weeks, one in Scotland near Balmoral, a second in the Lake District, on Lake Windermere, a third in Virginia, USA, in the Massanutten Mountains, and another in Val de Lobo, Portugal. We subsequently transferred one time-share week to each of the girls thus keeping all four within the family. With these, a chalet in Spain, and a flat in Famagusta – though the latter was still occupied by the Turks – we ensured that we would never be short of holiday accommodation. As a child I had learned to cook and it invariably fell to me to assume the mantle of chef whenever we were self-catering and Barbara would take a well-earned rest, while I managed the kitchen. I had always enjoyed cooking, and having nothing to do was not my idea of a holiday. I rarely found enjoyment in reading fiction: my holiday reading was generally a computer manual or a guidebook. We eventually sold our chalet in Spain in 1997.

In 1987 Barbara and I decided to revisit some of our old haunts in SE Asia and embarked on a round-the-world trip to take in Australia, where Caroline and her husband were dancing in Brisbane with an Australian company. Before leaving home we wrote to Singapore to the young Chinese girl we had engaged as our baby *amah* some forty years earlier and she insisted we should stay with her and her family. Consequently we found ourselves ensconced in a high-rise flat in the Chinese quarter and hanging out our laundry from the window on a long pole – something Barbara said she had always wanted to do! Our servants from the old colonial days took us out to a number of superb meals, to a family wedding and banquet and generously entertained us throughout our stay. It was touching that they said we had been good to them and they wanted to say 'thank you'. We found Singapore greatly changed, highly developed with skyscraper blocks and with vast highways and flyovers: many of the old colonial style buildings had gone, as had much of the character of the place we had known. Our visit took place just before the opening of their new underground railway system and the Government had decided that to ensure its smooth running, Singaporeans should be given the opportunity to use it entirely free of charge for a time, to familiarise themselves with ticketing and other procedures. We took advantage of this to explore a brand-new system graced with all the latest technology.

In a nostalgic moment we tried to find the hotel where we had stayed on the night of our wedding. We remembered it as being on the seashore but, to our surprise, it was now some distance inland. It was explained to us that in-filling with rock and ballast shipped from the Malay mainland had extended the shoreline. The islands we had known were now much closer to the shore and an overhead cable car had been constructed connecting Sentosa Island, which used to be some distance offshore.

Back in Singapore after a gap of forty years I recalled how apprehensive some of us in the office were at the time when Lee Kwan Yew was first elected. How would he turn out? We need not have worried. Today Singapore stands as a fine monument to his record. He proved himself a strong and determined leader, but he has also been guilty of many infringements of civil liberties. Even so, I doubt if history will judge him harshly for this. I rather think he will be seen to have adroitly managed to steer a course somewhere between the leader of a Western democracy and that of a Chinese emperor with considerable success.

A poignant reminder of the changes that had occurred in Singapore in the preceding forty years came with a telephone call we received from the daughter of our former Chinese cookboy. As a child she would have hesitated to enter our house from the adjoining servants' quarters where she lived with her parents. Now she was personal assistant to a leading

Japanese industrialist and travelled the world with him. She
wanted to meet us and invited us to take tea at the Singapore
Hilton. She reminded us of what she described as 'our many
kindnesses to her, her brothers and her parents' and of how we
used to take her and her brothers with us whenever we took our
own children to the beach or for a picnic: they had not
forgotten, and we were greatly touched by this reminder.

During our time in Singapore we managed to fit in a visit to
some of our Chinese friends in Kuala Lumpur. I had made the
journey from Singapore to KL in 1955 by train and we decided
to do this again. I've long been fascinated by trains and the
journey brought back many memories. We had the choice of an
air-conditioned first class compartment or an ordinary open
compartment with double bunks, but as neither of us liked
sleeping with air conditioning, we chose the latter. We were
late boarding and I took the last remaining top bunk and
Barbara had to settle for a lower bunk on the opposite side of
the compartment. I slept well enough, but when Barbara was
asked on arrival how she had slept, she announced that she had
'had a bad night with a big fat Sikh on top of me'. I had hastily
to explain the bunk situation.

I was disappointed to find that, since I left KL it had
changed beyond all recognition. I could not even find the office
where I had worked and only with the help of friends did I
locate the bungalow Barbara and I shared when we were first
married. K.L, like Singapore, had become another sprawling
city with masses of tower blocks, hotels, highways and
flyovers. In my time it had been a delightfully sleepy place.
This only confirmed my view that it is better never to return to
places you have loved: the past is best preserved as a memory.
We were taken to a Chinese banquet on the evening of our
departure but had to leave, somewhere between the sixth and

seventh course, in order to catch our return night train to Singapore.

Our next port of call was Brisbane to visit Caroline and her husband Sean and make the acquaintance of our first granddaughter, Natasha, who had been born a few months earlier. During our flight from Singapore we heard on the aircraft news service of the great storm of 1987 that caused extensive damage, especially in the South of England. A telephone call that night from our children brought news of the loss of some twenty large trees in our garden. Providentially, our thatched roof had survived hurricane force winds and no serious damage had been caused to our property. Neighbours moved the fallen trees from the roadway but they lay on the ground until we got home, for me to cut up and dispose of them: a task that took me over a year. Replacing all the fences and replanting the trees was a major task. We had a large garden by local standards and prior to the storm our cottage and garden had been completely screened by trees, after the storm it was open on all sides.

Sean's parents still lived in Brisbane and were able to show us around. We visited a wildlife reserve where I remember seeing the baby kangaroos (joeys), wearing little woollen jerseys, being fed from their bottles, and a colony of flying foxes resting in the trees on the riverbank. We were also taken for a boat trip on the Brisbane River with dinner on the *Kookaburra Queen*, a replica of an old paddle steamer, and we did our share of baby-sitting.

We flew on to New Zealand where we stayed with friends in Hamilton who took us to see the hot mud springs at Rotorua and other sights, before travelling on to Wellington, Christchurch and Queenstown in South Island. The beautiful scenery surpassed anything I have ever seen, with the sea an intense blue, surrounded by snow-covered mountains running down to the edge of the water. We spent a morning at its lovely botanical gardens before flying on via Hawaii – where it rained for most of our time there. Dr. Kyaw Myint, our Burmese doctor friend from our Rangoon days, met us. (It was he who had brought our daughter Nina into the world.) He had flown from Los Angeles to meet us and had hired a car in which he drove us around the island where he had bought a plot of land and was having a house built for his retirement.

We could not resist making a visit to Pearl Harbour, which had played such a significant part in World War II. There on the harbour bed lay the hulls of many of the great battleships sunk in the treacherous Japanese air strike of 1942. One of them we visited, along with groups of Japanese tourists and their new brides, had been preserved as a tomb. We thought it ironic that a visit to this scene of Japanese infamy should form a regular part of the itinerary for newly married couples. Far from being a solemn occasion, the journey to the memorial ship turned out to be hysterically funny. The barge provided to transport us to the sunken hull of the USs Arizona was manned by a female US naval crew. Whenever the officer shouted orders to the pilot – 'hard aport' or 'slow astern' – it appeared that the pilot had attended an unrelated training course, and she invariably steered the vessel in the wrong direction. Exasperated by all this, and having twice overshot our landing place, the officer-in-command shouted 'For Heaven's sake, when I say hard astern I b....y well mean take her backwards'. When we did eventually tie up, even though our faith in the US Navy had been undermined, we all stood together in silence on a deck constructed over the hull of the great battleship with its deck just visible below the surface of the water. The ship entombed the bodies of those who went down with her on that fateful day, the day that marked the entry of the USA into the war, and an event for which we in Britain had waited so long. I was acutely aware that some of those around us as we stood there in silent homage were likely to be descendants of those very people responsible for that shameful act. It was an impressive moment and my feelings as I stood there in silence with all those young Japanese brides and grooms were decidedly mixed.

We flew on to Los Angeles, where we enjoyed the hospitality of our Burmese doctor's brother who was married to an Indonesian lady, and were taken to Monument Valley and the Grand Canyon. We had been driving towards the canyon for some eight hours through the afternoon and evening and were hoping to bed down soon, when my host asked if I would take a turn at driving. When I enquired as to how much further we had to go, he informed me that it was only about another two hundred miles or so! Not surprisingly I dozed off more than once on that exhausting trip: driving at relatively low speeds, as required in the USA, did little to keep me alert.

We were also taken for a day trip to Mexico and on our return we visited San Diego and made a quick tour of the sights. Then, back in Los Angeles that night, we woke to find the bed shaking. Barbara shouted, 'What on earth are you doing' – she was not used to such activity from my side of the bed! I leapt out and heard our hosts shouting 'Earthquake, quick, get into the garden'. I noticed the light pendant swaying alarmingly as I grabbed my dressing gown and joined our hosts outside. It was soon over and little damage had been done, but we learned afterwards that the quake epicentre was almost exactly where we had been that afternoon in Tijuana in Mexico, with a force of 6.5 on the Richter scale. It was quite a big one but we were at least 100 miles away when the shock occurred. We were quite glad to be heading back to England and having our feet on firm ground.

A holiday we took in Morocco in 1989 with our daughter Nina was notable for the interest she aroused with young Arab men. Wherever we went I was accosted and asked if she was for sale. The price was always in camels to which I could not readily relate a value. I wondered how her husband would have reacted had I returned home to announce that we had sold her for 200 camels – the best price I was offered. To her surprise nobody put in a bid for Barbara, or for me for that matter.

We took another vacation to a time-share in North Carolina, taking with us my eldest and youngest brothers and my sister-in-law. It seemed that we were having some effect on the meteorology wherever we went. We now ran into hurricane Hugo. We watched the television portrayal of imminent disaster with some anxiety. Parts of the West Coast of South Carolina had been devastated and at one point the storm was heading straight for us. Local people could be seen packing and leaving, but we had nowhere to go and, in the event, the storm passed north of us. Although it was some 80 miles away it still managed to uproot a few trees on the golf course estate where we were staying and caused extensive damage further north

In 1994 we took a holiday in Canada and stayed at two different resorts in the Rocky Mountains. As we drove from Calgary towards Vancouver we could only marvel at the breathtaking scenery. Our love of railways led us to take a Canadian Pacific Railway train from Whistler, where we were staying, to Lilluet, an old gold mining village some miles to the north where we found a tiny local museum managed by a lady from Bradford! The railway line was so close to the edges of some of the lakes that looking out of the railway carriage one could easily imagine that the train was afloat. The reflections of great mountains in the waters of the lakes and the changing colours of the landscape created picture-postcard scenes we shall never forget. For much of the journey the train moved at a snail's pace as it meandered around the shores of huge lakes from one beautiful valley to the next. Slow though the train was, the driver slowed even more as we passed places of interest on the way – rivers where salmon were spawning, or where waterfalls were visible – so that passengers could get a better view. I tried to imagine my commuter train at home slowing down as we left East Croydon station while the driver announced that he was reducing speed so that passengers could see fish spawning or, more likely, Mrs. Bloggs hanging out the washing!

In 1997, just when the leaves were turning in the fall, we visited some distant relations of Barbara's in the USA and travelled extensively in Maine and New Hampshire. We found there was little to do there but admire the scenery that was every bit as spectacular as pictures we had seen, and had a lot of amusement looking through what the Americans tend to call 'collectables'. We found them selling, as eminently collectable objects, many ordinary household items we remembered from our childhood days, which had been long since discarded. Almost anything British and old commanded a high price.

We had for some time been collectors of what we called 'mystery objects' i.e. things familiar to some and not to others. The Americans call them 'Wotsits' and we discovered that in some towns in Maine they have 'Wotsits' societies where members meet periodically with their latest finds to discuss and identify their newest discoveries. We had used our mystery objects at several of our garden parties in England to amuse our guests or raise money for good causes, and wanted to add to our collection. We found a few new gadgets in the collectables stores and came home with a suitcase full of twisted wires and chunks of metal. One of our best finds in a shop near the motor museum in Stanley, was a heavy lump of metal we identified as a puncture repair outfit dating from the very first approach to this task. The heat from a bowl of charcoal at its centre welded the patch onto the tyre. Barbara was certain that we would never pass the security checks with a case full of metal objects but, in the event, no questions were asked and our suitcase full of 'Wotsits' – which could have been grenades or bombs – went through from Portland to London with no questions asked, and this at the height of the security scare that followed the Lockerbie air disaster.

We found ourselves taking a boat trip on our last evening in Portland, Maine. We had driven into the old town to take a quick look around before departing and managed to get ourselves thoroughly lost. We stopped to ask a resident how to find the town centre and, on hearing that we just wanted to see the sights, he invited us to park our car and join him on his speed-boat docked at the rear of his house. He took us for a grand tour of the harbour to see the old George Washington Lighthouse and a Russian fish factory ship to which the fishermen were just delivering and processing their catch. The area around the vessel was teeming with seals feeding from the scraps being thrown from the ship.

When the English channel tunnel was opened we took an early opportunity to make a trip under the water. We had crossed it so many times by ferry, and now wanted to make the journey beneath the seabed. Our wonderment at the engineering achievement was tempered by the failure of the designers to pay more attention to aesthetics. For a project that had cost so much it seemed to us a shame that more had not been done to make the points of arrival and departure more visually pleasing. The stations and the trains looked as though designed for cattle rather than people and the high wire fences reminded me of wartime concentration camps.

Although every day in retirement seemed fully occupied, I found time to develop an idea I had for a burglar alarm system. The crime rate in the UK had increased dramatically and we could no longer leave our home unattended for a moment, even while in the garden, without fear of becoming a victim. I had an idea for a small radio listening device within the home that would be activated by any intruder and would transmit a signal to a neighbour or neighbours. I took the idea to a leading firm who liked it and poured a lot of capital into its development. Then, just when it was ready to be launched, the firm was taken over by another. By this time developments in computer technology and electronics had caught up and it was abandoned. So much for my days as an inventor.

Barbara and I also joined the *'Friends of Ferring'*, a voluntary village organisation providing help and transport for those, mostly elderly folk, in need of services such as fetching and carrying to and from dental surgeries, hospitals and the like. I produced a directory of local organisations for the Friends, listing every village service, business, club and society. There seemed no end to the pursuits awaiting willing hands, but following the debacle over sports facilities I did little more for the village.

After a year overseas Caroline and Sean returned from Australia to Belgium and later moved to the UK where Sean started dancing in 'Phantom of the Opera' in London. In 1996, he set up a dance boutique in Worthing and I was soon brought in to assist with shop-fitting and later assisting as his

367

accountant. Caroline retired from her professional dancing career having performed in many parts of the world and purchased a well-established dance school in Worthing from the lady – Mrs. Jean Butterworth – who had first taught her, and Alison, to dance some twenty years earlier, and who was then retiring after teaching for over fifty years. I soon became involved with the school and when I was not dealing with administration, accounts, or designing and printing stationery, I found myself making stage props – everything from miniature Victorian prams to Noah's Ark. We watched with admiration and pride as her school flourished and her many pupils achieved their various successes in national examinations and at the Worthing and Brighton Festivals. Few occasions gave me more pleasure than watching the group dances she had choreographed and produced, in which so many youngsters obviously found delight and achievement.

After dabbling on the periphery of computers for years I was finally persuaded by the ever-increasing workload from the school and the shop to buy a word processor. I was soon to wish I had done this years earlier. It was not long before I upgraded and upgraded again to a powerful computer, which enabled me to match the growing demand from the dance school and, in particular, to compile our family tree and prepare an inventory of our cottage. The computer was by now an important part of my life and Barbara was telling her friends that if she wanted to speak to me she had to make an appointment.

Research into Barbara's family tree gave us a further insight into the days of the clipper ships. We still have souvenirs from this period, including the brass wash-hand basins from a captain's cabin and one from a first class cabin, also a poster announcing the departure of one of the Clipper ships from Liverpool with a list of the provisions and personal items that passengers were required to take with them. Another fascinating souvenir is a printed list of the stores passengers were allowed for each voyage. For example, in respect of the clipper ship the 'Star of the East' which sailed on 21st October 1856 for Melbourne (1st class fare £45). The Notice of Voyage reminded passengers that:

> 'Each will have to provide themselves with a knife and fork, I table spoon, I tea spoon, 1 tin plate, 1 drinking cup, 1 tin quart and pint pot, 1 slop pail and a keg or can for holding water........ The whole can be had in Liverpool for about £1. Cooks are provided for all passengers.'

The notice also reminded passengers of a strict dietary scale that would be applied:

> 'When fresh meat is issued 1 lb. to each adult per day will be allowed; there will be no flour, rice, raisins, peas, suet or vinegar during the issue of fresh meat'.

Under the heading 'medical comforts' there was 'an allowance of half a gallon of brandy per 200 passengers'. Hardly enough to cure the blues. It must have been something to see the passengers making their way up the gangplank carrying their quart pots and slop pails!

Another of our prized possessions, passed down from Barbara's great-grandfather, who was a peripatetic C of E minister, is his travelling font in Parian ware; barely twelve inches tall, which he carried with him on his travels, and used for numerous Christenings. His diaries, which we still have, show that he preached in a different church every Sunday for sixty years, taking a different text for each, presumably to avoid repeating his sermons, he carefully noted every one he

369

used.

In the autumn of 1996, finding that we had a friend of a friend living in Prague, Barbara and I decided to revisit the scene of my student battles of the 1950s, to see if we could trace any remains of the former International Union of Students. Following the collapse of communism in Czechoslovakia, the Prague headquarters had been forced to close when Soviet funding had ended, and we found only the deserted building. We also made contact with a group of students who had set out to re-establish an international student movement, but they knew little of the early history I was able to convey to them. They invited me to return and I may well do so if only to enjoy a fascinating city, steeped in history and full of memories for me.

To celebrate the new millennium we decided to spend a month in South Africa where neither of us had previously been. Barbara had a cousin living in Durban and an old friend in Louis Trichardt in the Northern Province. We flew to Cape Town where we took the cable car to the top of Table Mountain on a delightfully clear morning. There had been extensive bush fires throughout the district and much of the landscape was a mosaic of blackened, recently burnt vegetation. Some fires were still smouldering. We spent two days sightseeing in the area before taking the famous Blue Train to Pretoria. The scenery from the luxury of the train, in February when we travelled through the Karoo, was disappointing. The whole is said to be a sea of flowers – but only in September. We flew on to Pietersburg, where Barbara's old friend and her husband met us, drove us to their cattle farm in Louis Trichardt, and entertained us for a week. Again there was so much to see and so little time. I shall retain many memories, especially of the colourful tulip trees that line many of the roads and the gigantic and somewhat grotesque baobab trees with their cavernous trunks, appearing to have been planted up-side-down – we picnicked under one where General Smuts, the South African wartime leader, was reputed to have stopped on a number of occasions. I particularly liked the anecdote we were told about the origin of the baobab. The story goes that when God created the world he gave each of the animals a tree to plant. The hyena was the last in line and was so disgusted at having to wait that he planted his tree upside down.

We experienced a full-blown cyclone two days after we arrived which swept through the Northern Province destroying most of the bridges and flooding farmland. The neighbouring country, Mozambique, was already flooded by exceptional rainfall. Some two metres of rain had fallen in the month, greatly in excess of the norm. We saw the Limpopo River in full flood as its muddy waters roared relentlessly on to add to the destruction and misery of those already marooned in Mozambique. It was awesome. After being cut off for twenty-four hours we escaped by way of the last remaining road bridge, part of which had already been swept away by the floodwaters.

Leaving the cyclone and the devastation it had caused behind us, we flew back to Johannesburg and took an escorted tour of five days during which we visited the Kruger National Game Park, where we saw all the big game except the lion. Our guide could not resist the remark 'the lions are having a lie-in'. We also journeyed through Swaziland, where we visited a Zulu village – an experience that opened my eyes to the iniquities of that period of British imperialist expansion in Africa – (my previous knowledge of those events had been largely based on the heroics of the Brecon boys who won all those VCs in the

371

Zulu Wars) – and we spent a night in the Hluhluwe Reserve – more big game – before arriving in Durban, where we were met and generously entertained for our final week by Barbara's cousin and her husband. They took us for two nights to the Drakensberg Mountains to savour the grandeur of a magnificent landscape and to use as a base for a number of interesting excursions. I dearly wanted to visit Rorkes Drift, the scene of the epic battle of the South Wales Borderers, but that will have to wait for another time.

Prior to our visit I had not appreciated the similarities between the English and South African landscapes and was constantly remarking on the likeness of the countryside to the plains of Wiltshire, the lowlands of Scotland or the rugged Brecon Beacons. Much of the time it was difficult to imagine that one was in another and distant continent.

It was sad to see at close hand that South Africa is in such serious economic and social decline, and to learn that the future for those with white skin, who have contributed so much to the well-being and development of the country, is now in jeopardy. White people were departing in large numbers, leaving many key posts to be filled by inexperienced and often corrupt and incompetent individuals. Much of Africa is suffering from a crisis of leadership, and the consequences, especially the breakdown of law and order and the tide of rising crime, were already in evidence in those parts of the continent that we visited. Our hosts in Louis Trichardt had 1,500 head of cattle stolen recently in one night raid, and the police had failed to trace the culprits. It seems that many aspects of primitive tribalism are re-emerging in those parts of Africa where the colonial powers once provided stability.

We had much on which to reflect during our flight home

from Durban to Heathrow – a ten and a half-hour overnight flight - and were starkly reminded of the breakdown of law and order in South Africa when my suitcase rolled off the baggage reclaim carousel at Heathrow, taped together after having been rent open by a vandal's knife.

I finalised this book in May 2000 when it was too wet for me to be working in the garden we both loved. Barbara was still playing tennis in both winter and summer, but I was having a break, having sliced the end of a thumb on my saw bench two years earlier: an incident that enforced a temporary halt to my tennis days. It seems I have a proclivity for DIY and gardening mishaps, and have paid many a visit to the hospital accident and emergency department to be repaired. Fortunately, none of the damage has seriously interrupted my plans or caused me to waste much time.

In retirement we were fortunate in having many friends living close at hand. One was John Willson, a keen tennis player, a considerable prankster and a man with a most generous heart. Whatever project I undertook I could count on him to be the first to volunteer help. He had the rare ability to turn the most arduous task into a pleasure and often a joke. He was always teasing me about the time I spent levelling my tennis lawn and on one April fools' day I found a series of molehills strewn across it – he had brought in the soil over night. On another occasion he made a number of miniature road signs – 'Gradient 1:20'; 'Danger Old People Crossing'; 'Steep Climb Ahead', etc. – which he placed strategically over the court just before play was due to commence. Sadly, John died suddenly in 1999 and I lost a valued friend.

So often we hear of people in retirement complaining about being bored, and we know of many who have gone into rapid decline when they stopped their daily routines and filled out time with little more than watching television. I learned early in life that interest in almost anything grows with knowledge of the subject. People who do not appreciate art, music or sport invariably know little of them and miss so much. I have also grown to appreciate that life is never fair, and we brought up our children to understand and accept this: I think it has helped them to weather the storms of life.

Our thatched roof cottage near the sea, with its garden and a row of white fantail doves sitting on the roof, made very much the kind of home we had always wanted, and in retirement we made full use of the facilities we had. In the summer months our garden became the setting for a few large parties, and we had occasional open days for charity, for the local sports association, for croquet, for short-tennis for children and even for bowls. Each summer we also enjoyed the company of many good friends who came to play on our tennis court, or to swim with us in our pool. At the end of last season we counted that we had entertained over five hundred people during the year. The diplomatic way of life is not readily cast off.

If we have any more adventures, and I'm sure we will, they will have to be the subject of another book. Mine has been a full and varied life and it looks like continuing in much the same vein. For me it has always been a case of 'So much to do and so little time'. Perhaps now, as time moves on and the senses dim, it is more a case of 'So much still to do and so little time left to do it'. I'd better get on with it.

Ben's Boys – 1984.
L to R: Back: Self, David, Fred, Mervyn, Front: Leslie, Harry

Nina and
Andrew's
wedding –
Ferring
1983

Caroline and Sean's
wedding (Ah Yair in
Centre) – Ferring 1984

Nicola and Tom's
wedding – Ferring
1990

Willow Cottage, Ferring.
Our retirement home

Tending my
tennis court
with my
grandson
Oliver

Our four daughters. L to R: Nina, Alison, Nicola and Caroline – 1997.

Our six grandchildren – L to R: Oliver, Thomas, Joshua, Natasha, Ben.
Front: Emily – 1997

DIY – making stage props with 'assistance'
from Ben and Natasha.

The survivors
Barbara and Stanley – April 2000

So Much To Do
So Little Time

• • • • • • • • •

Epilogue

EPILOGUE

At the start of the second millennium, the old family firm of Benjamin Jenkins and Sons is still based opposite the Brecon barracks, having retained the old yard alongside the canal. It has passed down through the generations to a great-grandson of the original founder, but its core business has moved with the times and it has become essentially a plant-hire and builders' merchandising company.

When I first retired in 1978, five of my brothers were still living. The eldest, Leslie, qualified as a pharmacist and chiropodist and practiced from his own pharmacy. He married Bessie, and they had two daughters. He died in 1998. Harry, who joined the army from school, made his career in the Royal Corps of Signals, serving much of his time abroad. Late in life he married Joyce and adopted her son. He died in 1995. Mervyn - apart from an absence during the 2nd World War - continued in the family business. He married Valerie and they had three children. He devoted his spare time to working for the community as a councillor, an alderman, mayor of Brecon and magistrate, and was for many years chairman of the Bench, and of the local Conservatives. He was also a churchwarden. In 1984 he was appointed a CBE. Fred married Dulcie, and they had one son He made a career in the Royal Air Force where he served his country for thirty-nine years. On leaving school, David took a post with the National Provincial Bank and, after the war - he was commissioned in the Royal Engineers – he graduated at Cardiff University and later joined the Coal Board, rising to become a Director. He married Elaine and they had four children. On retirement he took an MA in history at Nottingham university.

As for our daughters, Nicola married Tom Kane a chartered surveyor and they settled in Henley-on-Thames with their two children, Emily and Oliver. Caroline married an Australian, Sean O'Brien. They live in Worthing, where she runs a dance school and he a dancewear boutique. They have two children, Natasha and Benjamin. Nina married Andrew Shrives, a businessman, and they live at Capel in Surrey. They have two boys, Tom and Joshua. Alison lives in London where she settled after a career in dancing that took her all over the world, and ended in 1996 with a knee injury. She works as an assistant to a few of the great and famous in the theatrical world.

Barbara and I have enjoyed a closely-knit family, with our four children, three sons-in-law and **six** grandchildren, all in good health and never far away. We have much to be thankful for.

'Today **six** slender fruit trees stand
Where yesterday were none;
They have been planted by my hand,
And they shall dazzle in the sun
When all my springs are done.

Two apples shall unfold their rose,
Two cherries their snow; two pears;
And fruit shall hang where blossom blows,
When I am gone from these sweet airs
To where none knows or cares.

My heart is glad, my heart is high
With sudden ecstasy;
I have given back, before I die,
Some thanks for every lovely tree
That dead men grew for me.'

Longfellow.

So Much To Do So Little Time

• • • • • • • • •

Appendices

APPENDIX A

Chapters 8-16 - Further background on students and the 'Cold War':

In 1947 the Communist Information Bureau, or Cominform, was created. In essence this was Stalin's response to the Marshall Plan which he saw as a threat to the Soviet Empire. It was then the intention of the Soviet Union that the world should be considered as being divided into two diametrically opposed camps: on the one hand, what they styled as the 'anti-democratic camp of America and its allies'; on the other the 'anti-imperialist and democratic camp of the Soviet union and its allies'. Collaboration and conciliation between these two powerful rivals was no longer deemed to be possible and the Cold War ensured.

The Cominform was not intended as a decision-making body nor an executive one; its functions were mainly to convey Soviet orders to all the countries and organisations under its control. Its relevance to my narrative is that it set up and controlled a number of 'front' organisations to further Soviet objectives throughout the world. One of these was the International Union of Students (IUS) and another the World Federation of Democratic Youth (WFDY).

APPENDIX B

Chapters 8-16 - The early history of the student movement.

The early history of the British and international youth and student movements, which involved such eminent personages as Prime Minister Harold Wilson, American Secretary of State Dean Acheson, Sir Stafford Cripps, Foreign Secretary Herbert Morrison and others, is well documented in a book entitled 'Students and the Cold War' written by a Belgian research student, Dr. Joel Kotek, published by MacMillan in 1996. Originally prepared for a Ph.D. thesis it details a number of the situations in which I was involved in the period 1948 through 1952 and I commend it to any serious student of the Cold War and student involvement in it. Some of the events recounted in my narrative are also the subject of a pamphlet published by the Batchworth Press, written in 1952, by Ralph Blumenau, an undergraduate at the time, who was closely involved. Also of direct relevance is a pamphlet written by John Clews entitled 'Students Unite' published in Paris in 1952 by the Congress for Cultural Freedom and written while he was serving as my proxy in Prague when I was an international vice-president of the IUS.

The International Union of Students was formed at a congress held in Prague in August 1946, when 300 delegates from 38 countries attended the inaugural meeting. 14 of the 20 British delegates were communists. The Czechoslovak prime minister attended and the meeting heard messages read from a number of world leaders including the Yugoslav Marshall Tito. From the outset the structure of the IUS ensured communist control – but this was never made to appear too obvious. A

British student, Dr. Thomas Madden, was elected general secretary and a Czech, Joseph Grohman, president – both were communists. When the IUS constitution was being approved any delegate who suggested a change that might limit communist control was shouted down and branded as "imperialist" or "fascist".

While many of those who attended the inaugural meeting were probably unaware of the background to the IUS, those in charge of it knew precisely what they were about. The Soviet Union attached great importance to the IUS, and its youth counterpart the WFDY, and their roles in subverting the youth of the West to communism.

APPENDIX C

Chapter 9 - Background to my first visit to Prague:

On 25th February 1948, following the communist coup in Czechoslovakia, and responding to a call from the president of the Prague university students union, some 10,000 students marched on Hradcany Castle in support of President Benes and ministers who had been forced to resign following the coup.

While a delegation of protesting students was still holding discussions with Benes inside the castle, the police forced the students outside back across Charles Bridge and dispersed them. There were no fatalities and only minor injuries, but 118 students were arrested. Afterwards the Czechoslovak students union president was arrested and some student leaders managed to flee the country. The IUS with its headquarters in Prague was at the centre of these dramatic events

After a series of show trials that followed, dozens of dissidents were hanged: induced confessions were all that were required to convict. Communist Action Committees then began to revive previously abandoned trials of 1800 cases against students accused of earlier collaboration with Nazi Germany.

APPENDIX D

Notes on personalities mentioned in the text.

Ralph Blumenau was NUS international vice-president in my NUS years. He went on to teach history at Malvern College for the whole of his career.

James Driscoll was leader of the Young Conservatives and University Conservatives 1949-51, and a NUS vice-president and executive committee member. He became Managing Director of British Steel and later Director of the Nationalised Industries' Chairmen's Group.

Martin Ennals, who headed the NUS Grants and Welfare Department, became general secretary of the National Council for Civil Liberties and general secretary of Amnesty International. He died in Canada in October 1991.

Fred Gee was president of University College London students union, after which he spent some years with the FCO, the Rank Organisation, the British Film Institute and the British Standards Institution, becoming a Member of the Royal Institution, a Fellow of the Royal Meteorological Society and a Fellow of University College.

Joseph Grohman, the Czechoslovak president of IUS, had to resign in 1952 when he was accused of spying for the Americans. He was saved from a worse fate by the intervention of Shelepin and was eventually rehabilitated in 1962. In 1969 he was appointed Deputy Minister of Education to the Czech. mission at UNESCO. He was arrested in 1976 after Brezhnev had removed Shelepin from the Politbureau in 1975, and spent nine years in prison.

Fred Jarvis was leader of the National Association of Labour Students Organisations (NALSO) and a member of the NUS executive committee. He became president of the NUS and later secretary of the National Union of Teachers and, at one time was chairman of the TUC.

John McNab was NUS Vice-President. After a career in the FCO he took early retirement and settled in Australia.

Alexander McLellan, my team-mate during the debating tour of the Indian sub-continent, became a Fellow of the British Institute of Management and was chairman of the Royal Overseas League in Scotland 1978-83. He spent much of his career in top positions in the world of education/management overseas, and has many educational publications to his credit.

Guthrie Moir became controller of education and religious programmes with Thames TV. He was a member of the General Synod from 1956-74 and sat on the Buckinghamshire County Council as an Independent for 20 years. In 1970 he became the first non-Roman Catholic to be awarded the Bene Merenti medal by the Pope, for services to religious and educational television. He died in 1995.

Alexander Shelepin, my principal adversary, was Stalin's man directing the IUS and WFDY 'front' organisations. He was appointed to the First Komsomol Secretariat in 1954 and became a member of the Soviet Supreme Praesidium 1961-1975. He succeeded Beria as chief of the Soviet Union's secret police and was closely linked with the purges and oppressions of the Cold War years. Under Khruschev's aegis he was appointed chairman of the Committee of State Security (KGB) in 1958 at the age of 40. He died in 1994. His obituary notice in *The Times* commented that he "was reviled in the West as a neo-Stalinist. Some even likened him to Himmler".

U Nu became prime minister of Burma in 1947, following the assassination of Aung San, the architect of Burma's independence. Following his deposition by General Ne Win's military junta in

1962, he was first detained, and then spent most of the 1970s abroad in exile. In his autobiography, written while imprisoned, he admitted with remarkable frankness that he spent his youth, lying, stealing, drinking, drug taking and womanising, until he discovered the spiritual truths of Buddhism. He died in 1995.

Frank Panton became a senior scientific officer in the Civil Service and an adviser on nuclear energy to the Cabinet.

Olaf Palme, one-time president of the Swedish National Union of Students became prime minister of Sweden and died at the hands of an assassin in 1986.

Bill Rust, who preceded me as NUS president, became principal of the West London Technical College and subsequently principal of Hammersmith and West London College. He was awarded an OBE on his retirement. He undertook several educational consultancies in the Middle East and has a number of educational publications to his credit.

John Thompson succeeded me as president of NUS and later became secretary of the International Union of Teachers. He died in a road crash in Hungary in the 1970s.

Reggie Underwood, my closest wartime colleague and life-long friend, became a chartered surveyor. He died in 1992.

John Watkinson became president of Sheffield university students union after which he spent a year with the Ministry of Supply before joining the BSA Group as Chief Research Metallurgist. He subsequently held directorships with Foseco-Minsep, Plessey and Rolls-Royce. He was also CE of OTIS Elevator plc, and of United Technologies (UK).